LORD,

GIVE ME A HEART
FOR YOU

LORD,
GIVE ME A HEART
FOR YOU

A DEVOTIONAL STUDY

on HAVING *a* PASSION *for* GOD

KAY
ARTHUR

WATERBROOK
PRESS

LORD, GIVE ME A HEART FOR YOU
PUBLISHED BY WATERBROOK PRESS
2375 Telstar Drive, Suite 160
Colorado Springs, Colorado 80920
A division of Random House, Inc.

All Scripture quotations, unless otherwise indicated, are taken from the
New American Standard Bible® (NASB), © Copyright The Lockman Foundation
1960, 1962, 1963, 1968, 1971, 1972, 1973, 1975, 1977, 1995. Used by permission.
(www.Lockman.org) Also quoted is the *King James Version.*

Italics in Scripture quotations reflect the author's added emphasis.

ISBN 1-57856-420-4

WATERBROOK and its deer design logo are registered trademarks of WaterBrook Press,
a division of Random House, Inc.

Printed in the United States of America

CONTENTS

INTRODUCTION

O h, to love God so very, very much, so much that every "whatever" in our lives would be for His sake and His alone—whatever pressure, whatever trial, whatever task. All would be leading us to have a heart for God—to be one whose sole passion is to please God.

I know, Beloved, that you probably picked up this book because that is your desire as well as mine.

For years I have longed to write a study—another "Lord" book or a Precept course—on the anatomy of a heart for God. What does a heart for God look like when lived out in flesh and blood in the daily circumstances of life? This is what I wanted to know, to study, to learn, and to live. And the perfect book from Scripture that seemed to demonstrate this was 2 Corinthians. Finally the day came, and I knew that God would have us study the subject in the form of another "Lord" book rather than a Precept course, for a "Lord" book allows more room for me to also pour out my heart, to share the things the Lord has taught, while at the same time helping you discover for yourself the wonderful truths of God's Word.

This has been such an incredible spiritual journey for me. Now you have in your hands the tangible result of it, and I am thrilled. Thrilled and honored! Thrilled that you want to have a heart for God and honored that I would have the privilege of walking with you through 2 Corinthians, Acts, and other portions of Scripture that will help you understand what it's like to have a heart like His.

I think this will be another revolutionary study in your life, precious one, for Paul reveals himself in this book of 2 Corinthians in a way that he does nowhere else. His vulnerability will touch your heart as you realize how much this great man of God is just like you in his battles, his fears, and his conflicts, as he deals with the inevitable pressures of seeking to serve God in a world opposed to God and among believers who don't always exemplify Jesus Christ.

It is my passion that whether you study this on your own or in a group, your heart will touch God's heart in such a way that it will beat in unison with His from this day forward. In 2 Chronicles 16:9, we learn that the eyes of God are looking for a man or a woman whose heart is fully His, that He might show Himself strong on that person's behalf. May His eyes fall on you! That is my prayer.

Now if there's a possibility that you are going to use this as a group study, you will want to read "Guidelines for Group Use" in the "Study Resources" section at the back of this book, where you'll find other valuable tools to enhance this study.

Also if you would like to develop your skills in handling the Word of God more accurately or in leading others in group studies designed to minister to people of all ages *at any level of commitment* while respecting the restraints on their time, Precept Ministries International can provide the training and materials. For more information, simply call our toll-free number (1-800-763-8280) and let one of our staff members help you. It would be their pleasure. We're known as "The Inductive Study People: everybody, everywhere, any time, any place, any language, any age. One message: the Bible. One method: inductive." We have numerous types of inductive studies, from forty-minute Bible studies that have no homework to others that average fifteen minutes of homework per day to others that require an hour of study per day. We have studies for children, teens, and adults. Please don't hesitate to call us. We exist to serve you.

Finally, let me share my vision—it's the possibility of a new avenue of ministry for you, Beloved of God…

A new beginning—
An avenue of ministry—
A sense of doing something that has eternal value

These are three things I think are so important for you and for me. There's so much to learn, to know, to experience, to do—and we never want to lose sight of that. To do so would be to miss what God has for us. To fall short of the tremendous potential of our lives—a potential that is ours because we are His, because we are children of the Creator of the

Universe, indwelt by His divine Spirit and given the mind of Christ. You and I, Beloved, are God's workmanship gifted by the Spirit of God and created in Christ Jesus unto good works that would absolutely stagger our minds if we were to see them before they ever happened.

And what has God put into your hands? What are you holding and reading right now? Is it an accident? A coincidence? No! You are holding a devotional study that first and foremost will be the beginning of a new depth of understanding about God and all that He is for you.

God is going to speak to you because, through this book, you're going to come face to face with the living Word of God—the Word that not only discerns the thoughts and intentions of your heart, but becomes the means of throwing His light on the direction your life is taking so you can know with absolute confidence where you are headed. If you listen to what He says—and by that I mean ordering your life accordingly—then there is, in a sense, a new beginning…of understanding, of purpose. A new level of Christlikeness is attained. You will be, as Paul would say, pressing on and attaining that for which Jesus Christ laid hold of you.

Which brings me to my next point—an avenue of ministry. What you have learned, God intends for you to share. I have a vision, and you, Beloved, are part of that vision. Our Lord's commission in Matthew 28 was that we make disciples of all men—that we teach them to observe all that He has commanded us. Acts 1 tells us that when we are saved and receive the Holy Spirit we become His witnesses—yet the question is often, "How?"

Here is the how. This "Lord" book contains truths every human being needs to know and to apply to his or her life. These are precepts for life; through them we will gain understanding and, as the psalmist says, "hate every false way" (Psalm 119:104). We hate it because it is false rather than true, and it is truth that sets us apart, sets us free.

So what is my vision for you, my friend? It is that you go to the Lord in prayer and ask Him to direct you to at least one other person—but preferably at least ten—and that you, along with them, study this book together. You may not be a teacher, but you can be the group's facilitator. You can take the questions you'll find at the end of each chapter and use them to stimulate a discussion among those whom the Lord has brought together in answer to your prayer. These are those who will be part of your crown of rejoicing in the presence of our Lord Jesus Christ. As you watch them learn and grow in the knowledge of God and of His Word, you will experience the humbling joy of knowing that you have been used of God. That what you have done has eternal value. That your life and God-given gifts have not been wasted. That your work will live on—that the grace of God poured out on you was not poured out in vain, for you have labored in the strength of His grace.

So as you facilitate a group using this book, you need to watch for and encourage others in your group to do as you have done—to take what they have learned and impart it to another as you did with them. Think of the multiplication that will happen! Do you realize, Beloved, that this is the way we can reach our neighborhoods, our communities, our nation, and beyond? Think of the transformation that will take place among all those people today who are so interested in "the spiritual" but won't step inside a church. Think—just think!—what is going to happen!

The time is now. The hour is short, so stop and pray right now, Beloved, and ask God what He would have you to do. He will show you, because He is God and because such prayers are in accordance with His will. As you step out and begin, just know that if you will step out in faith, God will give you an avenue of ministry, person by person or group by group, that will not only stagger your mind but absolutely delight your soul.

I cannot wait to hear what God does in and through you, my friend.

FINDING GOD'S COMFORT IN AFFLICTION

Have you ever become weary…
tired…
discouraged…
depressed…
defeated…
because—

because you've been so afflicted that you actually despaired
of life?[1]

because people accused you of not keeping your word?[2]

because your honesty caused sorrow and they missed the
fact that you had to say what you said because love
compelled you?[3]

Have you felt a little overwhelmed by conflicts without and fears
within[4]

because you're concerned for the well-being of someone you
dearly love—

a parent, a child, a mate?[5]

Or because of a tenuous relationship with another,
and you don't know where you stand?

Their once-warm heart has turned cold…

the company they keep has changed…

and deep down, gut-level, you believe these new
associates have turned them against you…[6]

Or perhaps you've been criticized, torn down, demeaned,
> due to some physical attribute that is less than perfect,
> or because of some "lack" in your personality,[7]
> or maybe because others have questioned your role, your
>> position, in respect to them,[8]
> or because you've been accused of treating someone
>> improperly.[9]

Are you stressed out, Beloved,
> because you fear that those whom you've loved, protected, cared
>> for, or ministered to
>>> have been led astray in their thinking?[10]

Or because you have a "thorn in your flesh" that God hasn't
> removed, though you've begged Him over and over to do so?[11]

Or because you know you may end up in a confrontation you
> don't want…but probably must have?[12]

You're in good company, my friend, for all that you just read is exactly what was experienced by one of the greatest men of God, the apostle Paul. For Paul, it was not just one of the above, but all of the above.

It's all recorded for us in the most intimate and personal of all of Paul's letters—2 Corinthians, the letter we're going to study. In it, you and I will see what I'll call the anatomy of a heart for God.

Wouldn't you like to know, my friend, that after going through the kind of circumstances I've just queried you on, you could still be able to say at the end of your life, as Paul did, "I have fought the good fight, I have finished the course, I have kept the faith; in the future there is laid up for me the crown of righteousness, which the Lord, the righteous Judge, will award to me on that day; and not only to me, but also to all who have loved His [Christ's] appearing"?[13]

Wouldn't you like to be assured that you could experience all the situations I've posed and still turn to others, as Paul did, and say in total sincerity and truth, without one drop of egotism: "Follow me. Be an imitator of me, even as I am of Christ Jesus. Look at the way I walk and know that if others do not walk this way, they aren't walking in a way pleasing to God."[14]

Can you imagine having such confidence? Confidence, not brashness. Confidence in the midst of cross fire. Confidence even if the government threatened to take your life for what you believed and lived. Confidence so sure that you could stand alone, even though others deserted you because they loved this present life more than the next.[15]

This is the heart I long for.

And what about you, Beloved? Surely, because you picked up this book with this title, we are kin—of a kindred heart.

On the day we see Jesus Christ face to face, to have missed having a heart like this will seem like the greatest of tragedies—especially when we see such a heart was indeed possible for the believing, for the learning, for the disciplined. God always hears the cry of His people, especially when they cry, "Lord, give me a heart for You—*give me a heart for You!*"

Why don't you close today by going back and reading through the questions and the "becauses" I posed at the beginning. (Each one of these, by the way, reflects real-life situations that Paul deals with in 2 Corinthians.) Put a star by each one that somehow pertains to you. Then, when you finish, take a few minutes to sit in the Lord's presence and talk to Him about your heart, just as countless others have done through the corridors of the centuries.

Then record below, for your own benefit, this prayer for your heart.

– D A Y   T W O –

His conversion was glorious—yet hard for some to believe. One moment he was adamantly persecuting those who were followers of Jesus Christ, whom he despised with a vehemence. The next moment he was prostrate on the ground saying, "Who are You, Lord?" to the resurrected, ascended Jesus Christ.

The brilliance of his encounter with this One he believed to be an enemy of God left him temporarily blind until a man by the name of Ananias came trembling into his presence.

Ananias had a right to tremble. Every follower of Jesus Christ trembled at the thought of encountering this banty rooster named Saul who was so cocksure of himself and his cause. No one wanted to be caught by this man of small stature who carried, so to speak, a very big stick—letters of permission from the chief priests in Jerusalem to imprison any of "those of the Way" and probably put them to death. Hadn't Saul consented to the death of Stephen after Stephen testified before the Sanhedrin? Saul joined with others in deeming these people to be enemies of the God of Abraham, Isaac, and Jacob. ("Those of the Way" is what these followers of Christ were called. The nomenclature probably came because Jesus had claimed with His own mouth to be "the way, and the truth, and the life" and declared that none could come to God, the heavenly Father, except through Him.[16])

Ananias went to see this murderer Saul, but only because he was convinced he had heard the Lord's command to go. Ananias had explained to the Lord the reputation of this one to whom he was being sent—but to no avail.

Just as difficult for Ananias as going to Saul was the message he had to deliver. The Lord had said to Ananias, "Go, for he is a chosen instrument of Mine, to bear My name before the Gentiles and kings and the sons of Israel; for I will show him how much he must suffer for My name's sake."[17]

After spending three sightless days, neither eating nor drinking, and seeing a vision of Ananias coming to him, Saul received his sight—and immediately he was out trying to convince others that Jesus of Nazareth was truly the Christ, the long awaited Messiah.

Years later, after beginning his first missionary journey, Saul became known as Paul. How this change came about we don't know, but never again does even Paul himself use his former name except when sharing the story of his conversion before a Jewish mob in the temple and later before King Agrippa. Saul was his Jewish name, while Paul is of Latin origin and means "little." I cannot help but wonder if Paul took on this Latin name not only as a way of more closely identifying with the Gentiles to whom he was called to minister, but also because of its meaning. For Paul saw himself as "the least of the apostles, and not fit to be called an apostle, because I persecuted the church of God."[18]

Although Paul described himself this way, and as "one untimely born,"[19] he became probably the greatest of the apostles. Not only were most of the New Testament epistles written by him, but the greater portion of Acts is devoted to the account of this man's three missionary journeys and closes with the account of his imprisonment and journey to Rome where, as a Roman citizen, he appealed to Caesar.

It was on Paul's second missionary journey that he went to Corinth. Let's take a look at how Saul of Tarsus, a Pharisee and "a Hebrew of Hebrews,"[20] ended up in Corinth, Greece, a city unrivaled for its immorality. To do that we need to begin with Acts 15:40–16:12. As you read through this passage (printed out for you below), mark the references to geographical locations by double underlining them. If you have a green pen, do it in green.

The reason I'm asking you to do this, Beloved, is to introduce you to a way to mark your Bible with standard or consistent markings so that it will be easy to spot various truths quickly. If you start marking your Bible in a purposeful way, you'll find yourself incorporating a learning skill that will help you better remember and retain what you learn. (See pages 265-268 in the Study Resources section for more information on marking your Bible.)*

---

* I am giving you the text printed out because I'm afraid, my friend, if you have never studied with me before, you might be hesitant to mark in your Bible. So as we get to know and trust each other, let's do it this way to begin with—then you'll become convinced on your own. Just remember that, more than anything else, God wants you to know and obey His Word. He wants you to study it, to handle it accurately so that when you see Him face to face you will not be ashamed. The Word of God is your textbook for life. His words are our counselors—Divine therapy for all that ails us. And the more time you spend studying His precepts and applying them to your life, the healthier and stronger you are going to become as a human being. His words are spirit and life—and as we study together you'll see how they'll breathe new life into your inner man.

As you read this passage, remember that this is Paul's second missionary journey. What was his purpose on this journey? We find it in Acts 15:36, where Paul to Barnabas, "Let us return and visit the brethren in every city in which we proclaimed the word of the Lord, and see how they are." As you mark *where* Paul and Silas go, observe what happens in the churches they established on the first journey.

◗ ACTS 15:40–16:12

40 But Paul chose Silas and left, being committed by the brethren to the grace of the Lord.

41 And he was traveling through Syria and Cilicia, strengthening the churches.

16:1 Paul came also to Derbe and to Lystra. And a disciple was there, named Timothy, the son of a Jewish woman who was a believer, but his father was a Greek,

2 and he was well spoken of by the brethren who were in Lystra and Iconium.

3 Paul wanted this man to go with him; and he took him and circumcised him because of the Jews who were in those parts, for they all knew that his father was a Greek.

4 Now while they were passing through the cities, they were delivering the decrees which had been decided upon by the apostles and elders who were in Jerusalem, for them to observe.

5 So the churches were being strengthened in the faith, and were increasing in number daily.

6 They passed through the Phrygian and Galatian region, having been forbidden by the Holy Spirit to speak the word in Asia;

7 and after they came to Mysia, they were trying to go into Bithynia, and the Spirit of Jesus did not permit them;

8 and passing by Mysia, they came down to Troas.

9 A vision appeared to Paul in the night: a man of Macedonia was standing and appealing to him, and saying, "Come over to Macedonia and help us."

10 When he had seen the vision, immediately we sought to go into Macedonia, concluding that God had called us to preach the gospel to them.

11 So putting out to sea from Troas, we ran a straight course to Samothrace, and on the day following to Neapolis;

12 and from there to Philippi, which is a leading city of the district of Macedonia, a Roman colony; and we were staying in this city for some days.

Good job. Now let's take a look at the map on the next page of Paul's second missionary journey and find out where these places are.[21] According to Acts 15:35, Paul and Silas left from the city of Antioch. This particular Antioch was in Syria (watch that, because a city of that name—known as Pisidian Antioch—is also mentioned in Acts). So beginning in Antioch of Syria, trace their journey on the map. Use a colored pen that will stand out so you can easily follow them.

On page 10 you'll see a chart showing the sequence of events in Paul's life after his conversion.[22] When you have time, you might want to scan this chart and notice the events in Paul's life that led up to his second missionary journey.

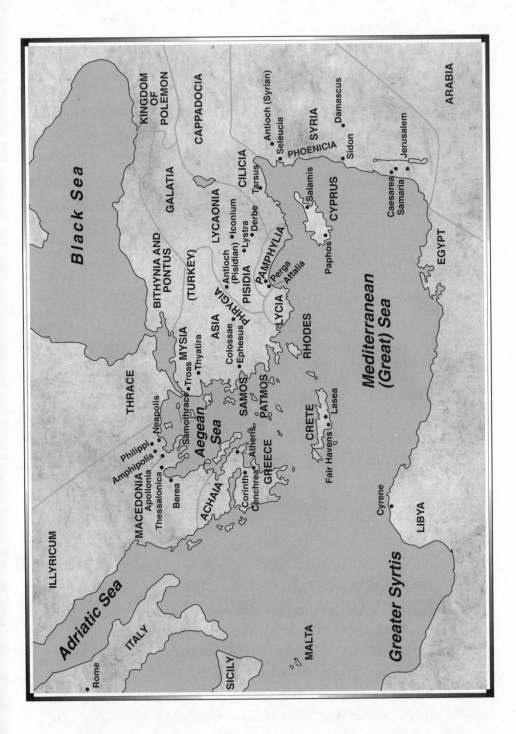

Well, Beloved, you've done a good day's work. Quite an accomplishment. As you read this portion from Acts, wasn't it interesting to see Paul's sensitivity to the leading of God? First Paul and Silas passed through the regions of Phrygia and Galatia because they were forbidden by the Holy Spirit to speak the word of God in Asia. Then, when they arrived in Mysia and wanted to go into Bithynia, the Holy Spirit again checked them. They went instead to Troas, where Paul saw the vision of the man of Macedonia asking him to come over and help them. And what did they do? The Word tells us that they sought to go to Macedonia immediately. No delay, no hesitation.

When your heart belongs to God and you will to do His will, you can rest assured, Beloved, that God will lead you by His Spirit, step by step. Your responsibility is simply to commit your way unto Him, and He will bring it to pass.[23]

Then you can walk in confidence knowing that "the steps of a man are established by the LORD, And He delights in his way."[24]

— DAY THREE —

From the beginning, God made it clear to Paul that he was destined to suffer. Remember the Lord's word to him through Ananias? "He is a chosen instrument of Mine, to bear My name before the Gentiles and kings and the sons of Israel; for [note the "for"] I will show him how much he must suffer for My name's sake."[25]

But suffering wasn't to be Paul's alone, precious one. When anyone unwraps the gift of salvation, he or she will find suffering tucked in with it. The two are inseparable. Paul would later write to the church he founded in Philippi, "For to you it has been granted for Christ's sake, not only to believe in Him, but also to suffer for His sake, experiencing the same conflict which you saw in me, and now hear to be in me" (Philippians 1:29-30).

At the very end of his life, as Paul prepared to die for his faith, he wrote his final letter to Timothy, his son in the faith (you remember Timothy, for you read yesterday in Acts 16 how he and Paul had met). Paul

Sequence of Events in Paul's Life After His Conversion*

Scripture	Year A.D.	Event
Acts 9:1-25	33–34	Conversion, time in Damascus
	35–47	Some silent years, except we know that Paul:
Gal. 1:17		1. Spent time in Arabia and Damascus ⎤ 3 years
Acts 9:26; Gal. 1:18		2. Made first visit to Jerusalem
Acts 9:30–11:26; Gal. 1:21		3. Went to Tarsus, Syria-Cilicia area
Acts 11:26		4. Was with Barnabas in Antioch
Acts 11:30		5. With Barnabas took relief to brethren in Judea, and Paul's second visit to Jerusalem
Acts 12:23	44	Herod Agrippa dies
Acts 12:25		
Acts 13:4–14:26	47–48	6. Returned to Antioch; was sent out with Barnabas by church at Antioch
		First missionary journey: *Galatians written(?)*
	49	Proconsul Sergius Paulus on Paphos is datable
Acts 15:1-35; Gal. 2:1		Apostolic Council at Jerusalem—Paul visits Jerusalem (compare Acts 15 with Galatians 2:1)
Acts 15:36–18:22	49–51	**Second missionary journey:** *1 and 2 Thessalonians written*—1½ years in Corinth, Acts 18:11
	51–52	Gallio known to be proconsul in Corinth
Acts 18:23–21:17	52–56	**Third missionary journey:** *1 and 2 Corinthians and Romans written*—probably from Ephesus
Acts 21:18-23	56	Paul goes to Jerusalem and is arrested; held in Caesarea
Acts 24–26	57–59	Appearance before Felix and Drusilla; before Festus, appeals to Caesar; before Agrippa—datable
Acts 27–28:15	59–60	Went from Caesarea to Rome
Acts 28:16-31	60–62	First Roman imprisonment: *Ephesians, Philemon, Colossians, and Philippians written*—2 years in prison
	62	Paul's release; possible trip to Spain
	62	Paul in Macedonia: *1 Timothy written*
	62	Paul goes to Crete: *Titus written*
	63–64	Paul taken to Rome and imprisoned: *2 Timothy written*
	64	Paul is absent from the body and present with the Lord (*Others put Paul's conversion about A.D. 35, his death at A.D. 68.*)

14 years, Gal. 2:1 (spanning A.D. 33–34 through 47–48)

reminded Timothy that "all who desire to live godly in Christ Jesus will be persecuted" (2 Timothy 3:12). Those who desire to live godly in Christ are those who have a heart for God. This, Beloved, is something you and I need to understand and remember as we pray, "Lord, give me a heart for You."

Strange as it seems, suffering is a precious gift when viewed from an eternal perspective, because suffering not only proves our faith but is used of God to make us more like Jesus. And believe me, when we stand some-day at the judgment seat of Christ, that's all that will matter.

Let's return to Acts and watch what transpires once Paul and Silas arrive in Philippi. As you read the following text from Acts, do the following:

- Double underline all geographical locations, as you did before.
- Mark every reference to the Jews with a blue star of David like this: (Remember that Paul was sent not only to the Gentiles, but also to the sons of Israel; we don't want to miss anything that has to do with getting the gospel to the Jews.)
- Color every reference to the synagogue blue or mark it with a symbol like this:
- Mark any reference to suffering of any kind with a red line over the appropriate words like this:
- Mark every reference to the Scriptures (such as *the word* or *the word of God*) like this:

(For a useful bookmark that you can use throughout this week's study, take a three-by-five card or a piece of paper, fold it into a long strip, and list on it these key words or things mentioned above that you want to mark and show how you're marking them.)

You're in for a fairly long read now, but I believe it will be so fascinat-ing that it won't be difficult. Since our quest is to gain a heart for God, and this is the major way it comes—by spending attentive time in your Father's Word—it should only inspire us to live more consecrated lives. Remember, Beloved, these words are pure truth, and God will use them to sanctify you—to make you holy even as He is holy. There's nothing better you could be doing.

As you begin, may I suggest that you pray and ask God to speak to your heart. These were real people living in real places, just like you.

◗ ACTS 16:13–17:34

13 And on the Sabbath day we went outside the gate to a riverside, where we were supposing that there would be a place of prayer; and we sat down and began speaking to the women who had assembled.

14 A woman named Lydia, from the city of Thyatira, a seller of purple fabrics, a worshiper of God, was listening; and the Lord opened her heart to respond to the things spoken by Paul.

15 And when she and her household had been baptized, she urged us, saying, "If you have judged me to be faithful to the Lord, come into my house and stay." And she prevailed upon us.

16 It happened that as we were going to the place of prayer, a slave-girl having a spirit of divination met us, who was bringing her masters much profit by fortune-telling.

17 Following after Paul and us, she kept crying out, saying, "These men are bond-servants of the Most High God, who are proclaiming to you the way of salvation."

18 She continued doing this for many days. But Paul was greatly annoyed, and turned and said to the spirit, "I command you in the name of Jesus Christ to come out of her!" And it came out at that very moment.

19 But when her masters saw that their hope of profit was gone, they

seized Paul and Silas and dragged them into the market place before the authorities,

20 and when they had brought them to the chief magistrates, they said, "These men are throwing our city into confusion, being Jews,

21 and are proclaiming customs which it is not lawful for us to accept or to observe, being Romans."

22 The crowd rose up together against them, and the chief magistrates tore their robes off them and proceeded to order them to be beaten with rods.

23 When they had struck them with many blows, they threw them into prison, commanding the jailer to guard them securely;

24 and he, having received such a command, threw them into the inner prison and fastened their feet in the stocks.

25 But about midnight Paul and Silas were praying and singing hymns of praise to God, and the prisoners were listening to them;

26 and suddenly there came a great earthquake, so that the foundations of the prison house were shaken; and immediately all the doors were opened and everyone's chains were unfastened.

27 When the jailer awoke and saw the prison doors opened, he drew his sword and was about to kill himself, supposing that the prisoners had escaped.

28 But Paul cried out with a loud voice, saying, "Do not harm yourself, for we are all here!"

29 And he called for lights and rushed in, and trembling with fear he fell down before Paul and Silas,

30 and after he brought them out, he said, "Sirs, what must I do to be saved?"

31 They said, "Believe in the Lord Jesus, and you will be saved, you and your household."

32 And they spoke the word of the Lord to him together with all who were in his house.

33 And he took them that very hour of the night and washed their wounds, and immediately he was baptized, he and all his household.

34 And he brought them into his house and set food before them, and rejoiced greatly, having believed in God with his whole household.

35 Now when day came, the chief magistrates sent their policemen, saying, "Release those men."

36 And the jailer reported these words to Paul, saying, "The chief magistrates have sent to release you. Therefore come out now and go in peace."

37 But Paul said to them, "They have beaten us in public without trial, men who are Romans, and have thrown us into prison; and now are they sending us away secretly? No indeed! But let them come themselves and bring us out."

38 The policemen reported these words to the chief magistrates. They were afraid when they heard that they were Romans,

39 and they came and appealed to them, and when they had brought them out, they kept begging them to leave the city.

40 They went out of the prison and entered the house of Lydia, and when they saw the brethren, they encouraged them and departed.

17:1 Now when they had traveled through Amphipolis and Apollonia, they came to Thessalonica, where there was a synagogue of the Jews.

2 And according to Paul's custom, he went to them, and for three Sabbaths reasoned with them from the Scriptures,

3 explaining and giving evidence that the Christ had to suffer and rise again from the dead, and saying, "This Jesus whom I am proclaiming to you is the Christ."

4 And some of them were persuaded and joined Paul and Silas, along with a large number of the God-fearing Greeks and a number of the leading women.

5 But the Jews, becoming jealous and taking along some wicked men from the market place, formed a mob and set the city in an uproar; and attacking the house of Jason, they were seeking to bring them out to the people.

6 When they did not find them, they began dragging Jason and some brethren before the city authorities, shouting, "These men who have upset the world have come here also;

7 and Jason has welcomed them, and they all act contrary to the decrees of Caesar, saying that there is another king, Jesus."

8 They stirred up the crowd and the city authorities who heard these things.

9 And when they had received a pledge from Jason and the others, they released them.

10 The brethren immediately sent Paul and Silas away by night to Berea, and when they arrived, they went into the synagogue of the Jews.

11 Now these were more noble-minded than those in Thessalonica, for they received the word with great eagerness, examining the Scriptures daily to see whether these things were so.

12 Therefore many of them believed, along with a number of prominent Greek women and men.

13 But when the Jews of Thessalonica found out that the word of God had been proclaimed by Paul in Berea also, they came there as well, agitating and stirring up the crowds.

14 Then immediately the brethren sent Paul out to go as far as the sea; and Silas and Timothy remained there.

15 Now those who escorted Paul brought him as far as Athens; and receiving a command for Silas and Timothy to come to him as soon as possible, they left.

16 Now while Paul was waiting for them at Athens, his spirit was being provoked within him as he was observing the city full of idols.

17 So he was reasoning in the synagogue with the Jews and the God-fearing Gentiles, and in the market place every day with those who happened to be present.

18 And also some of the Epicurean and Stoic philosophers were conversing with him. Some were saying, "What would this idle babbler wish to say?" Others, "He seems to be a proclaimer of strange deities,"—because he was preaching Jesus and the resurrection.

19 And they took him and brought him to the Areopagus, saying, "May we know what this new teaching is which you are proclaiming?

20 "For you are bringing some strange things to our ears; so we want to know what these things mean."

21 (Now all the Athenians and the strangers visiting there used to spend their time in nothing other than telling or hearing something new.)

22 So Paul stood in the midst of the Areopagus and said, "Men of Athens, I observe that you are very religious in all respects.

23 "For while I was passing through and examining the objects of your worship, I also found an altar with this inscription, 'TO AN UNKNOWN GOD.' Therefore what you worship in ignorance, this I proclaim to you.

24 "The God who made the world and all things in it, since He is Lord of heaven and earth, does not dwell in temples made with hands;

25 nor is He served by human hands, as though He needed anything, since He Himself gives to all people life and breath and all things;

26 and He made from one man every nation of mankind to live on all the face of the earth, having determined their appointed times and the boundaries of their habitation,

27 that they would seek God, if perhaps they might grope for Him and find Him, though He is not far from each one of us;

28 for in Him we live and move and exist, as even some of your own poets have said, 'For we also are His children.'

29 "Being then the children of God, we ought not to think that the Divine Nature is like gold or silver or stone, an image formed by the art and thought of man.

30 "Therefore having overlooked the times of ignorance, God is now declaring to men that all people everywhere should repent,

31 because He has fixed a day in which He will judge the world in righteousness through a Man whom He has appointed, having furnished proof to all men by raising Him from the dead."

32 Now when they heard of the resurrection of the dead, some began to sneer, but others said, "We shall hear you again concerning this."

33 So Paul went out of their midst.

34 But some men joined him and believed, among whom also were Dionysius the Areopagite and a woman named Damaris and others with them.

As you marked every reference to the Jews, synagogues, and the Word of God, did you notice that Paul had a strategy—an m.o. (method of operation)? He spells it out rather clearly in his letter to the church at Rome when he writes, "For I am not ashamed of the gospel, for it is the power of God for salvation to everyone who believes, to the Jew first and also to the Greek" (Romans 1:16).

Paul's strategy was first to find his own people, the Jews. In Philippi we know there were less than ten Jewish men, for it took a *minyan* (ten men) before a synagogue could be formed, and there was apparently no synagogue there. So Paul went instead to the Jewish place of prayer where he found those who were of the seed of Abraham. His strategy here as elsewhere was to begin to reason with them from the Scriptures, "explaining and giving evidence that the Christ had to suffer and rise again from the dead, and saying, 'This Jesus whom I am proclaiming to you is the Christ [Messiah]'" (Acts 17:3).

In every city on this journey, Paul suffered persecution in one form or another. And yet did you notice that he never deemed himself a failure, nor did he play the role of a coward and go home? He stood firm. You know, Beloved, it's easy to stand firm when you're absolutely convinced that you're right—and right where God wants you.

Think about it...then tomorrow we'll look at Paul's arrival in Corinth. You're going to see that everything you've studied these past few days is so foundational for your understanding of 2 Corinthians.

— D A Y   F O U R —

It has been an awesome experience for my husband, Jack, and me and the Precept Ministries International teaching team to travel each year to Philippi in Greece and teach the book of Philippians onsite to our brothers and sisters traveling with us. We then journey to Thessalonica, Berea, Athens, and Corinth, teaching Paul's epistles on location as we pray together and examine our lives in the light of these truths. Boarding a cruise ship, we sail across the Aegean to Ephesus and there do the same. It's an experience none of us forget—nor do we ever come home and read these scriptures again without seeing these places in our mind's eye. Now that's a vacation with a purpose! Then to top it all off, as we sail the Aegean Sea, we dock at the island of Patmos, where John had his vision recorded for us in the book of Revelation, and we teach that book in such a visual way that suddenly the events in Revelation fall into place and you begin to get a mental image. Unforgettable!

One of the tour's highlights to me is definitely Corinth. No city that we visit more typifies our culture today than that of biblical Corinth. The introduction to the book of 1 Corinthians in the *New Inductive Study Bible* tells us more:

Sin abounded in the cosmopolitan city of Corinth, the chief city of Greece. Corinth overlooked the narrow isthmus that connected the Greek mainland with Peloponnesus and received ships in its two harbors. The Corinthians were intrigued by Greek philosophy and captivated by the disciplined training and athletic events held at the Isthmus. At one time the city was home to at least twelve heathen temples. The people, then, desperately needed to hear the good news of Jesus Christ, the One crucified for sinners.

The worship ceremonies carried out by a thousand temple prostitutes connected with the temple of Aphrodite (the goddess of love) bred blatant immorality throughout Corinth—so much so that the Greek verb translated "to Corinthianize" meant to practice sexual immorality.

Prostitutes openly plied their wares, and meat markets thrived on sales from the sacrifices offered in the temples. The Corinthians ate well, satisfied their sexual urges without condemnation, flirted with the wisdom of men, and did all they could to keep their bodies as beautiful as those of the Greek gods. They loved to listen to great orators. For the 250,000 citizens there were almost two slaves per person. What more did Corinth need? Freedom. Freedom from sin and death. God met that need by blocking Paul at every hand on his second missionary journey until he received the Macedonian call, "Come and help us."[26]

Let's read our final portion of the account in Acts of Paul's second missionary journey and find out what happened in Corinth when Paul arrived with the good news that would set men, women, and children free from the shackles of sin.

As you read, follow the same marking instructions as you did yesterday. Use the bookmark you made. However, you need to add to it two more things. The first is the symbol for marking references to time. I use a clock like this: (⏰) I draw it in green ink over every reference in time. Do this as you do your assignment for today. Also, when you come to any reference to the judgment seat, <u>underline</u> it in red.

When you observe the Word of God, you want to learn to examine the text by asking the five *W*s and an *H*: Who, What, When, Where, Why, and How. So watch *what* happens to *whom* in Corinth, *when* it happens, *where* it happens, *why* it happens, and *how* it happens.

▶ ACTS 18:1-22

¹ After these things he left Athens and went to Corinth.

² And he found a Jew named Aquila, a native of Pontus, having recently come from Italy with his wife Priscilla, because Claudius had commanded all the Jews to leave Rome. He came to them,

³ and because he was of the same trade, he stayed with them and they were working, for by trade they were tent-makers.

⁴ And he was reasoning in the synagogue every Sabbath and trying to persuade Jews and Greeks.

⁵ But when Silas and Timothy came down from Macedonia, Paul began devoting himself completely to the word, solemnly testifying to the Jews that Jesus was the Christ.

⁶ But when they resisted and blasphemed, he shook out his garments and said to them, "Your blood be on your own heads! I am clean. From now on I will go to the Gentiles."

⁷ Then he left there and went to the house of a man named Titius Justus, a worshiper of God, whose house was next to the synagogue.

8 Crispus, the leader of the synagogue, believed in the Lord with all his household, and many of the Corinthians when they heard were believing and being baptized.

9 And the Lord said to Paul in the night by a vision, "Do not be afraid any longer, but go on speaking and do not be silent;

10 for I am with you, and no man will attack you in order to harm you, for I have many people in this city."

11 And he settled there a year and six months, teaching the word of God among them.

12 But while Gallio was proconsul of Achaia, the Jews with one accord rose up against Paul and brought him before the judgment seat,

13 saying, "This man persuades men to worship God contrary to the law."

14 But when Paul was about to open his mouth, Gallio said to the Jews, "If it were a matter of wrong or of vicious crime, O Jews, it would be reasonable for me to put up with you;

15 but if there are questions about words and names and your own law, look after it yourselves; I am unwilling to be a judge of these matters."

16 And he drove them away from the judgment seat.

17 And they all took hold of Sosthenes, the leader of the synagogue, and began beating him in front of the judgment seat. But Gallio was not concerned about any of these things.

18 Paul, having remained many days longer, took leave of the brethren

and put out to sea for Syria, and with him were Priscilla and Aquila. In Cenchrea he had his hair cut, for he was keeping a vow.

19 They came to Ephesus, and he left them there. Now he himself entered the synagogue and reasoned with the Jews.

20 When they asked him to stay for a longer time, he did not consent,

21 but taking leave of them and saying, "I will return to you again if God wills," he set sail from Ephesus.

22 When he had landed at Caesarea, he went up and greeted the church, and went down to Antioch.

Now before you read further, go back and reflect on what you've seen and marked. Use the following questions to help you do this. If you have time and want to write out the answers to these questions in a separate notebook, do so; otherwise just answer them in your mind:
- Who are the main characters in Acts 18:1-18?
- What happens to them?
- How is Paul received?
- What emotions does he have to deal with during this time?
- What do you learn from marking the time phrases?
- What do you learn about the judgment seat?

On our annual teaching tour of Paul's ministry locations, while we're in Corinth we visit the site of the judgment seat where Paul stood before Gallio, the procounsul of Achaia. Those of the group who wish to then move single file, one by one, past this place of judgment.

It's a sobering experience—a living reminder of a certain day to come, as you'll see with greater clarity when we come to 2 Corinthians 5.

I wonder what was going through Paul's mind when he stood before Gallio? Was he, too, thinking of the time to come when he would stand before Another, before the judgment seat of Christ? Did he whisper a prayer, as I and so many others have done as we stood there in Corinth, that we each would stand before Christ's judgment seat without shame and be able to say, even as Paul did to Timothy, "I have fought the good fight, I have finished the course, I have kept the faith"?[27]

Paul went through many trials and afflictions to get to Corinth, and his journey was not yet complete—but he knew that he knew he was in the will of God. Nothing, Beloved—absolutely nothing—brings greater peace in the midst of suffering than to know that you're where God would have you to be.

I love God's words to Paul in Acts 18:9-10: "Do not be afraid any longer, but go on speaking and do not be silent; for I am with you, and no man will attack you in order to harm you, for I have many people in this city."

Paul was afraid—the tense of the verb "do not be afraid" is present, which means he was in a state of fear. Have you ever thought of the great apostle Paul being fearful? No, probably not. We forget, don't we, that the heroes of the faith are people just like us, people who must battle the same emotions and deal with the same fears. The fear of man. The fear of shame. The fear of suffering. The fear of rejection. The fear of _____; you fill in the blank. What are you fearful of?

Paul was afraid! Thus he was given the Lord's imperative, His command: *Do not be afraid.* The Lord was telling Paul, "Stop being afraid—it's all right. Go on speaking. Don't let fear silence you. I am with you."

That's all Paul had to hear. Listen to the next words: "And he settled there a year and six months, teaching the word of God among them."

Just to know that you're in His will brings peace—and the ability to continue to do what He has called you to do. Without that knowledge there's either a confusion that can immobilize you or a harried scurrying about as you try to do more than God ever intended for you to do. I know, precious one, I know—after thirty-five years of walking with Christ, I know. There is nothing more valuable than knowing, "This is the way, walk in it."[28] It gives you the strength and confidence to settle in and persevere.

– D A Y   F I V E –

Has the pressure ever been so great that you thought you were going to die—or so stressful that you wish you would?

Maybe you're there right now. Or perhaps it's not as bad as that. Maybe it's just an unrelenting, incessant pressure that won't seem to go away. In fact, you're thinking that you're almost beyond your limit of endurance.

How are you going to make it, Beloved?

Although I am full of questions today, let me ask one more. Do you know anyone else who's been where you are—*and made it?* I'm talking about getting through it victoriously...someone who "made it" in such a way that it created a sense of awe when you heard about it or watched it?

Do you know *why* this person made it? *How* he or she made it? Why not ask?

Second Corinthians begins in an unusual way for one of Paul's epistles, for usually he seems reluctant to talk about his trials and difficulties. If you read his writings as a whole, you'll see that he states his emotions but never dwells on them. Yet he never begins any of his other letters the way he begins what we call the second epistle to the Corinthians. Take a few minutes and read through 2 Corinthians 1:1-11 so you can see what I am talking about. (The full text of 2 Corinthians is in the back of this book, beginning on page 235.)

As you read through the first eleven verses of this epistle, you'll find it most insightful if you'll mark three repeated key words. (And at this point, may I suggest that you begin a new bookmark of key words for 2 Corinthians.) Here are the key words:

- First, mark any reference to *affliction* or *suffering* (with a red overline, as you learned in Day Three).
- Second, mark every reference to *comfort.*
- Third, mark every reference to *death.* I usually draw a black tombstone and color it brown.

As you do this, ask the Lord to open the eyes of your understanding, as Scripture says, so you can behold wonderful things from His Word.[29] It's a good habit of dependence to develop whenever you read the Bible.

Now stop and look over the key words you marked in 2 Corinthians 1:1-11. Do you notice that when we undergo pressure, its purpose is the comfort and salvation of others? In other words, when others in similar situations of pressure can see that we can make it, that we're going to survive, it helps them. If we made it, so can they. And we make it, Beloved, because of what? That's right! We make it, because when we belong to God, whatever touches us also touches Him—and He is there as our Father God to comfort us. He's the Father of mercies and the God of all comfort.

I'll never forget when I sat down at a table opposite Ruth Graham and we talked about our prodigal sons, who now blessedly are no longer prodigals but bring joy to our hearts. But at the time of our conversation, there was nothing but pain associated with my beloved Tommy. Ruth had just finished writing *Prodigals and Those Who Love Them*. And although the book wasn't yet published, I knew it would be out soon. However, what was even better than the book was being able to share "mother to mother" with Ruth, to find the commonality of not only our horrendous burden but also how God enabled us to endure it, the way He comforted us.

Naturally I grieved that Ruth or any parent would have to go through such pain, but I couldn't help telling her how much it comforted me to know that she, too, had been there, that she understood, that she had endured. I wept with gratitude for my fellow sufferer who could comfort me with the comfort she had received from our precious Lord.

Paul wrote that the affliction he and his companions endured in Asia burdened them "excessively, beyond our strength" (2 Corinthians 1:8). It's one thing to endure something yourself as a leader, but when those who are with you also suffer, it makes it even harder.

What it was that Paul had to endure we don't know. We can try to guess, to surmise—but why? If we needed the specifics, God would have spelled them out.

I think it's best this way, because the word that Paul uses for "affliction," *thlipsis,* in the Greek means a pressure, a pressing; anything that burdens the spirit. Anything! If Paul had told us what it was, then we might have missed the point. The point is that whatever brings pressure, whatever burdens you—or to put it in modern-day terminology, whatever stresses you out—God is there with adequate comfort.

The text says in verse 4 that He comforts us in "all" our affliction. And the more intense the suffering, the more abundant the comfort. In other words, He assures us, precious one, that we can never "out-suffer" His comfort.

And what about those who shared in Paul's sufferings? They, too, shared in God's comfort. In other words, sharing suffering isn't bad, because without it you would miss the awesomeness of His comfort.

"That's all right," you may feel like saying; "I'll do without the suffering." It would be a natural response, wouldn't it? But also an uneducated one, a biblically illiterate one. Especially if you want a heart for God. Who is comforting you? God, of course! Has He suffered? Does God know pain? Oh yes, He knows.

In Genesis we read how "the LORD saw that the wickedness of man was great on the earth, and that every intent of the thoughts of his heart was only evil continually." Then we read his response: "The LORD was sorry that He had made man on the earth, and He was grieved in His heart."[30] Only one man—Noah—had remained righteous out of the whole lot. And God was grieved. Maybe you can relate, maybe those who are family or fellow workers are all living in ways that literally eat at your heart.

Later in the Old Testament we read these words that God spoke about His "wife," Israel: "How I have been hurt by their adulterous hearts which turned away from Me, and by their eyes which played the harlot after their idols."[31] Maybe your mate has committed adultery—maybe he or she lives in habitual immorality. *God understands.*

God watched His Son die the death of all deaths—have you lost a child to death? Or perhaps you're losing a child to death even now. *God understands.*

Have you thought your heart would break—burst wide open because of sin? Jesus' heart burst. This was proved by the blood and the water that gushed out when the Roman soldiers pierced his side to see if he was dead.[32] Jesus, God in the flesh, died of a heart broken by sin.

Without first experiencing the pressure, you would miss the comfort that God alone can give. The Greek word translated as "comfort" in this text is an interesting one: *parakaleo*. It means "to call near, or alongside," and it's the verb form of the same word Jesus used for the Holy Spirit as our Comforter[33]—the One whom He promised would indwell us after He ascended to the Father.

When you and I suffer affliction, the Lord draws near and He comforts us.

The second reason you wouldn't want to miss affliction is given in 2 Corinthians 1:4,6. It's a reason I've mentioned already, but it bears mentioning again so we don't forget it: *Our suffering always benefits others.* Think with me of just two worldwide ministries that have been born out of suffering, ministries that have brought untold comfort to many who might otherwise not have known it—the prison ministry of Chuck Colson and the ministry to those with disabilities by Joni Eareckson Tada. If Chuck Colson hadn't gone from the White House to prison, would he ever have understood what it's like to live behind bars? Would there have ever been a Prison Fellowship? And if my dear friend Joni had never become paralyzed as she dove from a raft one sunny afternoon, would she have even thought of the handicapped, let alone become a source of hope, encouragement, and practical help to them through Joni and Friends?

And what about that person you've been able to comfort, strengthen, and support because you understand, because you've been in a situation where you knew God in a way you had not known Him before you suffered? Others saw your example of endurance, and they endured.

What greater joy could there be, Beloved, than knowing that whatever trial or tragedy you experienced under the hand of your sovereign God was not wasted but used? This is what has brought such solace to the hearts of Bob and Diane Vereen, ambassadors at-large for Precept Ministries International. The tragic, seemingly unnecessary death of their twenty-three-year-old son in a careless traffic incident—and the way they dealt with it—has helped so many.

Bob and Diane endured what was beyond their strength to endure, which brings us to the third insight we can gain on affliction from this passage: God carries us beyond what we would otherwise be able to endure. As Paul says in 2 Corinthians 1:9, "We had the sentence of death within ourselves so that we would not trust in ourselves," and that's because of verse 8: "We were burdened excessively, beyond our strength." When we go beyond our limit, then we experience the supernatural intervention of God and we know that we know that it's God. And we'll never forget it. It will be an genuine experience that will always remind us of the total sufficiency of His grace—grace perfected, brought to completion in our weakness.

Severe affliction like this is a good reminder of our utter impotence without Him. That can be a very humbling experience—but whatever humbles us is worthy of embracing, for God draws near to the humble, but resists the proud.[34]

The fourth and final thing we want to notice that affliction like this produces is corporate prayer. One of the things I like to do as I read through my *New Inductive Study Bible* is mark every reference to prayer. I use the suggested marking and color the word pink. Then I sometimes write *Prayer* in the wide margin so that it really stands out. It's a wonderful way to get a biblical perspective on prayer. Paul writes in 2 Corinthians 1:10-11 that God "delivered us from so great a peril of death, and will deliver us, He on whom we have set our hope. And He will yet deliver us, you also joining in helping us through your prayers, so that thanks may be given by many persons on our behalf for the favor bestowed on us through the prayers of many."

Oh, the importance and power of prayer! Just from this verse alone we learn that we help others through our prayers. God is sovereign. He rules supremely over all. Yet we help others through prayer! His favor is actually bestowed upon people because of the prayers of others. How many stories I have heard of how people were suddenly led to pray for someone, sometimes across oceans and continents, without knowing that the person for whom they were praying was at that moment in great danger or need. The burden was there and they couldn't stop until the pressure to pray was gone. Later—sometimes hours later, other times days or months later—they would hear how the person's life had been sustained or preserved at the very hour they had been called to prayer by the Spirit of God.

This is grace—grace that, when appropriated, brings peace. Isn't that the greeting, or should I say blessing, that Paul pronounced as he began his letter? Won't you join me in asking our God to reveal this truth to our hearts?

> *O Father, make us ever mindful of Your grace—grace that*
> *brings to Your children all the comfort they'll ever need in*
> *any affliction. And may we realize that when we appropri-*
> *ate this lavish, extravagant grace You have poured out on*
> *us, our hearts will be at peace...for we have residing*
> *within the Prince of Peace.*

Be still, our souls—rest. The Father of all mercies and the God of all comfort is near.

MEMORY VERSES

Blessed be the God and Father of our Lord Jesus Christ, the Father of mercies and God of all comfort, who comforts us in all our affliction so that we will be able to comfort those who are in any affliction with the comfort with which we ourselves are comforted by God.

2 CORINTHIANS 1:3-4

SMALL-GROUP DISCUSSION QUESTIONS

1. As we begin our study from 2 Corinthians, we watch Paul move from city to city, taking along Silas and Timothy. Why did Paul make this second missionary journey? And how did he know which churches to visit?

2. How would you describe Paul's heart for the church?

3. What was Paul's method of operation when he arrived in a city? What did he do in the synagogues?

4. How did the people respond to Paul's ministry? What emotions does he experience?

5. What forms of suffering and persecution do we see in believers' lives today?

6. What is God's purpose in our suffering and persecution? What do we learn about this from 2 Corinthians 1:3-5?

APPLICATION:

7. How can you be sensitive to the leadership of the Holy Spirit and listen with your heart for His guidance?

8. Look at what the Lord told Paul in Acts 18:10. What can most help you not to be afraid to speak the truth or preach the gospel?

9. If you desire to live a godly life, and are faithful to proclaim the gospel where you are, and your prayer is, "Lord give me a heart like Yours"—what can you expect in how you are treated by other people?

10. How can you stand firm and persevere in the midst of persecution and affliction?

11. Where do you find comfort? Do you seek it from others, or do you run to the Father of mercies and God of all comfort?

12. Are you an encouraging example to others in how you look to God for comfort and in how you endure?

13. Spend time in prayer for one another, and for those who are suffering. Ask God to comfort them with His comfort and to take away every fear.

---

1. 2 Corinthians 1:8.
2. 2 Corinthians 1:15-18.
3. 2 Corinthians 2:4; 7:8.
4. 2 Corinthians 7:5.

5. 2 Corinthians 2:13. Here we see Paul without peace because of concern for someone he loved—in this case, his coworker Titus.
6. 2 Corinthians 6:11-14; 7:2; 11:13-14.
7. 2 Corinthians 10:7-10.
8. 2 Corinthians 11:5-6; 12:11-12.
9. 2 Corinthians 12:13.
10. 2 Corinthians 11:3-4.
11. 2 Corinthians 12:7-9.
12. 2 Corinthians 12:20–13:2.
13. 2 Timothy 4:7-8.
14. 1 Corinthians 11:1; Philippians 3:17-19, paraphrased.
15. 2 Timothy 4:6-18.
16. John 14:6.
17. Acts 9:15-16.
18. 1 Corinthians 15:9.
19. 1 Corinthians 15:8.
20. Philippians 3:5.
21. From *The New Inductive Study Bible* (Eugene, Oreg.: Harvest House, 2000), 1794.
22. From *The New Inductive Study Bible,* 1779.
23. Proverbs 3:5-6.
24. Psalm 37:23.
25. Acts 9:15-16.
26. *The New Inductive Study Bible,* 1848.
27. 2 Timothy 4:7.
28. Isaiah 30:21.
29. Psalm 119:18.
30. Genesis 6:5-6.
31. Ezekiel 6:9.
32. John 19:34.
33. John 14:16, KJV.
34. James 4:6.

c h a p t e r

2

RESOLVING CONFLICTS

– D A Y   O N E –

Relationships are the single most important thing in our lives. Money, fame, notoriety—apart from solid healthy relationships with others—are devastatingly empty achievements that cruelly imprison the soul in solitary confinement. Shut up alone, where there's no one to talk to except a self that cares about no one else except itself. What horrific companionship!

When I even sense there might be the slightest schism between myself and another, my mind has trouble focusing on anything else. Rehearsals of conversations and incidents, remembrances of a look, questions about how and what and when and why—all these bombard my mind.

I can be teaching from the platform, talking to a person on the phone, meeting with my peers, dealing with the business issues of the day with the office staff, taking a shower, putting on my makeup, talking to family, preparing dinner for Jack and myself and all the time be haunted by the crack—real or unreal—in a relationship.

Nothing brings peace or quietness in my inner man until I do what I can to resolve it. To find out the whys and wherefores, to explain, to lay the matter to rest. And until then there's no real peace in my soul. The praise of others, the plaudits of a task well done—even the affirmation of other relationships doesn't bring rest to my soul.

You would think at my age, at this period of my life in Christ, I would be able to handle it better—but I can't until I do what I can to resolve it. Can you relate, my friend? Or are you able to throw those things off—to put them out of sight and out of mind?

I wish I were able to do that…

How well I understand Paul's torment—his eagerness to hear from the Corinthians that all was well between them, his desire to explain, to resolve their differences. As I said in the preceding week's study, it helps to know that others have been where you've been—and to learn from how they dealt with it.

That's what we'll see this week as we study 2 Corinthians 1:12–2:17: handling broken relationships and people broken by their sin.

Some in the church at Corinth were openly opposed to Paul. They simply didn't like him, and they let it be known. Everything he did was suspect, and the slightest supposed failure became justification for their stance. It wasn't easy for Paul. Of all the churches he established, none caused him greater distress or demanded more of him than the church at Corinth. And yet the very thing that caused him such pain and torment is being used of God to bring instruction by example to those who are dealing with difficult relationships and the issue of forgiving and comforting those who have wounded you deeply yet eventually came to their senses.

I think at this point, Beloved, it will help for us to stop listening to me and see what I'm talking about in 2 Corinthians 1:12-18. Read through this portion of Paul's letter in the back of this book. As you do, this time color-code the following:

- Mark every reference to Paul (or to Paul and his companions, which means you would mark every *we* and *us* that refers to them). You might want to color these references blue.
- Mark every reference to the Corinthians in orange or another color of your choosing.
- Underline occurrences of *I wrote* and *we wrote*.
- Mark *proud confidence* in a distinctive way. Later you'll mark *boasting* the same way, as this is the literal meaning of this word in verse 12. You could box it in green and color it pink on the inside. (By the way, I simply make these suggestions because some like more guidance on how to mark.)

- Also mark every reference or indication of time, because sequence is going to be important in untangling this schism between Paul and the Corinthians.
- Put a circle around *understand*—after all, it's an important word when it comes to good relationships!

When you finish, review what you learned by marking these words. What do you learn about Paul? about the Corinthians? In what areas does Paul seem to be justifying himself? Think about it, and we'll look at this tomorrow.

– D A Y   T W O –

The misunderstanding that wedged itself between Paul and the Corinthians so consumed Paul that this and a resultant explanation of his ministry became the subject of the first seven chapters of this epistle. Only in chapters 8 and 9 does he turn to another issue, the issue of giving. Then in chapters 10 through 13 Paul goes back to their relationship, and this time he has to talk to them quite strongly regarding the authenticity of his apostolic authority—which some doubted.

In all this, you and I are going to discover some awesome biblical truths and at the same time touch on so many issues that hit us today right where we live and struggle in our quest for a heart for God.

Now what was the fracas in Corinth about? Some in the church had gotten the ears of the others (isn't that often the way it is in many churches?) and were telling them, in essence, "If you read any of Paul's letters, you'd better read between the lines because Paul doesn't say what he means or mean what he says. Just look! He said he was coming here to Corinth, but he didn't!"

That's why Paul wrote, "We write nothing else to you than what you read and understand" (1:13). In other words: "Don't read between the lines. My words say exactly what I mean and can be understood by simply taking them at face value."

The Corinthians don't have to be ashamed of Paul. In fact, Paul,

Silas, and Timothy are their reason to be proud (1:14). Paul and the others can literally boast that they didn't conduct themselves in fleshly wisdom toward the Corinthians. Rather, they had behaved in holiness and godly sincerity—in the grace of God before others and before the Corinthians (1:12).

The whole issue Paul's detractors were using against him was that Paul didn't keep his word and come to Corinth, as he had written that he was going to do.

And they were right. Paul didn't come as he said he was going to. But is that sufficient cause to demean the man? That's the question. And it's a question that must be investigated.

How quick our flesh is...

to believe the worst, or even to relish it!

to attribute bad motives rather than good motives!

to assume rather than investigate!

to look only at what a person does or looks like or acts like and miss that person's heart.

to say, "They'll never change. There's no hope."

Have you been there, Beloved—on either end? The judging or the being judged?

The question is, Have you learned anything?

I've been on both ends. Fortunately, as I have grown in my quest for a heart for God, I've learned about the "wrong" end—unbiblical judging. That's the end I can control.

But what do I do when I'm the recipient of the judging? I'm learning the right response from Paul...as you will also, I pray. For I know, Beloved, how hard it is for you to be misunderstood, unjustly condemned, wrongly perceived.

So let's look at how Paul handled this situation and what it was about him that enabled him to deal with it in such a way that he kept a clear conscience before God.

First of all, Paul faced the issue and dealt with it factually. He admitted that he did intend "at first to come to you, so that you might twice receive a blessing" (verse 15). He was going to pass their way "into Macedonia, and again from Macedonia to come to you, and by you to be helped on my journey to Judea" (verse 16).

When Paul wrote this, the Corinthians believed his intention was to come to them from Ephesus. If this is so, then trace on the map[1] on the next page the journey Paul would have taken. Take him all the way back to Judea. If he was going to Judea he would have sailed into the port of Caesarea, which was the only port in Judea at that time.

When Paul wrote the letter we call 1 Corinthians, what did Paul tell them regarding his plans to visit them? Read 1 Corinthians 16:5-9 and record your insights below.

Does this sound like a different plan from the one in 2 Corinthians? How?

Did you notice the distances Paul would have traveled? Is this why he changed his plans? Or did he write the Corinthians lightly, saying that this was what he was going to do without any intention of ever doing it? Or with the intention of doing it only if it seemed suitable at the moment?

Read through 2 Corinthians 1:15–2:4 and mark the text as you did yesterday. Only this time also mark…

- the word *affliction.*
- every reference to *sorrow.* You might want to mark these like a downturned mouth and color them red.
- any reference to the emotions Paul experienced.

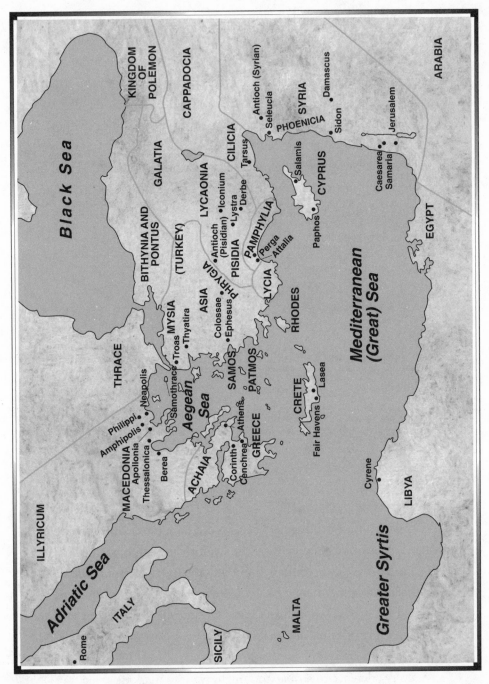

When you finish, list below what you see from the text about Paul's reason for not coming as he had planned.

What emotions did Paul experience in all this? List them below along with the verse number(s) that gave you this information.

We have some exciting, liberating things to see tomorrow. Things that if followed can bring peace to your soul in fractured relationships. Just be thankful, Beloved, that relationships are important to you.

— D A Y   T H R E E —

The whole situation with the Corinthians was stressful, bringing great anguish to Paul's heart. The valiant apostle who sang while chained in a Philippian jail now wept as he sat at a table with quill in hand writing to the Corinthians. It seemed easier to suffer beatings and imprisonment for the furtherance of the gospel than a broken relationship with a church he had birthed through the gospel. He expected animosity from the world but not from those who professed to love and serve the same Savior.

What sustained Paul? What kept him from writing off those who sought to trouble him? What restrained him from using his invested authority as an apostle?

First and foremost, it was a clear conscience. This was what gave Paul "proud confidence." Oh, Beloved, there is nothing that will bring you greater peace and confidence in difficult situations than a conscience that is totally clear, absolutely transparent before God. Nothing hidden. No wrong, fleshly motives. No deceptive or manipulative responses or behavior. But rather a Godlike sincerity. A holiness of behavior, knowing that you have done or will do whatever pleases the Father.

Homer Kent, in his commentary on 2 Corinthians, explains that the term translated "proud confidence"—*kauchesis* in Greek—

> emphasizes the action rather than the contents, so the thought is, "Our act of boasting should be understood in this way." Paul meant that when he and Timothy engaged in justifiable glorying regarding what God had been accomplishing through them, it followed the pattern which he next explained.... These faithful men could glory as they did because it was the testimony of their consciences that God had approved their conduct. The conscience is one's inner consciousness regarding the rightness of his actions. When Christians are enlightened by the Word of God and the Holy Spirit, and then walk in full harmony with that knowledge, their consciences will approve their actions.[2]

Paul's decision to change his travel plans was not one of fleshly wisdom. In this the Corinthians ought to have been proud. The one who established their church was not a man of whom they had to be ashamed; he conducted himself like a man of God.

Paul was so confident in his character and conduct in this matter that he knew that "in the day of our Lord Jesus" (2 Corinthians 1:14) he would be proud of the Corinthians, and they would be proud of him. This was a day ever before Paul, as well it should be before us. For if we kept the day of Christ always in mind, it would act as a purification filter for all our thoughts, words, and deeds.

We'll see later how Paul expounds on the details of that day in chapter 5; however, let's take a few minutes and look at how Paul uses this phrase "in the day of Christ" in other places in his letters. Look up each reference listed here and record what you observe from the text.

1 Corinthians 1:8:

1 Corinthians 5:5:

Philippians 1:6:

Philippians 1:10:

Philippians 2:16:

Paul wanted the Corinthians to "understand until the end" (2 Corinthians 1:13). "The end" is the day of Christ, when our precious Lord returns for His church. It's in this "day"—at this time—that we'll give an account at the judgment seat of Christ of the stewardship of all that our God has bestowed upon us in grace. It was *in* this grace that Paul, Silas, and Timothy conducted themselves in the world and especially toward the Corinthians (2 Corinthians 1:12).

A heart that belongs to God always moves in grace, in graciousness, and in favor toward others. That's the *second* thing you need to remember when you find yourself in divisive situations. Keep your conscience clear and move in grace. You are God's representative, and He is the God of all grace.

Third, as God's representative your yes must be yes—not yes and no. In other words you're never to say "yes" while in your heart you have no intention of doing it—if that's your thinking, then it's "yes and no." God's Word is never yes and no, and ours should not be either. God's yes is always and forever yes; He will never go back on His promises.

Do you realize what would happen in families if we didn't vacillate but said what we meant and followed up on our promises? What an example it would be to our children, and what confidence it would build in our relationships!

Yet, at this point, are you saying, "But, Kay, Paul didn't do what he said he was going to do"?

You're right, but there was another factor that came into play; a *fourth* thing we need to learn from Paul's example. Paul didn't go to Corinth as planned because it wouldn't have been the best for the Corinthians. Listen to his words: "But I call God as witness to my soul, that to spare you I did not come again to Corinth" (1:23). Paul didn't want to cause them more sorrow than he had already caused them, and if he came to Corinth that's what he would have done, because they had failed and Paul had to correct them. Something was wrong, and it couldn't be ignored or covered up.

Love—the agape kind that desires another's highest good—doesn't whitewash sin or allow wrong behavior to continue without confrontation. This is why confrontation—honest, gracious confrontation—is so essential to healthy relationships. A healthy relationship is one that is open. Things aren't buried, covered up, ignored, or denied, because when they are, decay sets in—putrefaction.

Jan Silvious and I have a radio program, *Precept Live with Kay and Jan,* which airs every Sunday evening and puts us into contact with people across the nation. I would guess that 90 percent of the issues we deal with have to do with broken or damaged relationships. After years of counseling, Jan is so strong on the fact that, if you want a relationship with a person, it will take the participation of both parties as well as total honesty. No covering up. If the other person won't do what is right, then you do what you can and move on. It's kind of like what Jesus told the seventy when he sent them out: If they weren't received, they were to shake the dust off their feet in condemnation against their resistance and move on.

There comes a time when you have to be willing to let go and give the "protagonist" time to decide whether or not they value the relationship enough to do what they need to do. Which is the *fifth* thing we need to remember. In 2 Corinthians 1:24 Paul wrote, "Not that we lord it over your faith, but are workers with you for your joy." You can do your part but you cannot force the other person to do his—at least not in a healthy relationship.

Paul was an apostle, he carried that authority, but it didn't make him lord over others. Each of us has but one Lord—and it isn't our pastor, but rather the Great Shepherd of the sheep. Our elders and our pastors are there to work with us and beside us in the process of maturity, but not to dictate to us.

Ray Stedman, a dear brother who before he went to be with the Lord established Peninsula Bible Church in Palo Alto, California, and set up a plurality of teaching leaders there, said that in essence Paul was saying,

"Look, I'm not your boss. If I had come to Corinth the way I had originally planned, after having already paid you a painful visit, it's very likely that my powerful personality, my strong will, my position as a respected apostle would have put such pressure upon you that you would have obeyed me—but without the conviction that I spoke for the Lord. So I did not come, in order that you might preserve freedom to do what God wants, not what I want."

Paul sees himself as a fellow worker, standing alongside them, helping them to understand what God wants so they would enter into the joy of the Lord. But he is not their boss. Leaders in the church are not bosses. This is a common misconception. Many churches look to *the* pastor but you never see that term in Scripture. There are pastors, but never *the* pastor. Churches are not to look to the pastor for authority, for permission to exercise spiritual gifts.

We do not have to ask our pastor whether we can teach in our home or not. We do not have to go to the pastor to get permission to use our spiritual gifts. The pastor does not give them to us. The Lord does, and we are responsible to him for the exercise of the spiritual gifts, not to the pastor. The pastor is our helper; he is there to encourage us and to help us understand these gifts, how to recognize them, but we are not responsible to him for exercising them. He is responsible to his Lord to help us put them with others and to maintain unity within the church, but not to govern what ministry we have. That comes from the Lord himself. He is the head of the church, the body. Peter says that elders are not to be "lord over God's heritage" (1 Peter 5:3, KJV).[3]

Healthy relationships are not built on dictatorships. God is God and He is to be supremely obeyed. However, even our relationship with God isn't that of a dictatorship—rather, it's a familial relationship, a covenant relationship. We have a choice to make, a free will that we exercise. However, we do need to realize that while a sovereign God allows us to choose our way, we will be held responsible for that choice. We cannot choose the consequences. God, because He is God alone, does that.

Graciously, however, He lets us know what the consequences are before we make our choice. They're written in the Word. How clearly this is seen in the book of Deuteronomy where God says to His covenant people, "I have set before you life and death, the blessing and the curse. So choose."[4]

So how did Paul handle the fact that, before God, he knew it was best not to go to Corinth as he had planned and said he would? Remember there were no telephones to pick up, no planes to hop. Travel was long and arduous. Therefore if "in person" was impossible, communication had to be by letter. A letter that he trusted would be read and understood for exactly what the words meant. We'll look at that tomorrow.

And how, Beloved, should we bring this day to a close? First, we need to remember this is not a comprehensive study on dealing with difficult relationships; we're dealing only with the text at hand. Second, it might be good to simply look at the points I've numbered for you in the text, and list them below. Then read through 2 Corinthians 1:12–2:4 and think on these things in the light of your relationships. Is there anything you've seen that you need to apply to your own life? If so, note it in some way, then talk to your God about it. He is the expert on relationships.

— D A Y   F O U R —

Changing your plans is so much easier if it doesn't affect others, but when it does, you leave yourself wide open for criticism.

This is what Paul had to deal with, as do many in leadership positions. It goes with the territory. Although leaders may profess to believe in Jesus Christ and desire to serve Him, they don't always walk in the Spirit. When people who work under a leader are dissatisfied, disgruntled, given to griping, or they're not particularly pleased with the way the ministry or business or organization is being run, then any change in plans becomes grounds for complaint, an opportunity for accusations, an occasion for murmuring, and an opportunity to undermine the leadership.

It took real courage before the Lord for Paul to change his plans, and it cost him great anguish of soul. He loved the Corinthians and couldn't bear to bring more sorrow. So instead of visiting them, he wrote them. So where is that letter? And when was it written?

The letter is not to be found—it's lost, no longer in existence, because in His sovereignty God did not include it in the canon of Scripture. Yet we can understand something about the time of that letter and its chronological relationship to 1 and 2 Corinthians. So let's put the puzzle together so that you'll possibly better understand the occasion of 2 Corinthians and why Paul bares his soul in this epistle like he does nowhere else in any of his preserved epistles.

Let's begin by looking at the following brief passage from 1 Corinthians. As you read the text, underline the phrase, "I wrote."

▶ 1 CORINTHIANS 5:9-11

⁹ I wrote you in my letter not to associate with immoral people;

¹⁰ I did not at all mean with the immoral people of this world, or with the covetous and swindlers, or with idolaters, for then you would have to go out of the world.

11 But actually, I wrote to you not to associate with any so-called brother if he is an immoral person, or covetous, or an idolater, or a reviler, or a drunkard, or a swindler—not even to eat with such a one.

If you were numbering the letters Paul says he wrote to Corinth, where would you put 1 Corinthians in relationship to what you just observed?

Next read 2 Corinthians 2:1-4, which is printed out below and again mark the phrase "I wrote." Also, box in the phrase, "I would not come to you in sorrow again."

◑ 2 CORINTHIANS 2:1-4

1 But I determined this for my own sake, that I would not come to you in sorrow again.

2 For if I cause you sorrow, who then makes me glad but the one whom I made sorrowful?

3 This is the very thing I wrote you, so that when I came, I would not have sorrow from those who ought to make me rejoice; having confidence in you all that my joy would be the joy of you all.

4 For out of much affliction and anguish of heart I wrote to you with many tears; not so that you would be made sorrowful, but that you might know the love which I have especially for you.

Now the question is this: Is what Paul wrote in these verses a reference to 1 Corinthians or to another letter now lost?

From the content of 1 Corinthians, which was a response to letters Paul had received from the house of Chloe regarding the divisions and quarrels within the church,[5] as well as a response to specific questions the church had written to him about,[6] it appears that 1 Corinthians is not the letter Paul referred to in 2 Corinthians 2:3-4. Which means we now have a third letter in the mix, plus the letter we know as 2 Corinthians. Where does it fit? Write out your insight by putting these four letters—(a) our book of 1 Corinthians, (b) our book of 2 Corinthians, (c) the letter Paul refers to in 1 Corinthians 5:9-11, and (d) the letter he refers to in 2 Corinthians 2:3-4—in the order in which you think they were written.

Now let's see if we can piece together what happened. Although it may not be the most exciting thing you'll read, this is good information. It helps put Paul's relationship with the Corinthians in context, it broadens your knowledge, and it also helps you see just how much anguish this conflict caused Paul.

Here's an outline to follow as we look at the possible order of events:

1. Acts 18:1-17 records Paul's first visit to Corinth.
2. Paul wrote the letter mentioned in 1 Corinthians 5—a letter now lost—telling the Corinthians how they were to deal with immoral people who call themselves Christians. This we'll call Letter Number One.
3. The church wrote back to Paul with questions.[7] This letter was apparently delivered to Paul by Stephanas, Fortunatus, and Achaicus.[8]
4. Paul answered their questions and addressed the problems in Corinth with a letter preserved for us in the Word of God as 1 Corinthians (Letter Number Two). We believe it was written from Ephesus.[9]
5. Paul made a second trip to Corinth, in all probability on his third missionary journey. Although a visit to Corinth is not specifically noted in the account of this journey in Acts, we do read that Paul "came to Greece."[10] This short visit seems to be alluded to in

2 Corinthians 2:1—"But I determined this for my own sake, that I would not come to you in sorrow again." This could not refer to Paul's first visit to Corinth because that was not in sorrow. The sorrow came later, probably in the second visit, when opposition to Paul would have been aroused by those Paul referred to later in 2 Corinthians.

6. Paul then wrote what we'll call Letter Number Three (since it was actually the third letter we know of that he wrote to the Corinthians). As we've seen, Letter Number Three is referred to in 2 Corinthians 2:3-4.

This is the very thing I wrote you, so that when I came, I would not have sorrow from those who ought to make me rejoice; having confidence in you all that my joy would be the joy of you all. For out of much affliction and anguish of heart I wrote to you with many tears; not so that you would be made sorrowful, but that you might know the love which I have especially for you.

Apparently Letter Number Three was taken by Titus to Corinth, a conclusion based on the following scriptures. Look up each one and see what you learn about Titus and the timing of Paul's letters. As you read these verses, make sure you underline every time you see, "I wrote."

2 Corinthians 7:6-8:

2 Corinthians 7:12-13:

2 Corinthians 12:14 (This is an important verse, as it tells you how many times Paul visited Corinth.):

2 Corinthians 12:18 (Notice the verb tenses in this verse.):

Then (and this is where you see the anguish of Paul's heart) read 2 Corinthians 2:12-13 as one sentence, not as two separate verses. (As you look at this sentence, check out Troas on the map again.) Note what opportunity in Troas Paul mentions in this passage—and what happened.

7. After Paul found Titus and received his wonderful report of the Corinthians' response to Letter Number Three, he took quill in hand again and wrote the letter we're now studying, the one chosen by our Father to be included in His Word as the book of 2 Corinthians.

And why did Paul have to write a letter like Letter Number Three that caused them so much sorrow? We'll see the reason as we continue our study, since the first seven chapters of 2 Corinthians deal with this whole situation.

As we bring this day to a close, Beloved, I want us to see another example in Paul of a heart for God:

Who was right—and yet sought out the hurt brothers and sisters?

And who moved first in reconciliation—

the one who was right or those who were wrong?

The one who was right!

Paul communicated to the sorrowful Corinthians through a letter delivered by Titus. It was really just like what His Lord taught His disciples on that day on the mount overlooking the Sea of Galilee: If they remember that their brother has something against them, then they're to leave their offering at the altar and first go and be reconciled to that brother.[11] This is why Paul bypassed the opportunity for ministry in Troas, took his leave of them, and went on to Macedonia looking for Titus; his relationship with the Corinthians was foremost in his heart.

And what about us, Beloved, when we know that another person has something against us? Just how important are they—in God's eyes and in ours?

> *O Father, in 1 John 4 You tell us that herein is love, not that we first loved You, but that You loved us first and sent Your Son to us. May I, may my friend, have a heart like Yours; may we move toward others in love. For Jesus' sake…and for the sake of others… Amen.*

— D A Y   F I V E —

Would you pray, "Lord, give me a heart for You," if it meant you had to forgive someone who hurt you in one way or another? This is what we want to look at in our final day of study this week as we look at the rest of the second chapter in 2 Corinthians.

Read through 2 Corinthians 2:1-11 again today. Continue to mark every reference to *sorrow, love,* and *comfort,* as you did in 2 Corinthians 1. Also mark "I wrote" and any reference to *forgiveness* or *forgiving.*

When you finish, come back to this page and summarize in your own words the situation Paul is dealing with in these verses.

Now, even though you may have just written it out above, list below exactly what you observe from marking the verses on *forgiveness*. Number your insights: 1, 2, 3, etc.

Paul is very cautious in what he says—here again we see his heart for God. God's heart is never to discourage a person so they can never recover. Rather, reconciliation and restoration are always on God's heart. He is the God of all comfort, the God of all hope. His mercies are new every morning, and His compassions fail not.[12]

Consider verse 5:

But if any has caused sorrow, he has caused sorrow not to me, but in some degree—in order not to say too much—to all of you.

It seems that the guilty man who now needs assurance of forgiveness had attacked Paul in some way, and in attacking Paul he committed an offense against the Corinthians.

Yet the matter was over as far as Paul was concerned. The majority in the church at Corinth apparently punished the man according to the rule of church order, and the man received his punishment and learned from it. What the man did we aren't told, and Paul isn't about to rehash it. The man's sorrow is great enough.

Isn't that grace? To let it go, to not continue bringing it up? This shows a true heart for God as does Paul's instruction that they're to forgive the person and comfort him. Why? Hear again Paul's heart: Paul doesn't want this man to be "overwhelmed by excessive sorrow" (2:7). Excessive sorrow over sin can demoralize a person and cripple him emotionally so that he believes he can never hope to be used of God again in any capacity.

Some of the sweetest words in the world, no matter what language, are those that say, "I forgive you." It's really another way of saying, "I love you with the love of the Lord," as we can see in Paul's instructions to the Ephesians to "be kind to one another, tender-hearted, forgiving each other, just as God in Christ also has forgiven you. Therefore be imitators of God [have a heart like God's]...and walk in love, just as Christ also loved you and gave Himself up for us, an offering and a sacrifice to God as a fragrant aroma."[13]

Paul imitated Christ and forgave this man, and the Corinthians were to do the same. And they were to do it in a tangible way—not just saying in their hearts or with their mouths that they would forgive. Rather they were to comfort him. They were to reaffirm their love for him. In other words, to go to him and let him know that they really did love him with God's agape love that desires another's highest good.

When Paul wrote Letter Number Three, it was a letter that would put the Corinthians to the test to make sure this situation was dealt with in a way pleasing to the Lord and befitting those who call themselves His followers. Would they be obedient? We'll look at this more closely when we get to 2 Corinthians 7.

This whole issue of forgiveness was not, however, just for the sake of the man who needed forgiving, but for the church who also needed to forgive. Listen to Paul:

> For to this end also I wrote, so that I might put you to the test, whether you are obedient in all things. But one whom you forgive anything, I forgive also; for indeed what I have forgiven, if I have forgiven anything, I did it for your sakes in the presence of Christ, so that no advantage would be taken of us by Satan; for we are not ignorant of his schemes. (2 Corinthians 2:9-11)

When we refuse to have a heart for the God who commands us to forgive, then we're open targets for Satan's schemes. His devices are to divide. To cut us off from one another that he might devour us in sorrow or bitterness and to cut us off from the blessing of God that comes when we forgive as God would have us forgive.

When we don't forgive, Beloved, rest assured Satan will take advantage of our disobedience and move in like a roaring lion. Not only that, but when we refuse to forgive—as God not only commands us to do but also modeled for us in our redemption—then God will not forgive us.

I know that sounds tough and maybe not like God, but those are the words of His Son Jesus Christ in Matthew 6:14-15. Listen:

> For if you forgive others for their transgressions, your heavenly Father will also forgive you. But if you do not forgive others, then your Father will not forgive your transgressions.

Sometime, maybe later today, you might want to read Matthew 18:15-35. The conclusion—the point of Jesus' illustration—is verse 35, so don't miss it:

My heavenly Father will also do the same to you, if each of you does not forgive his brother from your heart.

And in the parable Jesus gave, what happened to the one who wouldn't forgive? He was turned over to the torturers! This is exactly what happens when we don't forgive—we're tortured! Forgiveness withheld does the greatest damage to the one who refuses to give it.

When you forgive, remember and rest assured, Beloved, that this does not release the offender from the offense; they still have to answer to God. But it does release the offended. Satan will have no foothold there, because you're being so like God.

Well, my friend, what are you going to do with what you've learned this week? May I suggest that we lift up our hearts to God in prayer and ask Him to cleanse us with the washing of His Word, that we might be presented to Him someday without spot or blemish.

Before God, you might ask yourself the following questions (and perhaps write the names of those whom God brings to your mind). Ask God if there is…

- anyone you need to move toward in restoring or rebuilding a relationship.
- anyone to whom you promised something and didn't fulfill it as you should.
- anyone you didn't deal with graciously, as God would have you do.
- anyone whom you need to forgive.
- any place where the enemy has taken advantage of you because you haven't moved in forgiveness toward another, although the offense was not directly against you.
- anyone you need to comfort because of excessive sorrow over sin.

Whatever God shows you, Beloved, act upon it. It will bring such cleansing and peace.

MEMORY VERSES

For if I cause you sorrow, who then makes me glad but
the one whom I made sorrowful? This is the very thing I
wrote you, so that when I came, I would not have sorrow
from those who ought to make me rejoice; having confidence in you all that my joy would be the joy of you all.
For out of much affliction and anguish of heart I wrote
to you with many tears; not so that you would be made
sorrowful, but that you might know the love which I
have especially for you.

2 CORINTHIANS 2:2-4

SMALL-GROUP DISCUSSION QUESTIONS

1. From what we see in 1 Corinthians 16:5-9 and 2 Corinthians
   1:12-18, what seems to have happened between Paul and the
   Corinthians?
2. What was Paul's reason for not coming to Corinth as he had planned?
3. Last week we saw an emotion in Paul—fear—that may surprise us.
   In 2 Corinthians 1:15–2:4, what other emotions do you see Paul
   experiencing?
4. Why does Paul deal with forgiveness in 2 Corinthians 2:1-11?
5. What part does forgiveness have in our difficult relationships?
6. What does Ephesians 4:32–5:2 teach us about forgiveness? How are
   we to forgive?
7. According to Matthew 6:14-15, what is the result of unforgiveness?
   What does it produce in a person's life?

APPLICATION:

8. Paul had a clear conscience before God. From what you see in
   1 Corinthians 1:8 and 5:5 and in Philippians 1:6,10 and 2:16, what
   can we keep in mind to help us keep a clear conscience before God?

9. Briefly discuss the points in this week's lesson that can help us deal with being misunderstood.
10. How can we handle difficult relationships that will show we have a heart for God?
11. Are you experiencing a difficult relationship that is breaking your heart? What can you do about it?
12. Why is it important for you to keep your word, instead of saying one thing and meaning another?
13. Do you know of any situations in which you have said that you forgive someone, but you have continued to bring up the issue that caused the sorrow? If you want a heart for God, what must you do about this?

------

1. From *The New Inductive Study Bible* (Eugene, Oreg.: Harvest House, 2000), 1794.
2. Homer A. Kent Jr., *A Heart Opened Wide* (Grand Rapids, Mich.: Baker, 1982), 38.
3. Ray C. Stedman, *Expository Studies in 2 Corinthians: Power Out of Weakness* (Waco, Tex.: Word, 1982), 25-26.
4. Deuteronomy 30:19.
5. 1 Corinthians 1:10-11.
6. 1 Corinthians 7:1.
7. 1 Corinthians 7:1.
8. 1 Corinthians 16:17.
9. 1 Corinthians 16:8.
10. Acts 20:2.
11. Matthew 5:23-24.
12. Lamentations 3:22-23, KJV.
13. Ephesians 4:32–5:2.

FINDING ADEQUACY IN CHRIST

– D A Y   O N E –

I *nadequate!* Is that a word you dread? A word that always takes you down another peg, closer and closer to nothingness? A word, my friend, that you *feel?*

I could have done better...
   I should have tried harder...
      I didn't give it my best...
         If only I had worked at it more...
            Maybe if I had only...
   I want so badly to have succeeded...
         to have pleased them more,
         to make them happy,
         to have it work out differently,
         to make them proud,
         to be used of God.
   I wish I could go back and do it again.
      Why didn't I think of that sooner?
         Why did I wait so long?
            Why didn't I get my act together?
Why am I passed over? Unrecognized? Ignored? Unvalued? Not respected?
      Why him and not me? Why her?
      Why didn't they ask me? Why wasn't I chosen?

Why, when
    I've tried so hard and every way I know, didn't I at least
    make the team?
        Inadequate.
If only they had asked…
    had cared…
        had considered…
            had done what I asked them to do…
        would have listened…
    would have taken the time…
  then maybe it would have been different.

But it's not different—and it probably never will be, no matter how hard I try. No matter what recommendations, commendations I get from others it will probably never happen—because…
        I guess I'm just inadequate.

Do you know how many people battle this sense of inadequacy? I am among them when I forget the truths I'm about to share with you. And you know what? As I get to know people or learn about their lives, I'm shocked at how many others there are who even after achieving great things in the eyes of the world and in the eyes of Christendom still battle feelings of inadequacy.

I cannot help but wonder what would happen if they could sit down and grasp the awesome *truths* laid out in 2 Corinthians and other books of the Bible and find out what God says about any child of His being inadequate—truths written under the divine inspiration of the Sovereign God of the universe.

I have been before Him on my knees, in tears asking Him to forgive me for forgetting these truths, for failing to live in the light of them, for looking to man rather than to God, for allowing what I see, feel, and think is necessary or advantageous or strategic to overtake what I know is truth. *I am adequate because I am a child of God.* And nothing, absolutely nothing else matters but to walk in the knowledge of that adequacy. To live accordingly in total dependence upon Him alone. If I do that—and if that alone is my one passion, my single goal—then I'll have succeeded in the eyes of the *only* One who really counts, almighty God. And I will not be found inadequate.

He alone is the one to whom we answer. Oh, it may not seem like that, and the world and the people in it don't want you to even begin to think that, because the whole world lies in the power of the Evil One who would destroy us with his lies. But it's true.

Pure truth. Unadulterated. Absolute. Unchanging. Eternal.

And my prayer, Beloved, is that you'll have at least a glimpse of it through this study.

> *O Father, how I long that You would use Your servant now to minister to this precious one so that he or she might understand our adequacy in You. Free this beloved soul from the pressures of conformity to the world; show this son or daughter of Yours how to stand against all the wiles and schemes of the Evil One and to detect his lies, to bring every thought captive to the obedience of Jesus Christ.*
>
> *Open this dear one's eyes and heart to Your truths expressed through the life of Paul. May we remember that he's a man, human just like us, yet a man who so succeeded in cutting through all the worldly lures, pain, suffering, and rejection that, despite his struggles, he lived a life that he knew was pleasing to You.*
>
> *I thank You that I have been heard and that my adequacy is from You. You have made me adequate and called me to this task, and therefore I am not alone. You are my adequacy. How I thank You for hearing and answering me through the name of our Mediator of the New Covenant, our Lord Jesus Christ.*

Now, just to put you into context as we begin this rich week of study, may I suggest that you take a few minutes to read through 2 Corinthians

2:13–3:6 and mark in a distinctive way every occurrence of the word *adequate* or *adequacy.*

When you finish, make a list below of what you learn by observing and marking the use of this key word in the text. Watch for Paul's question—and his answers.

In the midst of a distressed heart and an anxious spirit, as Paul was looking for Titus, longing for a word from him about the Corinthians' response to his letter, unable to walk through the door opened in Troas because he had to find Titus, Paul's depression and desperation are suddenly brought into perspective as he remembers that he and the others with whom he colabors walk in God's triumph.

Whether this comes before or after he finds Titus and hears of the Corinthians' response to his letter written in tears, we cannot be absolutely certain. Some commentators hold that it was before he found Titus, others after. It seems to me Paul's burst of triumph comes when he finds Titus. However, that it not the issue for us now. The issue is *triumph*—Christ's triumph that we participate in even as the soldiers who walked in the train of their general's Roman *triumphus* (triumph).

Even though at this stage in his life, Paul had maybe never seen such a triumphal entry by a Roman conqueror, maybe he had read of it or heard from another firsthand what it was like. Yet he caught the feeling. As a citizen of Rome, he could not help but sense the drama.

Having formed clearly in Paul's mind, the picture now bursts forth in all its great pomp and majesty as Paul sees that he's led in the triumph of Christ! He's part of the victor's train of triumph. Hallelujah—praise be to God, for the rest of the story *will* be told, no matter what: God *always* leads His own in His triumph in Christ.

Although played out on the streets of Rome—a paltry rehearsal with extras from humanity's stage—it's a vivid, indelible vision of what is yet to come for the church.

Imagine with me the scene Paul may have envisioned: the Roman conqueror coming home to the triumph the Senate bestowed upon all its conquering heroes. Streets overflow with young and old eager to catch a glimpse of the one who broadened their empire and brought home the spoils of war. Trumpets blare, sweet incense and burning spices permeate the air as the priests of their pagan gods lead the triumphal procession, swinging their pots of incense. Flowered garlands decorate the victor's path, their delicate, scented beauty in sharp contrast to the iron chains hobbling the conquered enemies as they followed the chariot of the triumphant hero. The spoils of war, these prisoners are strong men with glistening muscles soon to be torn limb from limb in the arenas, pierced through as they fight one another with ball and chain, sword, or spear, or are executed in some other way that might entertain an increasingly bloodthirsty populace. To the prisoners, the smell of incense is the aroma of death.

The conqueror rides his chariot with pride. He has won the battle, subjugated the enemy, enhanced the treasuries of Rome. A laurel wreath surrounds his brow. His nostrils, once ablaze in war, are now softened by the sweet aroma of life, for he has proven himself adequate to his task.

And in the train of his glory march his valiant warriors as the procession leads them to the temple of Jupiter Capitolinus.[1] There they will make sacrifices to their god.

In Paul's outburst—his eulogy of triumph—this may have been the human illustration he had in mind. Regardless of the details of that image, Paul knew that God would always lead His people in triumph in Christ. Some battles might be lost along the way, but the war would be won. And wherever the battle was fought, God would manifest through His own the sweet aroma of the knowledge of Himself. To those who would be saved by their witness, these believers would be a sweet fragrance of life unto life. To those who refused to believe, who refused to be conquered by the gospel of Jesus Christ, these believers would be a fragrance of death unto death. The dead men refused life and thus someday will partake of the second death, the lake of fire where the worm does not die and the fire is not quenched. But either way—a fragrance either of life or of death—the Christian soldier would be a sweet fragrance in the nostrils of His Commander-in-Chief, because he exuded the fragrance of God's Son, the Lord Jesus Christ.

And who is adequate for these things? You are. I am. Anyone who believes in and receives Jesus Christ is adequate, as we'll see tomorrow.

Ten thousand blessings, Beloved.

— D A Y   T W O —

Who is adequate for victory, for triumph—to be the fragrance of Christ to God? To have Him see and sense again the pleasure that His Son brought Him, the One with whom He was well pleased? Paul was adequate, and he wants us to see that we are too!

Listen to him. Paul is not like many, who simply see a good thing and get on the bandwagon and clean out men's coffers. He doesn't peddle the Word of God, selling what is popular and ear-tickling for the sake of gain. Paul handles the Word of God with sincerity.

The Greek word for sincerity is *eilikrineia* and means clearness. The two parts of this word were derived from *heile,* the sun's ray, and from *krino,* which means "to distinguish." Thus this word has the connotation of being judged by sunlight and tested as genuine. Understanding this word gives us quite a picture, doesn't it, of the purity of Paul's teaching? This is good to know, because what you're about to see is pure truth—reality. And in it, Beloved, you'll discover why you are adequate, where the adequacy comes from, and how it happens.

At this point in his letter—from 2:14 until 7:2—Paul takes an awesome digression and leads us into invaluable truths, incredible insights that not only sustained him but will sustain you. I urge you to embrace them and know the inexpressible sweetness of a life lived in His adequacy.

Read through 2 Corinthians 3:1-11. This time do the following:

* Color every reference to the recipients of this letter in a specific color. Use orange if you like, which is the color suggested in the *New Inductive Study Bible* for the recipients of all the epistles.

- Also mark every reference to the Spirit like this: ⟋ Spirit⟍ As a suggestion, you may want to outline it in purple (the color of royalty) and fill it in with yellow—remembering that we walk in the light of God.
- Mark *new covenant* (I color mine red and outline it in yellow) and any synonyms you find for it.
- Finally mark *tablets of stone* and *letter* in the same way. Use this symbol ⌒ for it is a reference to the tablets of stone on which God wrote the Ten Commandments. Also mark any synonyms that pertain to it.

Don't rush your assignment. It's important for you to be familiar with the text so you won't get lost as I share these truths with you. When you finish your assignment, review what you observed yesterday by marking the words *adequate* and *adequacy.*

Record your observations below.

It's interesting that right after Paul's triumph of praise, he wonders aloud, "Are we beginning to commend ourselves again? Or do we need, as some, letters of commendation to you or from you?" (3:1).

Had someone suggested that it might help Paul in proving his apostleship and work in the kingdom for a letter of commendation to be sent to the Corinthians from others, or that letters be sent from the Corinthians that might help Paul be better accepted elsewhere? This frequently happens to me: People want me to write letters on their behalf recommending them to others. I have to admit that I don't like to write such letters. Are letters of commendation from others something that we really need?

Such letters were not what Paul wanted, needed, or would use. He didn't have to. He had living epistles of commendation, flesh and blood that testified of the effectiveness of his ministry. Epistles of his adequacy in bringing home the spoils of war from the devil's domain. He had charged into the basest of cities, Corinth, and had brought down the strongholds of the enemy with the sword of the Spirit, the glorious gospel of Jesus Christ. They—the church at Corinth—were not a letter of commendation from man but from Christ Himself! Not a letter written with ink but a letter written by the Spirit of the living God. A letter not written on tablets of stone as was the Old Covenant, the Law; rather they were letters of Christ written on the tablets of their hearts. Their confidence came through Christ. The work He had done in them was apparent to all!

Paul had earlier told the Corinthians, "Do not be deceived; neither fornicators, nor idolaters, nor adulterers, nor effeminate, nor homosexuals, nor thieves, nor the covetous, nor drunkards, nor revilers, nor swindlers, will inherit the kingdom of God. Such were some of you; but you *were* washed, but you *were* sanctified, but you *were* justified in the name of the Lord Jesus Christ and in the Spirit of our God."[2] Many in Corinth fell into the categories of sin just stated, but they weren't left that way. God, through the glorious message of the New Covenant, the gospel of Jesus Christ, had transformed them. They were made new, clean.

When Paul first took the gospel to Corinth, the Spirit of God did not call "many wise according to the flesh, not many mighty, not many noble." Instead, as Paul reminded them, "God has chosen the foolish things of the world to shame the wise, and God has chosen the weak things of the world to shame the things which are strong, and the base things of the world and the despised God has chosen, the things that are not, so that He may nullify the things that are, so that no man may boast before God."[3]

There was nothing adequate about "this lot" in the eyes of the world—nor probably in their own eyes, if the Corinthian believers were totally honest. But God was going to make them adequate, and that would be all they would need to be. For by God's doing they would be "in Christ Jesus, who became to us wisdom from God, and righteousness and sanctification, and redemption." So if any boasting were to be done, it would be "as it is written, 'Let him who boasts, boast in the LORD.'"[4]

Thus Paul reminds them in 2 Corinthians 3:5 that we are not adequate in ourselves to consider anything as coming from ourselves, but our adequacy comes from God.

Oh, my dear friend, do you see it? All that I listed at the beginning of this week, all the feelings of inadequacy with their various reasons, are always true of us if we're trusting in ourselves or in any other human creature or means, in any measure. Our adequacy comes from God and God alone. And when we stop and remember this truth delivered by Paul in all his purity, then we'll have a heart for God. God as our source, our sufficiency, and hence our adequacy. Adequacy for any and every situation.

Think about this, meditate on it. Talk with our Father about it…or if He's not yet your Father, talk to Him anyway, as God. Ask Him to show you what it means to be a participant in this glorious New Covenant of grace.

– D A Y   T H R E E –

Do you realize that one of the main reasons we tend to focus on our inadequacy, even though we're truly born of God, is because we forget what it means to be a letter of Christ, written by the Spirit of God? We slip into our old ways, our old thinking—performance-based, affirmed or disallowed by the measure of man.

Or we come under the influence of those who would seek to make sure we stay on that straight and narrow path and therefore give us their list of the dos and don'ts of holiness. They forget the work wrought in our hearts by the Mediator of the New Covenant through His death and resurrection. Consequently the veil taken away in Christ is tried on for size from time to time.

Yesterday you read through the first eleven verses of 2 Corinthians 3 and marked the references to *tablets of stone, letter, the Spirit,* and *new covenant.* Read through this text again and review your markings. Then list what you learned from marking the following:

When you observe the text, it becomes clear, doesn't it, that we're made adequate only one way: through the New Covenant and the ministry of the Spirit. Our adequacy will never come from ourselves. Did you see that, precious one? Let me say it again and you can underline it: Your adequacy will never come from anything you can ever do or be apart from Christ. Your adequacy will come only from God.

Let's go back and look at what God promised the children of Israel, as they were about to face the consequences of trying to live outside God's holy law. In Jeremiah 31:31-34 we read:

▶ JEREMIAH 31:31-34

31 "Behold, days are coming," declares the LORD, "when I will make a new covenant with the house of Israel and with the house of Judah,

32 not like the covenant which I made with their fathers in the day I took them by the hand to bring them out of the land of Egypt, My covenant which they broke, although I was a husband to them," declares the LORD.

33 "But this is the covenant which I will make with the house of Israel after those days," declares the LORD, "I will put My law within them and on their heart I will write it; and I will be their God, and they shall be My people.

34 "They will not teach again, each man his neighbor and each man his

brother, saying, 'Know the LORD,' for they will all know Me, from the least of them to the greatest of them," declares the LORD, "for I will forgive their iniquity, and their sin I will remember no more."

Now go back and read this passage again. This time mark the word *covenant* as you did in 2 Corinthians 3. Also mark these words: *law, heart, sin,* and *iniquity.*

What are the two covenants being contrasted here?

Isn't it exciting to see how this parallels 2 Corinthians 3? Both passages refer to the Old Covenant, the Law, and the New Covenant—the covenant of grace that forgives our sins, remembers our iniquities no more, and writes the Law in our hearts instead of on tablets of stone! Awesome!

It is *awesome* (a word, by the way, that's used a significant number of times in the Old Testament) to watch God at work. Here in Corinthians, right after Paul's exclamation of triumph, we have a contrast of the Old and New Covenants that serves as our best explanation of them in the New Testament, apart from the extended treatment we find in the book of Hebrews.

Paul was a servant, a minister of a new covenant. Not the old, but the new. Not of the letter, which killed—a ministry of death that could only condemn, because it could not make those under it adequate when it came to righteousness.

The Law could only set the standard, a righteous standard of holiness. Under the Old Covenant—the Law, written in tablets of stone—you did the best *you* could. But the New Covenant enables you to keep the standard set by the Law.

This is because God removes your heart of stone and gives you a heart of flesh. Listen to God's promise through Ezekiel: "Moreover, I will give you a new heart and put a new spirit within you; and I will remove the heart of stone from your flesh and give you a heart of flesh. I will put My Spirit within you and cause you to walk in My statutes, and you will be careful to observe My ordinances."[5]

The letter—the Old Covenant—kills because even if you keep the whole law and break it in only one point, then you're guilty of all. You sinned and must suffer the consequences. Therefore Paul also calls the Law "a ministry of death," a "ministry of condemnation." The Old Covenant can only condemn unrighteousness. The New Covenant provides righteousness, and the Spirit gives life. He takes us from death to life, never to die again. Under the Old Covenant we try to *earn* favor, but under the New we *receive* favor and are made adequate by His adequacy. Awesome, isn't it?

We who were totally inadequate are made adequate, just like Paul. Adequate to do the work of God under the power of the Spirit of God. Adequate as ministers of the New Covenant, also referred to as "the ministry of the Spirit," for it is the Spirit of God who is given to us as the guarantor of this New Covenant. He seals us in Christ until the day of our redemption, when this mortal body puts on immortality and this corruptible flesh puts on incorruptibility, as Paul has already explained to the Corinthians.[6]

The Law came with glory, but it wasn't a glory that would last. Why? Let's explore that.

Read through 2 Corinthians 3:7-18 and mark every occurrence of the words *glory, veil,* and *Spirit,* plus any reference either to the Old or New Covenants. Then we'll look at it together and call it a day. It should be a good day because of the good news we've seen.

Why couldn't the children of Israel look on Moses' face? Why did he put a veil over his face when he went out before the people after he received the Law? It was because God would replace the Old Covenant by the New. As we read in Hebrews, "When He said, 'A new covenant,' He has made the first [the Law] obsolete," and Jesus "takes away the first in order to establish the second."[7]

The Law was given for two reasons, according to Galatians 3. First, it defined our transgressions. It revealed our sin—our total inadequacy to keep the Law, to be righteous on our own. Second, it acted as a schoolmaster, a tutor, to keep us in line, to deal with us when we did sin by executing the ordinances God set down in the Law. The Law served as a tutor to bring us to Christ—Christ who would give us what we needed through the gift of His indwelling Spirit. The Spirit within would provide all that we needed to overcome our flesh. He would make us complete in Christ, adequate for every good work.

This is why Moses kept the veil over his face when he went before the people. It covered the glory that came as Moses received the Law, because the glory wouldn't last. It couldn't last because it could not make us perfect, and consequently we would never see heaven, we would never become children of God. So God sent His Son to earth, the Lamb of God to take away the sins of the world, and we beheld His glory as of the only begotten of the Father, full of grace and truth! Grace! Grace! Grace! Glory! Glory! Glory! Liberty! Liberty! Liberty! We are made *adequate*. And so we stand with unveiled faces beholding in a mirror the glory of the Lord and in the process—the wonderful awesome process of sanctification—we're being transformed into the same image from glory to glory, just as from the Lord, the Spirit.

We are complete in Him. Our adequacy is of God.

Doesn't that make you want to get on your knees? Do so now and ask God to show you which covenant you're living under. Have you really been forgiven and given the Spirit of God within your heart? Ask God to show you whether you have a religion under the Law or relationship under the New Covenant.

If you know that you know you're His under the New Covenant—because of the witness of the Spirit and the change in your life that evidences His power to free you from sin's power—then worship Him for all He has done. You'll be led in triumph!

— D A Y   F O U R —

Those who have found their adequacy in God can now speak with great boldness. Grace and truth have been realized in Jesus Christ. There is liberty. This is a permanent covenant never to be replaced.

And you, Beloved, like Paul, have a ministry: the ministry of the New Covenant. As you have received mercy by being brought into His kingdom, don't lose heart even if the gospel remains veiled to some. Don't fear the afflictions that will come your way. His grace is sufficient.

Don't look at the things that are seen.

He leads us in triumph, for He leads us…

> *not* to some god that has eyes but cannot see,
> ears but cannot hear;[8]
> *but* to the almighty sovereign Ruler of the universe,
> whose arm is not short that it cannot save
> and whose ear is not deaf that it cannot hear,[9]
> and whose eyes run to and fro throughout
> the whole earth looking for men and
> women whose hearts are fully His, that
> He might show Himself strong on their
> behalf.[10]

Our joyful task for the next two days will be to look at 2 Corinthians 4 and gain practical insights into our ministry under the New Covenant.

Read through this chapter now in the back of this book, and this time mark every occurrence of the word *we,* plus all the synonyms and pronouns that go with it. As you do, think about who is included in this plural pronoun. Also mark any key repeated phrase concerning the heart and put a big red heart over it!

Every child of God receives a spiritual gift from God, many times more than one. These gifts given by the Spirit are what make us adequate for the work He has for us. Paul taught this very clearly in 1 Corinthians 12–14, when he explained that there are varieties of gifts but the same Spirit, varieties of ministries but the same Lord, and varieties of effects (results) but the same God who works all things in all persons. What we are given we are given not for ourselves but for the common good.[11]

What does this mean practically? It means that we aren't to compare ourselves with each other. We aren't in competition with one another. We belong to one body. "If the foot says, 'Because I am not a hand, I am not a part of the body,' it is not for this reason any less a part of the body.…

God has placed the members, each one of them, in the body, just as He desired."[12]

If we remember this and that God is sovereign and that we're valued by God and have a ministry, then we'll stop feeling inadequate. We'll stop wondering, "Why him or her and not me?" We'll stop seeking our own promotion and leave that to God—if and when and how it's good for the work of the kingdom and therefore good for us. There's so much self-seeking today—seeking our own ministry, our own welfare, our own recognition in one way or another—when all God would have us seek is *His* heart, *His* will. When we do this and stay on this path, we'll know contentment, a peace that passes all understanding, although we're "delivered over to death for Jesus' sake."[13]

Paul's gifts were great—many in fact—but so was the task to which God appointed him. Magnanimous in its scope and in its suffering. When he wrote his final epistle to Timothy, his beloved son in the gospel, he exhorted him with these words:

> Join with me in suffering for the gospel according to the power of God, who has saved us and called us with a holy calling, not according to our works, but according to His own purpose and grace which was granted us in Christ Jesus from all eternity, but now has been revealed by the appearing of our Savior Christ Jesus, who abolished death and brought life and immortality to light through the gospel, for which I was appointed a preacher and an apostle and a teacher. For this reason I also suffer these things, but I am not ashamed; for I know whom I have believed and I am convinced that He is able to guard what I have entrusted to Him until that day.[14]

Did you see it, Beloved? Isn't it liberating! God called us not according to our works—not according to our own degree of adequacy but according to His own purpose and grace. It's a purpose and grace *granted* to us, *bestowed* upon us from above and for all eternity. This is what makes us adequate, able to do the work of ministry. Paul knew what God appointed for him, just as you are to discover what God has appointed for you.

So where do we begin? First, you must resolve that you will not "lose heart" or give up. The Christian life is not one chain of successes, victories, and triumphal marches. It's warfare against the forces of the Evil One. It's not for the faint-hearted, the lily-livered, but for those who are strong and courageous with a strength and courage that come from knowing the truth, which is what you and I are doing now—learning truth.

Second, if you'll look at the "we's" you marked, you'll see that we're to renounce the things hidden because of shame. Our lives are to be lived openly. We're to hide nothing because we have nothing to hide. The past was totally forgiven, we were declared righteous. Now we are to live accordingly. This certainly has *not* been modeled for us in many of our political leaders, nor unfortunately even in people who profess Christ. But it's to be modeled in your life, and it *can* be because of the power of the Spirit bestowed on you through the New Covenant in His blood.

We are not to walk in craftiness. We don't have to. We are adequate, and there's nothing to cover up or compensate for because we don't have to be anyone else for anyone else. We only have to be what God would have us to be. Paul was confident in this knowledge even though his detractors accused him of being a "crafty fellow" who was taking in the Corinthians "by deceit."[15] Neither Paul nor Titus took advantage of the Corinthians. Paul did not adulterate the Word of God.

Nor are we to adulterate the Word of God. We are not to mishandle it, twist it, or distort it for our own perverted pleasures or affirmations or gain. We're to hold nothing back. We are not to focus on pet or favorite doctrines. Paul told the elders from Ephesus, as he left for Jerusalem where chains awaited him, "I did not shrink from declaring to you anything that was profitable, and teaching you publicly and from house to house.… I did not shrink from declaring to you the whole purpose of God."[16]

Woe to us if we mishandle the Word of God, especially for our own gain or popularity. And there will be woe to so many. It's obvious, easy to see, if you hold to the integrity of doctrine and the holiness of God, that there's no shortage of contradictory doctrines taught on Christian television. This is why, Beloved, you must know God's Word for yourself so that your life, your counsel, your teaching, your instruction, your presentation of the gospel is a manifestation of truth that commends you to every man's conscience in the sight of God. In other words, you don't violate another's conscience by your presentation of the truth in your teaching and in your living. You realize you cannot escape God's scrutiny. Pray that your passion will be to handle it accurately, that you might be approved unto God, a workman unashamed,[17] earnestly contending for the faith once for all delivered to the saints.[18]

And what if everyone you talk to doesn't believe? Is it your fault? A result of your inadequacy? No, the gospel is veiled. Moses had a veil over his face, Israel had a veil over their hearts, and the unbelieving have a veil over their minds. They are blinded by the god of this world, the ruler of this world who is cast out, dethroned by Christ's payment for man's sin, thereby canceling the debt of sin, which is death.[19] The New Covenant, when entered into by faith, removes us from Satan's domain and transfers us into the kingdom of God. Until this happens for others, they remain blind in their mind, walking in darkness, unable to see the light of the gospel of the glory of Christ—Christ, who is the image of God and the radiance of His glory and the exact representation of His nature.[20]

Those who refuse to believe are not to be despised but pitied, for they are moving from death to death. But it's *not* your fault. Let me say it again: When others you talk with do not believe, it's not because of your inadequacy in the gospel, in the ministry, or in your witness. When you walk as Paul says he does in 2 Corinthians 4:2—renouncing things hidden because of shame, not walking in craftiness or adulterating the Word of God, but manifesting truth—then you can know that *you* are not the stumbling block in their salvation. Rather, it's the dark veil over their minds.

Despite this, you'll know peace as long as you remember you are the servant, not the savior. The same God who in the beginning spoke and said, "Let their be light," thus bringing light out of darkness, is the only One who brings the light of the knowledge of Jesus Christ into people's hearts. Isn't that liberating?

There's only one Savior, only one Lord, and we are bond servants of

His people for His sake. That's why Paul says, "We do not preach ourselves but Christ Jesus as Lord." We cannot do a thing to save anyone—only God can. Therefore when we present the gospel, we must let the hearers know that we cannot help them in any way except to assist them in finding God. Only God can save them. Only God can rescue them permanently.

How I love the following words from Isaiah! The Spirit of God led Isaiah to begin with the fact that God is the Creator. (You'll see the parallel in 2 Corinthians if your precious eyes have not already lit up in recognition once you read this.)

> For thus says the LORD, who created the heavens
> (He is the God who formed the earth and made it,
> He established it and did not create it a waste place,
> But formed it to be inhabited),
> "I am the LORD, and there is none else.
> "I have not spoken in secret,
> In some dark land;
> I did not say to the offspring of Jacob,
> 'Seek Me in a waste place';
> I, the LORD, speak righteousness,
> Declaring things that are upright.
>
> "Gather yourselves and come;
> Draw near together, you fugitives of the nations;
> They have no knowledge,
> Who carry about their wooden idol
> And pray to a god who cannot save.
> Declare and set forth your case;
> Indeed, let them consult together.
> Who has announced this from of old?
> Who has long since declared it?
> Is it not I, the LORD?
> And there is no other God besides Me,
> A righteous God and a Savior;

There is none except Me.

Turn to Me and be saved, all the ends of the earth;

For I am God, and there is no other."[21]

He is God and there is no other—and if they do not turn to Him, if they do not recognize Christ Jesus as Lord, they will surely perish. The lake of fire prepared for the devil and his angels will be their eternal dwelling place as well.

The fact that Paul preached Jesus as Lord, and never as Savior alone, is most important, Beloved, because Jesus must be recognized as God, one with the Father, like the Father. Possessing the same attributes as His Father, He is, as I quoted previously, "the exact representation of His [God's] nature."[22]

God spoke of His Son in these terms: "Your throne, O God, is forever and ever, and the righteous scepter is the scepter of His kingdom."[23]

And how does Paul say a person is saved? We find it succinctly stated in his letter to the church at Rome. As you read these verses, underline every occurrence of the word *Lord.*

● ROMANS 10:9-13

9 That if you confess with your mouth Jesus as Lord, and believe in your heart that God raised Him from the dead, you will be saved;

10 for with the heart a person believes, resulting in righteousness, and with the mouth he confesses, resulting in salvation.

11 For the Scripture says, "Whoever believes in Him will not be disappointed."

12 For there is no distinction between Jew and Greek; for the same Lord is Lord of all, abounding in riches for all who call on Him;

13 for "Whoever will call on the name of the Lord will be saved."

The word translated "Lord" is *kurios,* which means "supreme in authority." It comes from *kuros,* which means "supremacy." When used as a noun, *kurios* is a controller. Jesus is God, supreme in authority. As He said to His disciples before He ascended to the Father, "All authority has been given to Me in heaven and on earth. Go therefore...."[24]

And how critical is the acceptance of Jesus' deity to one's salvation? Listen to His own declaration: "Therefore I said to you that you will die in your sins; for unless you believe that I am He, you will die in your sins."[25]

In this passage, the word *He* has been added by the translators. Literally Jesus said, "For if you do not believe that I Am, you shall die in your sins." He used the very title, the very name that God used when Moses asked Him what he should say to the children of Israel when they asked who sent him. God replied "I Am." This, God said, was His memorial name to all generations.[26] Jesus is God, and if a person refuses to believe this, he or she will die in their sins. Lost forever.

But how does a person come to this realization? How did I come to that great and glorious day in my life, when this immoral woman fell on her knees and told God He could do anything He wanted with her? I came to that moment only because of the incomprehensible grace of God, who by Himself was shining in my heart to give me "the Light of the knowledge of the glory of God in the face of Christ" (2 Corinthians 4:6).

I didn't understand all the theology behind what I did, but I bowed the knee before God. No longer would I run my life and dishonor God. I surrendered—totally, completely. And I told Him to take control. Light shone out of the darkness of my slavery to sin, and I became His creation in Christ Jesus, even as God spoke and brought light to His creation on the day He created the heavens and the earth.

Oh, Beloved, what have you learned today that you need to thank God for or that you need to take to Him in prayer? Don't simply close this book and get up and walk away. Take a few minutes, close your eyes, and think about what you have seen in His Word—and in your life. Have you recognized that Jesus is Lord—God—and that there's no other who can save you? Or have you been looking to some man, some woman, some substitute parent, some lover, to fill that void within? Dear friend, it will never happen. You are a vessel made to contain God, and until you contain Him, you'll never find fulfillment, satisfaction. For none can satisfy except God.

What would you say to God at this moment? Write it out so you'll have it to remember and read again.

— D A Y   F I V E —

You are a vessel, precious one, made by God to contain God. What a glorious calling! Who could ask for any higher privilege? Who could dream of attaining such heights of glory? You—you, a human being—indwelt by God!

That is the height of glory. Yet how is that height of glory seen? How is it manifested to others?

It is manifested in the most difficult of situations. It is manifested in the difficulties of life that all humanity faces and deals with on one level or another. It is manifested when we experience "death"—death to a dream, a hope, an ambition. Death when we are despised, rejected, scorned. But because of the presence of God within us, because of the power of God, it's a death that brings life to others.

But before I say more about it, you must stop for yourself and read through 2 Corinthians 4:7-18 again. This time, mark every reference to the Corinthians. Color them whatever color you used before. Also mark the word *death*. You might want to do it with a tombstone and color it brown.

There are several contrasts that you don't want to miss in these verses, so watch carefully for them. When you see them, list them below.

What a heart for God Paul reflects! I weep when I read these verses. How I long to have a heart like this for my precious God! To be poured out for Him on the altar of sacrifice for the sake of others. To live with eternity stamped on my eyes so that I look at every difficulty in life as an opportunity for people to see the sufficiency of His truth and His power. How I long to remember that whatever I'm enduring is temporal. Eternity awaits, and how I handle this situation will bring me an eternal weight of glory far beyond all comparison. How I long for a heart like this!

As you read, did you note the parallel with the way Paul began this letter to the Corinthians? His affliction was for their comfort. Now again you see that his death is for their life. Always God, always others—others before him. Why was this Paul's attitude and mind-set? Because this is what it means to be like Christ. All that our blessed Lord and Savior endured, He endured for us and for the Father, that we might see the Father's heart. Oh, to be free from self! From selfish motives, ambitions, desires, promotions!

And how does that freedom from self come? It comes through death. "Death works in us, but life in you" (4:12). Remember what Jesus told His disciples when His hour had come?

> And Jesus answered them, saying, "The hour has come for the Son of Man to be glorified. Truly, truly, I say to you, unless a grain of wheat falls into the earth and dies, it remains alone; but if it dies, it bears much fruit.[27]

Fruit is born out of death—death produces life. Sounds strange, doesn't it? But you see, precious one, only through our difficulties of life, which are so similar to the difficulties of those who don't know Jesus, can others see that there's something, someone—some power, some knowledge—that enables us to handle it in a way that they could not. And when they see this, the first thing they recognize is that this isn't normal. It isn't natural.

So what is it? It can't be us, because we are human, just like them! So what is it?

And when they ask, they find out it is God. Then who gets the glory? God! They see His grace—which is power, which is sufficient—and this brings glory to the One who fills the vessel rather than to the vessel itself. They see our adequacy is of God.

What's the most important thing anyone could ever see in you in the middle of a trial, stress, suffering, rejection? It is Jesus. His life. He is seen and not you. And when that happens, Beloved, He alone gets the glory.

Do you battle with the fleshly desire?

Wanting people to know…

what part you played in the equation?

what you contributed through…

your effort?

your diligence?

your prayers?

your prowess?

your careful and wise handling of the situation?

your manipulation?

your understanding of the person?

your savvy?

your cleverness?

I do. I'm ashamed to say it, but I must be honest. I battle with these desires. But I don't want to. I want a heart like Paul's…who had a heart like Jesus…who had a heart for His Father.

So what can I expect, what can I know, if I pursue this course of holiness?

First, I can be assured of several things.

- You and I can be afflicted in any way—pressured, stressed, crowded by the circumstances of life—but we cannot be crushed. Why? Because there's a stronger power within us than without. It's God's power. Why don't you stop right now and go back to 2 Corinthians 4:7 and mark that word *power*. I draw a stick of dynamite like this ⬛⬛—outlined in black and filled in with red.

- When we're perplexed—unable to find our way out of a situation, at a loss mentally as to what we're to do—we are not to despair, lose hope, give up. His power is there. *He* is there. We are simply the vessel having within us the God of all hope.

- When persecution comes—and we've already seen that it *will* come in one form or another—you and I need to remember that we are not forsaken. As vessels we are never left empty once we believe and receive the Lord Jesus Christ. Our bodies are the temples of the Holy Spirit who is in us, sealing us until the day of our redemption.[28] The writer of the powerful epistle to the Hebrews reminds the suffering saints that "He Himself has said, 'I will never desert you, nor will I ever forsake you,' so that we confidently say, 'The Lord is my helper, I will not be afraid. What will man do to me?'"[29] We can rest assured that we're never alone in any persecution, never abandoned, never powerless.
- We may be struck down, brought very, very low, but we will never be destroyed. We will not perish. Even physical death cannot destroy the child of God, for death merely frees us from this body of flesh and puts us immediately into the presence of Christ. A joyful truth we'll study next week.

These, Beloved, are our assurances recorded and preserved forever in the Word of God. This is our legacy in the difficulties of life. But what's the purpose? We've touched on it, but let me move through the text with you so that the waves of these precious truths might wash over any dry shores of our soul.

There's one reason, and only one reason, that we experience these things: so that His life might be dramatically seen in our deathlike circumstances. Listen to His life-giving words again, "For we who live are constantly being delivered over to death for Jesus' sake, so that the life of Jesus also may be manifested in our mortal flesh" (2 Corinthians 4:11).

It reminds me of another favorite assurance from the book of Romans. As you read this passage, underline the phrases that mean the most to you. Also mark the word *love*.

❯ ROMANS 8:36-39

36 Just as it is written, "For Your sake we are being put to death all day long; we were considered as sheep to be slaughtered."

37 But in all these things we overwhelmingly conquer through Him who loved us.

38 For I am convinced that neither death, nor life, nor angels, nor principalities, nor things present, nor things to come, nor powers,

39 nor height, nor depth, nor any other created thing, will be able to separate us from the love of God, which is in Christ Jesus our Lord.

Dear friend, isn't it touching to see that all these things are for *His* sake? Oh, to love Him so very, very much so that every "whatever" in our lives would be for His sake and His alone! How I long to be so focused, to remember this in the midst of the mundane pressures and pettiness of life as well as in the gigantic trials.

When sheep are slaughtered, there's no noise, no bleating complaint. But slaughter a hog and the noise is awful. If we know our trial is for His sake, we won't murmur or complain. We won't scream, rant, rave, and carry on like someone who has no power within.

As you read those verses from Romans 8, did you underline the part that says we can overwhelmingly conquer? We are overcomers, Beloved. Some believe that overcomers are an elite group of Christians, the super-spiritual. But a careful study of the use of the word in Scripture shows that every true child of God is an overcomer.

To me, this passage especially makes that clear:

For whatever is born of God overcomes the world; and this is the victory that has overcome the world—our faith.

Who is the one who overcomes the world, but he who believes that Jesus is the Son of God?[30]

"So death works in us, but life in you" (2 Corinthians 4:12). And whatever it costs us to take the gospel and to defend it, it is worth it. Therefore Paul will hold fast to the truth. What he believes he will speak with great assurance. He knows without a shadow of a doubt that "He who raised the Lord Jesus will raise us also with Jesus and will present us with you" (4:14).

Paul has eternity stamped on his eyes: the resurrection and the judgment seat of Christ. And because of that, he doesn't lose heart. The outer man may be decaying, but his inner man is being renewed day by day.

I pray this is happening as we do this study and as we cry out, "Lord, give me a heart for You." Surely He hears and welcomes that cry. And of course it will mean that affliction will come. And when it does, remember, precious one, that whatever the affliction is, it's momentary. It will not last forever. Every trial has a beginning and an end, according to 1 Peter 1. It is momentary and light. Light in comparison to the eternal weight of glory that awaits you and me.

> *O Father, beloved, beloved Father, how I thank You for this precious one who is so faithfully studying Your truths, longing for a heart like Yours. Wrap Your dear children in the security of these truths. Hold them tight, that with their heads on Your breast they will hear the beating of Your heart and know that nothing, absolutely nothing will be able to separate them from Your love. Whisper in their ear, "It's all right, My child, I am here—I will always be here. We have eternity together as a family. Rest—it will never be more than you can bear."*

MEMORY VERSES

How do I choose one verse from all that we've studied? May I give you several that I think will minister to you in the days to come. As you read them, ask our Father what He wants you to remember, then memorize them in the confidence that this is God's Word for *you* where you are now.

Not that we are adequate in ourselves to consider anything as coming from ourselves, but our adequacy is from God.

2 CORINTHIANS 3:5

But we have this treasure in earthen vessels, so that the surpassing greatness of the power will be of God and not from ourselves.

2 CORINTHIANS 4:7

For we who live are constantly being delivered over to death for Jesus' sake, so that the life of Jesus also may be manifested in our mortal flesh. So death works in us, but life in you.

2 CORINTHIANS 4:11-12

For momentary, light affliction is producing for us an eternal weight of glory far beyond all comparison, while we look not at the things which are seen, but at the things which are not seen; for the things which are seen are temporal, but the things which are not seen are eternal.

2 CORINTHIANS 4:17-18

SMALL-GROUP DISCUSSION QUESTIONS

1. According to 2 Corinthians 3:5-6, what was Paul's attitude concerning his adequacy?
2. What does it mean to be a "letter of Christ," as Paul uses the term in 2 Corinthians 3:1-3?
3. Discuss the contrast between the Old and New Covenants. (Be sure to discuss *who* each covenant is between, and the result of each covenant.)

4. In what the Bible teaches about the New Covenant, what do we learn about the Holy Spirit?
5. Why was the Law given?
6. From what we see in Jeremiah 31:31-34 and Ezekiel 36:26-27, does being part of the New Covenant mean you no longer have to keep the Law? Explain your answer.
7. How can we manifest the glory of God?
8. How does understanding spiritual gifts help our feelings of inadequacy?
9. Why is it so important to know the Word of God for yourself?
10. What encouraging truth can we learn in 2 Corinthians 4:16-18 about the purpose of affliction in our lives?

APPLICATION:
11. How do we become adequate in the same way Paul was?
12. Who is reading your "letter"? What do they see? Are you a sweet fragrance of life unto life to those around you? What do you think others would say about you in this regard?
13. How can you be diligent to seek the good of others for *their* sake instead of for your own comfort?
14. What does it mean for you personally to be willing to defend the gospel no matter the cost?

---

1. *Expositors Bible Commentary* (Grand Rapids, Mich.: Zondervan, 1976), Volume 10, 332.
2. 1 Corinthians 6:9-11.
3. 1 Corinthians 1:26-29.
4. 1 Corinthians 1:30-31.
5. Ezekiel 36:26-27.
6. See 1 Corinthians 15:51-54, KJV.
7. Hebrews 8:13; 10:9.
8. Psalm 115:5-6.
9. Isaiah 59:1.
10. 2 Chronicles 16:9.

11. See 1 Corinthians 12:4-7.
12. 1 Corinthians 12:15,18.
13. 2 Corinthians 4:11.
14. 2 Timothy 1:8-12.
15. 2 Corinthians 12:16.
16. Acts 20:20,27.
17. 2 Timothy 2:15.
18. Jude 3.
19. John 12:31, Hebrews 2:14-15.
20. Hebrews 1:3.
21. Isaiah 45:18-22.
22. Hebrews 1:3.
23. Hebrews 1:8.
24. Matthew 28:18-19.
25. John 8:24.
26. Exodus 3:14-15.
27. John 12:23-24.
28. 1 Corinthians 6:19; Ephesians 4:30.
29. Hebrews 13:5-6.
30. 1 John 5:4-5.

STANDING AT THE JUDGMENT SEAT OF CHRIST

– D A Y   O N E –

The note arrived today, written in pencil. It's an extraordinary note printed on a small sheet of an ordinary blank white notepad.

January 2001

Now taking radiation treatments for the same old breast.
Cancer showing in the brain.
Pray for Bob. Thanks!

→

Seeing the arrow, I turned the paper over...

I read the end of the Book. We win.
Pray it will be well done for God's glory!
Love to all.

I know Charlotte and Bob Holmes well. We stayed with them four different times on our trips to Japan. We lived in their beautiful apartment in Tokyo, where Bob served as an executive for United Airlines. The company paid the salary for a job well done, but Bob and Charlotte were well aware that God had opened the door to Japan for a much higher purpose—the ministry of the New Covenant—and they pursued this purpose well. An executives' club was established where Japanese would gather with the Holmes in their spacious apartment to hear the Word of God. Charlotte taught English to Japanese women using the Bible as her text. The leaders of the chapel in the New Otani Hotel had the faithful assistance of this couple.

And then Charlotte and Bob opened their home to strangers like Jack and me, sending us off as dear friends.

Every morning when we entered their kitchen, there on a chalkboard would be a verse for the day. On the table would be a devotional on the names of God that they used as their manna in the morning. In the evening they would often play the piano and sing a hymn or two. Frisky, childlike Charlotte once danced an Irish jig. I can see her now in my mind's eye as I write through my tears.

On our last visit to Japan, we had a "girl day" together. Charlotte had to go shopping; the cancer had returned and she was losing weight. It was an opportunity to put her into some smart-looking outfits. I'll never forget how she pranced in front of her husband, showing off her new look and enjoying the delight in his eyes.

We haven't been back since then. The cancer progressed so much that they had to return to the States—afflicted but not crushed, perplexed as to the reason for the cancer's return but not despairing. They went to visit their daughters and their families on the mission field and then began the arduous round of cancer treatments.

We kept in touch by e-mail. But today, for you as well as for me, the handwritten note came just as I was preparing to share 2 Corinthians 5 with you. Oh, the sovereignty of God! What better illustration could I have for you than Charlotte's note. Although it brings grief to my heart, it also brings joy to my soul. Charlotte is going to die soon, but she knows we "win" because she knows "the Book"—God's book. She has read the end as well as all the beginning and middle. She knows that "if the earthly tent which is our house is torn down, we have a building from God, a house not made with hands, eternal in the heavens" (2 Corinthians 5:1).

Charlotte's brushes with death have been frequent these past years. And yet her request for herself and Bob would always be that God would use all this in the lives of others. Because their relationship with God is so strong and they're secure in their relationship with themselves, their concern is always for others. That's why I'm sure that, as she requested, all that they have to do *will* be done well—and it will be done for His glory.

In 2 Corinthians 5, Paul—who thought he would see the return of the Lord and lived in the expectancy of it—now has had such a close brush with death that it seems he believes he could die before the Lord returns.

Do you remember what he wrote in the opening paragraph of his letter to the Corinthians? Let me refresh your memory:

> For we do not want you to be unaware, brethren, of our affliction which came to us in Asia, that we were burdened excessively, beyond our strength, so that we despaired even of life; indeed, we had the sentence of death within ourselves so that we would not trust in ourselves, but in God who raises the dead. (2 Corinthians 1:8-9)

Paul thought he might die. Yet whatever would bring death would be, as we saw last week, "a momentary, light affliction" that would produce something far beyond all comparison in the future that lay just beyond death's door.

Take time to read through 2 Corinthians 4:16–5:8. As you read, mark again every *we*—and know this, Beloved: The *we* includes you if you belong to Christ.

When you finish reading, why don't you list below what you have learned from the text about the earthly tent that is our house now and about the house that is a building from God—the house Charlotte will soon put on in all its glory.

THE EARTHLY TENT   THE HEAVENLY BUILDING

Now, my friend, stop and think of where you would be emotionally...spiritually...mentally...if you were in Charlotte's shoes and about
to walk through death's door. What would you be dealing with? feeling?
fearing? Why don't you write it out, then you can see how God answers.

– D A Y   T W O –

Have you ever thought what your dying words will be? One of the things
I love to do is read the biographies of men and women who have gone
before us, people of faith who lived in a different time, in a different religious atmosphere where there was a sense of the awesome holiness of God
and of the awfulness of their sin. So many who went on to be mightily
used of God really wrestled with their sin. There was a holy fear of dying
apart from Christ—and of the judgment that awaited beyond the grave.

There was a sense of eternity—and of the gravity of facing a holy
God—that's missing today in our teaching and evangelism.

We're so quick to try to get people into heaven that I think many
times we go after a profession of faith rather than allowing the Holy Spirit
to bring...

> *conviction of sin* because they have not believed on Jesus.
> *conviction of righteousness* and their great need for it, for with-
> out His righteousness they will miss heaven.

We fail to let others grapple with their total inability to save themselves through their good deeds, religious sacraments, and impotent
wrestling with fleshly desires.

We fail to allow them to be *convicted of judgment.* We want to present
the blessings of belonging but fail to let them know the consequences of
rejecting.

The prince of this world *can* be cast out;

> people *can* move from death to life,
> > from the power of Satan to the kingdom of God.

But if they don't know where they are, if they don't recognize the danger lying before them beyond death's door, why should they believe? or see a need for change? or run? or flee for their lives?

We're in such a hurry to "get them saved" (as if we ourselves could save them) that we don't wait for God to shine His light into the darkness of their souls.

The great Shepherd of the sheep is not going to lose one single lamb that He wants in His fold. He promises this in the following passage. Listen carefully; it's the voice of the Shepherd. In fact as you read, why don't you mark every reference to the sheep, including the pronouns *them* and *they.*

▶ JOHN 10:27-30

27 My sheep hear My voice, and I know them, and they follow Me;

28 and I give eternal life to them, and they will never perish; and no one will snatch them out of My hand.

29 My Father, who has given them to Me, is greater than all; and no one is able to snatch them out of the Father's hand.

30 I and the Father are one.

I think it will help you if you'll take a minute and list everything you've learned about the sheep in these three short verses. Let me get you started on a list that's longer than three points:

1. They are Jesus' sheep.
2. They hear His voice.
3.

Did you see it? I'm sure you did! It's wonderful, isn't it? They shall *never* perish. *No one* can snatch them out of Jesus' hand. They have eternal *life*. Life, not death!

This is the hope beyond death's door for those who are His sheep. And when I read the biographies of those who have gone before, so often I learn how they died, what their last words were. In the last hours on earth of D. L. Moody, that uncouth shoe salesman who was used so mightily by God in America and England as a great evangelist, his final words included these: "Earth recedes; heaven opens for me" and, "This is my coronation day!"[1]

Can you imagine calling death our "coronation day" when we do all we can to stay alive? Maybe it's because we don't have the perspective that these saints of old had, because they lived in the Word instead of television. Maybe it's because the entertainment and noise and busyness of life—cell phones, faxes, e-mails, constant noise—was not so available, so incessant, so loud, so available, so taxing.

We're so occupied with today that we take no thought for our future and eternity—that is, until somehow we're brought face to face with the specter of death. Maybe it's a doctor's report, maybe it's a sudden pain, maybe it's a subtle wasting away, and you suddenly become conscious of your clothes hanging looser. Whatever, suddenly we're confronted with death. And how do we greet it? Do we know what faces us, what the process will be? I think if we really understood it biblically, as did the well-known D. L. Moody and as does the little-known Charlotte Holmes, we would have memorable truths to leave our loved ones as we stepped into eternity.

Let's see what Paul can teach us about death for the believer.

Paul was a tentmaker. This is the way he supported his missionary work. He knew how temporal tents were. He understood that buildings were much to be preferred. Yes, tents were portable, easily put up and taken down. And that's how he saw our bodies. They are temporal—put up at birth and taken down at death. And then what?

Continuing his metaphor, there's a building waiting in the heavens for the child of God; not a temporal structure but an eternal one. A building not made with hands, as Paul made his tents. This is an edifice constructed by God. It's the body we long for—so much so that when we understand what that body is like, we simply groan until we get it. It's not that we want to be without a body—for it's so hard to think of that, to conceive such a thing—but it's that we know there's a better body coming than this old tent.

I love the way Solomon describes this old tent in his book of wisdom, Ecclesiastes. Read a portion of it below and see if you can make the connection to the various parts of the body and what happens to them with age. If you're young, this might be harder for you to decipher, but if you're older, having probably experienced some of these things, you'll recognize them quickly.

> Remember also your Creator in the days of your youth, before the evil days come and the years draw near when you will say, "I have no delight in them"; before the sun and the light, the moon and the stars are darkened, and clouds return after the rain; in the day that the watchmen of the house tremble, and mighty men stoop, the grinding ones stand idle because they are few, and those who look through windows grow dim; and the doors on the street are shut as the sound of the grinding mill is low, and one will arise at the sound of the bird, and all the daughters of song will sing softly. Furthermore, men are afraid of a high place and of terrors on the road; the almond tree blossoms, the grasshopper drags himself along, and the caperberry is ineffective. For man goes to his eternal home while mourners go about in the street. Remember Him before the silver cord is broken and the golden bowl is crushed, the pitcher by the well is shattered and the wheel at the cistern is crushed; then the dust will return to the earth as it was, and the spirit will return to God who gave it.[2]

As you grow older, things grow dimmer. You like more light; you need more light. The clouds roll in and life isn't as easy, because old age brings its infirmities. You're not as steady as you once were. Your hands tremble more, your feet seem to stumble more easily. Your back begins to stoop a little. Some of your teeth don't want to hang around any longer, so the "grinding ones" are fewer. The vision grows dim, even as Isaac's did in Genesis 27:1, and the shades on your eyes droop more. You find it harder to hear—"the sound of the grinding mill is low." When you could sleep more because your duties are fewer, you find yourself rising with the birds, yet you have to turn up the radio and the television and sit in church with your hand cupped over your ear. Not only is the volume gone in your hearing but also your voice is softer. The exuberance, the song is softened—the volume turned down.

You find you aren't as adventuresome as you used to be. You grab hold of the railing, watch your balance, and yet flinch as you drive at the sound of a horn on the road, quickly jerking your car in fear.

The almond tree, which blossoms earlier and longer than the other trees, shows off its white head of hair. The grasshopper drags himself along. Things take longer to do; they're a greater chore. The caperberry speaks of desire, which dwindles with age. Desire to be, to go, to do, and to enjoy your sexuality—all these desires diminish with time, making it easier for people as they get older to be content with a slower, less exciting pace of life.

Now at this point I have to tell you that at age sixty-seven I feel like there's a young woman trapped inside my body—one who still feels marvelous, full of life and energy. But then my mother is eighty-nine, and grandma died at age one hundred! And right now I want to serve the Lord up to the minute He takes me home.

The earlier passage from Ecclesiastes was Solomon's counsel probably from an old man to those youths who would listen to him. He wanted them to understand that youth is a time to expend all your energies on matters of eternal value, to remember God, to know that death will come. Our dust shall return to the ground and our spirit to God.

It's interesting to note that right after Solomon talks about old age and dying, he closes his book with these words of wisdom, following even a pattern we'll see in 2 Corinthians 5.

The conclusion, when all has been heard, is: fear God and keep His commandments, because this applies to every person. For God will bring every act to judgment, everything which is hidden, whether it is good or evil.[3]

While death awaits all of us, except for those still living when Christ returns, judgment is certain for every human being, even the child of God. As we'll see later, this is a point Paul brings home quite strongly in 2 Corinthians. Before we go there, we must first see how we can be sure that when death comes and we walk beyond that door, we'll be home with the promise that "what is mortal will be swallowed up by life" (2 Corinthians 5:4).

How do we know this? What's our guarantee? Or is there nothing more than the printed word, which really, in essence, is enough? The indwelling Spirit is our guarantee given to us by the Father Himself. Remember Paul wrote: "For indeed while we are in this tent, we groan, being burdened, because we do not want to be unclothed but to be clothed, so that what is mortal will be swallowed up by life. Now He who prepared us for this very purpose is God, who gave to us the Spirit as a pledge" (5:4-5).

We've already seen how the Holy Spirit is given to us in fulfillment of the promise of the New Covenant, but let's go for a minute to the book of Ephesians and see what Paul wrote there in respect to the Holy Spirit.

In the following passage, mark every reference to the Holy Spirit, along with relative pronouns. I've already shared a way to mark the Spirit, but to save you looking for it, simply let me do it again: /Spirit. I draw a purple triangle in my Bible when I want to mark a reference to the Father, and then I color it yellow. You remember why: God is light! Then I use the left base of the triangle to represent the Holy Spirit and color it in the same way.

▶ EPHESIANS 1:13-14

13 In Him, you also, after listening to the message of truth, the gospel of your salvation—having also believed, you were sealed in Him with the Holy Spirit of promise,

14 who is given as a pledge of our inheritance, with a view to the redemption of God's own possession, to the praise of His glory.

Now then, go back and note the progress of events that are mentioned in this passage. What happens and in what order? You may want to mark them in the passage with a 1, 2, 3, etc., or list them below:

What did you learn about the Holy Spirit from marking these verses? List your observations below:

The Greek word for "pledge," used both in the Ephesians passage above and in 2 Corinthians 1:22 and 5:5, is *arrhabon*. It's a word of Hebrew origin and means something like a down payment, part of the purchase money or property given in advance as security for the rest. The *King James Version* of the Bible uses the term "earnest." In other words, the One who guarantees that you'll have a brand-new body is the Spirit of God, whom God gave you after you listened to the message of salvation and believed it.

This is why my precious friend Charlotte and so many others among my beloved friends can face death with such confidence. This is why they can be so courageous, as Paul tells us to be. It's because we know that we know that while we're in this body we are absent from the Lord—and we know this because we walk by faith, not by what our eyes can see. At the same time, we know that the very minute we walk through death's door we'll be at home with our Lord.

Isn't that incredible! Jesus took the sting out of death when He was made sin for us, and because of this we can actually "prefer rather to be absent from the body and to be at home with the Lord" (2 Corinthians 5:8). This is why Paul wrote to the Philippians, "For to me, to live is Christ and to die is gain."[4] If you're living for Christ, why would death be gain? Because at death you are living *with* Christ!

If to live is Christ and to die is gain, then what should be our ambition? Listen to the passion of Paul's heart: "Therefore we also have as our ambition, whether at home or absent, to be pleasing to Him" (2 Corinthians 5:9).

I know what D. L. Moody's ambition was—the same as Paul's. I know what Charlotte's ambition is—the same as Paul's. What's your ambition, Beloved?

Mine is the same: to be pleasing to my God.

— D A Y   T H R E E —

What follows death? Judgment.

Judgment not only for the unbeliever, but judgment for the believer. Why?

Because God is totally equitable, always absolutely just and righteous in all His ways. Nothing about our life escapes His notice. Books are kept, even a book of remembrance.

In Malachi, that last book of the Old Testament, we read,

Then those who feared the LORD spoke to one another, and the LORD gave attention and heard it, and a book of remembrance was written before Him for those who fear the LORD and who esteem His name.[5]

Remember Solomon's conclusion in Ecclesiastes? "God will bring every act to judgment, everything which is hidden, whether it is good or evil" (12:14). Paul tells us the same. Take time to read 2 Corinthians 5:1-11.

I know you have already read and marked the first eight verses, but now mark any reference to *the judgment seat of Christ.* Then list below what you have learned about the judgment seat from this passage.

Now let's go to Romans 14:10-12. Read and mark this passage as you did the verses from 2 Corinthians 5. Then add to your list above anything you learn about the judgment seat of Christ from this passage that you didn't learn from 2 Corinthians 5.

▶ ROMANS 14:10-12

10 But you, why do you judge your brother? Or you again, why do you regard your brother with contempt? For we will all stand before the judgment seat of God.

11 For it is written, "As I live, says the LORD, every knee shall bow to Me, and every tongue shall give praise to God."

12 So then each one of us will give an account of himself to God.

Who is being addressed in both these passages? Believers or unbelievers?

Now then, in light of what you just read and saw with your own eyes, and in light of your earlier observations, can you understand Paul's ambition to be pleasing to God? Can you understand his desire in the midst of afflictions to keep his mind on eternal things? Can you understand, Beloved, what might be part of the "eternal weight of glory far beyond all comparison" (2 Corinthians 4:17)?

Do you think it would be just of God to reward everyone equally when some were willing to suffer more for the gospel than others? When some served Him with all their heart, mind, body, soul, and strength, while others simply "jogged" through their lives, entangling themselves with the affairs of this life rather than enduring hardship as a good solider of Jesus Christ? Do you think they ought to receive the same reward?

What's the connection between 2 Corinthians 5:1-8 and 9-11? As you answer this below, remember that the word *fear*, in this context, doesn't mean "to draw back in terror" but rather "to respect God as God, to honor Him as God."

Paul reminded Timothy that "bodily discipline is only of little profit, but godliness is profitable for all things, since it holds promise for the present life and also for the life to come."[6] While godly living brings blessing by virtue of what it produces and in the peace of mind and soul it brings, it also benefits us in the life to come. In other words, what you do now—how you live, how you appropriate all that God has given you through the New Covenant—will be judged at the judgment seat of Christ, and rightly so! We're stewards of God's Word, of His gifts and grace, and it's only right that stewards give their masters an accounting of their stewardship.

The judgment seat of Christ is part and parcel of the day of Christ that we studied earlier. Paul reminded the Corinthians that this is the day when they would be his reason to be proud.[7] Proud because he diligently shepherded them as one who would give an account. That's why, as we'll see later in our study, Paul's ambition was to present them to Christ, their heavenly bridegroom, as a pure virgin.

When Paul wrote to the Thessalonians, that faithful, suffering church, he referred to them as his hope, joy, and crown of exultation in the presence of our Lord Jesus Christ at His coming.[8] His prayer for the believers in Philippi was that they would be sincere and blameless until the day of Christ—the day that would include Christ's judgment seat.[9] He urged them to hold fast the word of life, so that in the day of Christ he might have cause to glory that he did not run in vain or toil in vain.[10]

When Paul knew death was finally coming at the hands of Rome, he wrote Timothy in the confidence that he had fought the good fight, finished the course, and kept the faith, and that "in the future there is laid up for me the crown of righteousness, which the Lord, the righteous Judge, will award to me on that day; and not only to me, but also to all who have loved His appearing."[11] Did you note the description he gave our Lord? A righteous *judge!* Did you see the phrase "award...on that day"? What day? There could be no other, for there's no other mentioned but the day of Christ and His judgment seat.

Paul had already stood at one judgment seat before Gallio, the proconsul of Achaia, when he visited Corinth.[12] That was a small matter compared to standing before a Judge with whom you have no recourse, argument, or defense, because all things are naked and open in His sight. His judgment can only be just. No court of appeal is necessary.

And Paul knew that. This is why the governing ambition of his life was to fulfill the purpose of his creation—to be pleasing to God in life and in death. The judgment seat is not to deal with our sin—that was paid for in full by Jesus Christ on Calvary's cross. Rather it's there as a matter of reward or loss of reward. It's a time to recompense our deeds according to what we have done, whether good or bad. How that all measures out isn't explained in 2 Corinthians 5 or in Romans 14, but we can go to 1 Corinthians 3, where I believe we can gain more insight.

In 1 Corinthians 3, Paul is dealing with the immaturity of the believers, those who hadn't grown up and who thus were still on milk when they should have been taking solid food. Instead of studying the Word for themselves and consequently going on to maturity so they could discern good and evil, they wanted others to feed them. And each group had their "pet teacher." It's at this point that Paul makes it clear that teachers—he and Apollos in particular (Apollos was the eloquent one whom many favored above Paul)—were to do what God called them to do, being faithful in the planting and watering of the seed of God's Word. One would plant (that's what Paul did in Corinth), the other would water (that's what Apollos did in becoming their teacher after Paul left), but it was God who caused the growth.

At this point in his discourse, as he stresses the gravity of the teacher's work, Paul switches metaphors, moving from planting and watering to laying a foundation and building on it. He speaks not only of the one who lays the foundation—by introducing them to Christ, as Paul did in Corinth—but also of the one who comes along and builds on that foundation, as Apollos did.

I think it would help you greatly to read a portion of what Paul wrote in 1 Corinthians regarding this. To me, it throws additional light on the judgment that awaits the servants of God. See what you think.

As you read the following text, watch the contrasts—the different kinds of building materials and the fate of each. Mark the following words and phrases so you don't miss them: *the day, reward, each man's work.*

◗ 1 CORINTHIANS 3:10-15

10 According to the grace of God which was given to me, like a wise master builder I laid a foundation, and another is building on it. But each man must be careful how he builds on it.

11 For no man can lay a foundation other than the one which is laid, which is Jesus Christ.

12 Now if any man builds on the foundation with gold, silver, precious stones, wood, hay, straw,

13 each man's work will become evident; for the day will show it because it is to be revealed with fire, and the fire itself will test the quality of each man's work.

¹⁴ If any man's work which he has built on it remains, he will receive a reward.

¹⁵ If any man's work is burned up, he will suffer loss; but he himself will be saved, yet so as through fire.

Now this may seem a little strange, but I am going to ask you to do it—and then you can decide if you will or not. I really want you to do this so you "get the picture."

Using stick figures or whatever, draw this scene that Paul paints for the Corinthians in verses 12-15. You might want to approach it from the angle of two different persons with contrasting building materials. Just note that the building can have only one foundation—Jesus Christ. That's the foundation Paul laid when he brought the good news of the New Covenant, that ministry of life, to Corinth.

As you do this, note the "fate" of each person.

After Paul writes what he does in 1 Corinthians 3, he then deals in 1 Corinthians 4 with the way the Corinthians were judging him. In doing so, he admonishes them to stop what they're doing:

Therefore do not go on passing judgment before the time, but wait until the Lord comes who will both bring to light the things hidden in the darkness and disclose the motives of men's hearts; and then each man's praise will come to him from God.[13]

Paul knew he would be judged; he realized that the motives of his heart and of the hearts of the Corinthians would be exposed. Does that cause you consternation, Beloved? It does me. And it causes me to stop immediately and tremble when I know there isn't a pure motive behind what I am doing or saying. It isn't just the outward deed that's inspected —it's the motive behind the deed. Sobering, isn't it? It should be, for the judgment seat of Christ is a sobering event.

We shall stand before Him, one by one, and there He will distinguish what was good from what was not. He will look not at the quantity of our work, but the quality. Have we built with gold, silver, precious stones— treasures that cannot be created by the works of man? Or have we built with what is bad—worthless?

And what is worthless? Anything produced by the flesh for the flesh! Gold, silver, and precious stones can only be discovered and mined, but with the work of our hands and the sweat of our brow we can grow our own wood, hay, or straw. The building may go up quickly, it might even be impressive to those who look at it, but the fire of God will consume it. What we do in the flesh profits nothing. Oh, we will be saved—the foundation remains—but only as through fire!

I think this illustration that Paul gives in 1 Corinthians 3 was primarily to warn those who would come along as teachers and ministers in the church that they couldn't do God's work in the flesh and get away with it. There's a day of reckoning, the judgment seat when everything hidden in darkness will be brought to His pure light.

The other apostles, in their writings, also remind readers of the rewards to come and the crowns that await. The beloved apostle John writes in his second epistle, "Watch yourselves, that you do not lose what we have accomplished, but that you may receive a full reward."[14]

The saved will stand at the judgment seat of Christ; the lost will stand at the Great White Throne judgment, which will come, according to Revelation 20:10-15, at least a thousand years later, if you take literally (as I do) the words "one thousand years" mentioned six times in the first seven verses of that chapter.

Let's bring today's study to a close by reading this passage from Revelation so there'll be no confusion in your mind, precious one, as to the differences in these judgments. It's always a good idea to read for yourself any Scripture passages that you hear taught, so that you can check out the teacher as well as see truth for yourself. Yes, the teachers—the builders—will give an account for what they teach,[15] but you will also give an account, if you don't study and handle the Word of God accurately.[16]

▶ REVELATION 20:10-15

10 And the devil who deceived them was thrown into the lake of fire and brimstone, where the beast and the false prophet are also; and they will be tormented day and night forever and ever.

11 Then I saw a great white throne and Him who sat upon it, from whose presence earth and heaven fled away, and no place was found for them.

12 And I saw the dead, the great and the small, standing before the throne, and books were opened; and another book was opened, which is the book of life; and the dead were judged from the things which were written in the books, according to their deeds.

13 And the sea gave up the dead which were in it, and death and Hades gave up the dead which were in them; and they were judged, every one of them according to their deeds.

14 Then death and Hades were thrown into the lake of fire. This is the second death, the lake of fire.

15 And if anyone's name was not found written in the book of life, he was thrown into the lake of fire.

Examine this text in the light of the five *W*s and one *H:* who, what, when, where, why, and how.

Who are the principal characters in this event?

What is happening? List the specifics. What is the basis of their judgment?

When is it happening?

Where is it happening?

Why? What is the purpose of this judgment? Aren't they all ending up in the same place?

How is it happening?

If you're feeling creative, why don't you draw a sketch of this judgment?

A SKETCH OF THE GREAT WHITE THRONE JUDGMENT

This, Beloved, is the fate of all who pass through death's door without the presence of God's Spirit within them, without the Spirit who is given to believers as the promise of redemption. Those who appear before the Great White Throne judgment are people from all walks of life, people for whom Jesus died, but who refused to believe that truth and acknowledge Him as Lord.

They refused to bow, to submit, to believe on the Lord Jesus Christ. Consequently, after the millennial reign of the Lord Jesus Christ, the sea will give up the dead (dead in their trespasses and sins) and Hades will empty her ever-expanding borders where she has contained the living dead for this day and hour, and they will stand one by one before God Almighty. The books will be opened, but none of those standing there will find their names in the Book of Life. Their names will have been removed from the book because they did not choose life by coming to the Father through Jesus Christ, who is the way, the truth, the life. Instead they remained with their father the devil, the one who was a liar and a murderer from the beginning. Now they shall join him in the lake of fire, where they will stay for all eternity. There is no annihilation. As eternal life is forever, so is the lake of fire forever—eternal punishment, according to Matthew 25:41-46.

But why, you may ask, if they're all going to the lake of fire anyway, is there a need to judge them for their deeds? That's a valid question that I believe we find answered for us in our examination of the judgment seat of Christ.

Everyone who stands before the judgment seat of Christ is going to heaven—will be in heaven eternally with the Father. Yet God is just, fair, and righteous in all His ways. And because He is equitable, everyone will be judged according to his or her deeds—whether lost or saved. You've seen what happens to the saved in terms of reward and loss of reward, so let's look at the Great White Throne judgment. Those there are judged "according to their deeds."[17] Consequently, I believe from this and from two other passages that there are degrees of punishment. All are punished eternally, but at different heights or depths, shall we say.

Listen to Jesus' teaching, as recorded in Matthew. Mark the "woes," plus the word *tolerable* and the phrase *the day of judgment.*

▶ MATTHEW 11:20-24

20 Then He began to denounce the cities in which most of His miracles were done, because they did not repent.

21 "Woe to you, Chorazin! Woe to you, Bethsaida! For if the miracles had occurred in Tyre and Sidon which occurred in you, they would have repented long ago in sackcloth and ashes.

22 "Nevertheless I say to you, it will be more tolerable for Tyre and Sidon in the day of judgment than for you.

23 "And you, Capernaum, will not be exalted to heaven, will you? You will descend to Hades; for if the miracles had occurred in Sodom which occurred in you, it would have remained to this day.

24 "Nevertheless I say to you that it will be more tolerable for the land of Sodom in the day of judgment, than for you."

These are sinners who refused to repent and believe despite what they saw with their own eyes. What will happen to them? How will their punishment compare with Sodom and Gomorrah's? Why? Write your insights below.

Listen to what Jesus tells His twelve disciples as He sends them out as His ambassadors to the surrounding cities:

> Whoever does not receive you, nor heed your words, as you go out of that house or that city, shake the dust off your feet. Truly I say to you, it will be more tolerable for the land of Sodom and Gomorrah in the day of judgment than for that city.[18]

This has been a sobering lesson, hasn't it, Beloved? I remember the first time I heard someone talk about the judgment seat of Christ. I was but a babe in the Lord, and to be honest, it just didn't sound right to me that Jesus would have taught something like this. So I studied it on my own and found it to be true—and far more sobering than when I first heard it.

As Paul said, "Therefore, knowing the fear of the Lord, we persuade men, but we are made manifest to God" (2 Corinthians 5:11).

I'll be with you tomorrow, precious one. I am praying for you as I write. Would you pray for me since teachers shall receive the greater judgment?

God, grant us pure hearts that we might see You with
utmost clarity. May our driving passion be to be pleasing to
You in what we do and why we do it.

— D A Y   F O U R —

I'll never forget how God used one of the verses we're about to study today to keep me from fulfilling a desire that would have kept me, I'm sure, from the ministry I'm now involved in. It was a temptation I had wrestled with before I ever married Jack. In the midst of this great testing as a young Christian, God brought to my remembrance these words:

> For the love of Christ constraineth us; because we thus judge, that if one died for all, then were all dead: and that he died for all, that they which live should not henceforth live unto themselves, but unto him which died for them, and rose again. (2 Corinthians 5:14-15, KJV)

What I wanted, what I longed for, I couldn't have. The love of Christ "constrained me." I could not live for myself again. My heart for God—and the fear of facing my Lord at the judgment seat of Christ and having to hang my head in shame for the sake of temporal happiness—kept me on that straight and narrow path of obedience.

At the time I had no inkling of what God would do in the future, that there would ever be a Precept Ministries International working in more than 118 countries and 70 languages. Being a registered nurse, it never occurred to me that I would ever write a book or do many other things that I do now in ministry, although I have no formal degree or training to qualify me in the eyes of others.

In the *New American Standard Bible* that verse begins, "For the love of Christ controls us." Controlled by love! The Greek word translated as "control" means "to hold together, to confine, to shut in to one purpose." It was used of laying siege so that escape was impossible. That's what the love of God did for me; He held me back from sin. It makes me cry to think of it. I want to fall on my face in eternal gratitude for His restraining, constraining love that He poured out in me that I might give back to Him in love's obedience. What a fool I would have been not to be controlled by love!

Oh, how I love the verses you and I are going to study today. They're liberating. They're God's key that unlocks the shackles of our past that would keep us from moving out boldly for God, shackles that chain us to the lie, the conviction that we'll never really amount to anything for God because of where we've been and what we've done.

Read 2 Corinthians 5:11-17 before we continue further into our time together. As you do, mark the following: every occurrence of the word *died,* the phrases *according to the flesh* and *new creature.* Remember, this passage was written for you, and this is truth. Truth that sets us free, that sets us apart. Truth that will never alter. Truth that will never find an exception.

Now, Beloved, what did you see about yourself in these verses? According to God, what is true about you? What does He say? Write it out in your own words.

Paul has been made a minister of the New Covenant, even as we all have, although not necessarily in the same role, and he takes his calling seriously. He is aware of his stewardship, of his accountability. That's why, out of the fear of the Lord, his respect for Him as God, Paul seeks to persuade the Corinthians to believe on Jesus Christ and live accordingly.

In the midst of saying all this, once again you find him pleading with the Corinthians—for although Titus has brought word of their love, their problems aren't fully resolved. There's a contingent in the church at Corinth that is still against Paul. Therefore as he writes this portion of his letter, lest they think he's trying to commend himself to them, he clears the air immediately. No reading between the lines! What Paul says, he says so that the Corinthians can be proud of him. Proud rather than ashamed of him, as some detractors would try to convince them to be. These detractors are people who take pride in appearance but not in heart. In other words, the outside may look good, but the inside is rotten.

So, however Paul is acting, writing—if he seems to be "beside himself," insane, out of his wits—it is for God. If he seems to be of sound mind, it is for the Corinthians. Paul is doing what he's doing because he's controlled by the love of Christ. That's Paul's only motivation. That's what holds him, what causes him to endure, what keeps him on the path of holiness.

Paul understands that if Jesus died for all, then all died. They are therefore no longer to live for themselves. They're to live for Jesus, because it was Jesus who died for them and who rose from the dead for them. Everything Jesus did, He did on behalf of others—and Paul's heart was to have a heart like Jesus. Paul was going to imitate Jesus.

And what does this mean to our relationships? to how we look at others? to how we deal with others? It means that we're no longer to look at them in a fleshly way. We're to view them as they are in Christ—sins forgiven, brand-new creatures.

Listen to his words, let them go deep inside, running down like oil softening any calluses that have formed in your heart against people you don't like or appreciate for any reason—whether it be a personal matter or some prejudice that you hold against "people like that."

> Therefore from now on we recognize no one according to the flesh; even though we have known Christ according to the flesh, yet now we know Him in this way no longer. Therefore if anyone is in Christ, he is a new creature; the old things passed away; behold, new things have come. (5:16-17)

No person's past is ever to be held against him. A death and a resurrection have taken place. Paul no longer views Jesus as a baby in a manger, a son in His mother's arms, a tortured body hanging on a cross, a wrapped body in a tomb. He doesn't think of Christ in the flesh any longer. Jesus is raised and seated at the right hand of the Father. His work of redemption given Him by His father is finished—complete. The next time we see Him we'll see Him as King of kings and Lord of lords coming in righteousness to judge the world. And when we see Him, "we will be like Him, because we will see Him just as He is!"[19]

If we see Jesus as complete, then we must see His work of redemption complete in every person who believes on Him. And what are we to see and believe? That every redeemed person in Christ is a new creature; the old things have passed and the new things have come. Hallelujah! We aren't what we used to be!

I have friends who were formerly involved in lesbianism, homosexuality, adultery, thievery, etc., but who were washed, sanctified, justified. I no longer look at them as they once were, nor do they look at me and think "adulteress." I was once, but I am not that now. I am a brand-new creature. Old things have passed away. I no longer live, think, or act as I use to. Yes, I am in process—pressing on, being transformed from glory to glory into His image, and a lot remains to be done. I have not attained, but I know that all things have become new because I have been reconciled to God. I am a new creature enabled by the work of the sanctifying spirit to press on to Christlikeness. Whereas that was not possible before, it is now, and it will come to pass. This is the glorious message of hope Paul had to bring to people.

O precious one, have you allowed your past to keep you from serving God? Have you thought because of where you've been, what you did, that you would always be a second-class citizen in the kingdom of God? Are you afraid someone will find out what you were? Expose you?

If they did, they would have to open up a coffin, for that's where the old you lies—dead! Romans 6 tells us that your "old man" died and that a new you has been raised from the dead to walk in newness of life.

"All these things are from God," Paul says (2 Corinthians 5:18), so if anyone is going to come against you, they're going to have to do battle with your Covenant Partner.

And if God is for you, who is against you? He who did not spare His own Son but delivered Him over for you, how will He not also with Him freely give you all things?*

---

* I've changed the pronouns in Romans 8:31-32 from "us" to "you," precious one, because I don't want you to miss the point: God is saying this to you!

Who will bring a charge against God's elect? God is the one who justifies; who is the one who condemns? Christ Jesus is He who died, yes, rather who was raised, who is at the right hand of God, who also intercedes for us.[20]

Don't buy the lies of the enemy, Beloved, as he uses the tongues of men. Listen to God, believe God. 2 Corinthians 5:17 is one of the major verses that has given me the freedom to share my past so openly. I know who I am in Christ—I am a new creature. And I know that because I am not what I used to be.

The same is true for you if you're truly His child. Just remember it's the same for all His children, so treat them accordingly. Don't hold a "past" against anyone whom God in His great mercy has redeemed. Would you make yourself greater than God?

— DAY FIVE —

I think it would be so good if every morning, before we ever put our feet on the floor or rise from our bed, we would make the conscious decision that this day, no matter what the discipline, the cost, we are going to live for Christ. It would be the first commitment of the day, spoken aloud—a confession with our mouths from our hearts.

I say that because habits like this help us keep our focus. In 2 Corinthians 5:15, Paul says that Jesus died for all, that they who live should no longer live for themselves but for Him who died and rose again on their behalf. As we rise, we rise to live a resurrected life as new creatures for the resurrected One.

To know that we're no longer to live for ourselves and to obey this is to have a heart for God. The most miserable and wretched people are those who live for themselves. Not only are they never satisfied and terribly discontented, they also usually make everyone else that way simply by their presence. And what is their problem? They need to be reconciled to God and walk in the fullness of that reconciliation.

But how can this happen? That, dear one, is where *we* come in. Despite the differences in our spiritual gifts, our talents, our personalities, our denominations—and I could go on and on—every child of God has one ministry in common: the ministry of reconciliation. Not reconciliation between two parties living here on earth, but between One who resides in heaven and another who resides on earth.

But let me have you see that for yourself before I go any further. Read 2 Corinthians 5 all the way through this time. I want you to go back and read what you've already studied and marked because I want you to have Paul's flow of thought. Actually, it would be best to go all the way back to 4:16 and begin there.

When you come to 5:18, you're going to see a new key word that will be repeated in varied forms: *reconciled, reconciliation, reconcile.* Mark this word, whenever you see it, in a color or way that makes it stand out on the page. I used red and a symbol like this: ⋈

It would also be good to mark every reference to God the Father. Remember the triangle?

When you finish, list below what you have learned about God from 2 Corinthians 5:18-21. Make sure you're thorough in recording all that the text has shown you.

Now, Beloved, what did you learn about yourself from these scriptures? Don't answer this hurriedly. Think through the text. Give your indwelling Tutor the opportunity to lead you and guide you through these truths.

I know this is going to sound tacky, but believe me it wasn't tacky at the time. I was traveling by myself after a very formal occasion. When I returned to my hotel room to get my things and pack for my flight home, I started to change my shoes. Who travels on planes in rhinestone shoes? They were gorgeous—classy slings, a gift from my dear friend Grace Kinser, who took it upon herself to dress me and keep me in style when I had no money to do so. I had one shoe off and was about to take off the other when a conviction came into my heart that I was to wear those rhinestone shoes home. Thinking that was ridiculous, I slipped my bare foot into the more sensible travel shoe. But it didn't stay there long. I *felt* that for some reason I was to wear the rhinestone shoes.

What I didn't know at the time was that God was working on a "rhinestone cowboy" who needed to be reconciled to Him and who would come across my path.

The plane landed, but for some reason the door didn't open for a long time. So there I stood, packed in line, all of us eager to get off the plane. Suddenly this deep male voice behind me said, "I sure do like your rhinestone shoes." Smiling and turning to thank him, I saw his big grin and his ten-gallon hat. Although I didn't look, I was sure there were cowboy boots to match.

This was years ago; I was much younger and the man was a flirt. But even flirts need the gospel, so I began to pray and redeem the time. In the back of my mind I thought the door might continue having problems until God said what He wanted to say to this man.

The conversation turned rather quickly to the usual: What do you do? I first asked him about himself, trying to find the door God wanted to use to this man. Then in turn he asked me, "What do you do?"

Smiling, with all the dignity I could muster, I said, "I'm an ambassador."

"An *ambassador!* You're kidding!"

He was almost laughing, yet there was delight in his laugh. I think he was probably hoping I was telling the truth so he'd have something to tell his buddies. "Hey, you'll never believe it, but I met this lady ambassador on the plane!"

His next question came quick: "An ambassador for who?"

"A king."

"A *king!* Wow! What king?"

He asked, so I told him: "The King of kings—His name is Jesus Christ, and this is what He has done…"

With or without rhinestone shoes, even barefoot, if we belong to the King, we're ambassadors of the King. Whenever, wherever, we always have an ongoing ministry. The ministry of reconciliation. We have the message that every man, woman, child, and teenager needs.

From the down and out to the up and out and everyone in
between,
no matter the color of their skin,
the language they speak,
the culture they live in,
the gods they worship—
they must be reconciled to God, or they will perish.

God has done all that will ever be done on their behalf. They just don't know it, and it is your calling and mine to let them know the truth.

God so loved them right where they are—enemies, helpless, sinners, without God and without hope—that in the fullness of time He sent His only begotten Son from heaven to become flesh and blood, like us, so that Jesus might taste death on our behalf.

After demonstrating to all humanity through the life of His Son how God had intended for us to live, God then took His Lamb—without spot or blemish—and sacrificed Him for our sins.

Blood had to be shed, for without the shedding of blood there can be no remission of our sins.[21] But the blood that was shed could not be tainted by sin; it could not have one drop of Adam's blood in it, for it was by this one man, Adam, that sin entered into the world and death by sin. Death was the lot, the fate of all men, because all sinned.[22] There was no righteous man on the face of the earth who lived apart from sin until God sent forth His Son, born of a virgin,[23] born not of Adam's seed but of God's, by the power of the Holy Spirit.[24]

God could not redeem us with corruptible things like silver and gold from this empty way of life inherited from our forefathers. Redemption could come only one way: with the precious blood of a lamb unblemished and spotless, the blood of Christ.[25]

So after He was tempted of the devil, tried, tested, and in all ways tempted such as you and I are[26]...and after proving that He was the Christ, the Son of God, through His miracles and signs[27]...and after proclaiming to the multitudes the good news of the kingdom of God... Jesus continued in obedience, continued to yield Himself into the hands of His Father. And God took His Son, nailed Him to a cross, and there...

made Him who had never sinned
to be sin for us (2 Corinthians 5:21).

God laid on Jesus Christ the iniquity of all mankind—every human being from the time of Adam and Eve through the millennium yet to come. The oceans of sin flooded His soul, sucking Him down into the bowels of hell.

And He cried, "My God, My God, why have You
forsaken Me?"[28]

He was forsaken, Beloved, that you might never be forsaken. He was made sin so that you, in exchange, might have His righteousness, might become the righteousness of God *in* Him. In Jesus—nowhere else.

God in Christ did this for you, not by counting your sins, your trespasses against you, but against His innocent Son.

This is the message of reconciliation that you and I are stewards of. Having received it, having believed it, having embraced it and been saved by it, we now have a stewardship, a calling, a ministry, a message to a dying world:

"Be reconciled to God" (2 Corinthians 5:20).

To be reconciled means to take two who are at enmity with one another—enemies—and reunite them. We were the enemies, we were the ones who turned our backs on God, who said we wanted to be our own gods, to live our own lives, to set our own standards, to believe what we wanted to believe. *We* moved from God; God never moved from us.

But when we moved, God moved. He stretched out His arms in redemption and nailed them to a cross, showing us how much He loved us even when we were sinners.

Now it's our turn to move. God is in heaven. Jesus sits at His right hand interceding for us. And God has committed to us the word, the message of reconciliation. He has ordained us as ambassadors for Christ. We represent the King, the sovereign Ruler of the universe, almighty God. His kingdom. We're called, commissioned, and endued with power from on high by the Holy Spirit who indwells every believer.

We're to move wisely, fearlessly, prayerfully into the nations and kingdoms of this world with the word of reconciliation, not fearing the temporal powers but rather laying down our lives for the sake of the gospel of Jesus Christ, as servants of the New Covenant. Not excusing ourselves from duty because of a sinful unworthy past, because He has made us new creatures in Christ Jesus, equipped with power from on high and standing in the lavish grace of God that supplies our every need according to His riches in Christ Jesus our Lord. We're not to fear the threats of men. Nor are we to fear death.

The grave will never contain our soul, for we'll be immediately absent from the body and present with the Lord. The flames of hell will never lick our feet, for we shall immediately walk His streets of gold. The tears will quickly be wiped away by the finger of our God as He says, "Welcome home! Well done, My good and faithful servant!"[29] Mourning and sorrow with pass away, for in His presence there is fullness of joy.[30] And who will be our joy, our crown of rejoicing? It will be those to whom we took the word of reconciliation. Whether we sowed it, watered it, or were present at the reaping, we'll have done what God who gives the increase would have us do as His ambassadors.

What higher calling could we have than to be ambassadors for Christ? To reconcile men to God is to have a heart like His. This is why He sent His Son into the world, and why His Son sends you into the world!

MEMORY VERSES

Therefore we also have as our ambition, whether at home or absent, to be pleasing to Him. For we must all appear before the judgment seat of Christ, so that each one may be recompensed for his deeds in the body, according to what he has done, whether good or bad.

2 CORINTHIANS 5:9-10

SMALL-GROUP DISCUSSION QUESTIONS

1. From what you see in this week's Scripture passages, what keeps us from losing heart in difficult circumstances?
2. What truth is Paul teaching with the tent metaphor in 2 Corinthians 5:1?
3. How does the Holy Spirit enable us to face death with confidence?
4. How should our present behavior be affected by knowing that after death we will be "at home with the Lord"?
5. What did you learn from this week's passages about the judgment seat of Christ? What is the purpose of the judgment seat of Christ? Who will be there, and why? And what will be revealed there?
6. What is the danger of rushing someone into a profession of faith? (How does John 10:27-30 help us with this question?)
7. Since Jesus died for all, how are we then to live?
8. What does being a new creature in Christ mean? How should that affect the way we see others?
9. How exactly is a person reconciled to God, and what is the result of that reconciliation?

APPLICATION:

10. What does it mean to you to belong to Jesus and to hear the Shepherd's voice?

11. What does it mean for you to make it your ambition to be pleasing to the Lord?
12. What does it mean for you to have the love of God control you?

---

1. As noted by Lyle Dorsett in *A Passion for Souls: The Life of D. L. Moody* (Chicago: Moody, 1997), 380-81; and A. P. Fitt in "The Shorter Life of D. L. Moody" in *The D. L. Moody Collection,* ed. James S. Bell Jr. (Chicago: Moody, 1997), 96-97.
2. Ecclesiastes 12:1-7.
3. Ecclesiastes 12:13-14.
4. Philippians 1:21.
5. Malachi 3:16.
6. 1 Timothy 4:8.
7. 2 Corinthians 1:14.
8. 1 Thessalonians 2:19-20.
9. Philippians 1:10.
10. Philippians 2:16.
11. 2 Timothy 4:8.
12. Acts 18:12-16.
13. 1 Corinthians 4:5.
14. 2 John 8.
15. James 3:1.
16. 2 Timothy 2:15.
17. Revelation 20:12.
18. Matthew 10:14-15.
19. 1 John 3:2.
20. Romans 8:33-34.
21. Leviticus 17:11; Hebrews 9:22.
22. Romans 5:12.
23. Romans 3:9-18,23; Matthew 1:23.
24. Matthew 1:18-23.
25. 1 Peter 1:18-19.
26. Hebrews 4:15.
27. John 20:30-31.
28. Matthew 27:46.
29. See Matthew 25:21-23.
30. Revelation 21:4; Psalm 16:11.

SUFFERING AND SEPARATION THAT BRING HOLINESS

— D A Y   O N E —

W hen you have a heart for God and His ministry, the things of His kingdom more and more will ever be before you. There will be an increasing hunger, a longing, a greater desire for holiness, so that you give no cause for offense in any aspect of your life.

Does this seem foreign to what you see and know experientially about the Christian life today? I would assume so, for such passion, zeal, sacrifice, discipline is a rarity—especially in the Western world, where we still haven't paid a great price of suffering for bearing the name "Christian." But our day of suffering for Christ may come, and if so—what then?

I am convinced that God in His gracious response to all the prayer and fasting of His people has given us a reprieve from persecution. With that reprieve, my passion and prayer is that we will seize the day—

that we will take advantage of the times,

that we will prepare ourselves by cleansing ourselves from all defilement of flesh and spirit,

perfecting holiness in the fear of God.

This is the acceptable time, the day of salvation, and it must be seized or we'll miss the day and live to bitterly regret it.

As we study 2 Corinthians 6 and 7 this week, it's critical that you realize Paul was dealing with a church that had great problems, particularly all sorts of divisions. These people came from a society that had taken the name of their city and used it to describe a lifestyle. The phrase the Romans coined was "to corinthianize," which meant to live in moral debauchery, without restraint. It would be like someone being asked, "Well, what did you do last night?" and answering, "Not much, just the usual corinthianizing."

As you can see from this map,[1] Corinth was the connecting city between Achaia and Greece, with Macedonia to the north. It was on an isthmus where a canal had been built to connect two bodies of water, thus saving ships the dangerous trip around the Peloponnesus. Corinth became a melting pot of diverse cultures, gods, philosophies, and customs. It was a city where you did what was right in your own eyes, and as long as it didn't interfere with Roman law or disturb the peace, you could get away with it.

In Corinth there were almost two slaves for each of the 250,000 citizens who lived there. There were twelve heathen temples in which the Corinthians could worship various gods—including Asclepius, the god of healing. It's believed that his temple was built later than the others; they needed a god of healing because sexually transmitted diseases were bringing all sorts of bodily afflictions. Excavators at the site of this temple in Corinth have uncovered a storeroom containing a staggering number of clay figurines of the male sexual organ that apparently had been laid before this god's altar by men pleading for healing.

The church in Corinth included not only many slaves but also many who had been involved in all sorts of sexual activities forbidden by the God of Abraham, Isaac, and Jacob—fornication, adultery, perverted effeminacy, and homosexuality, not to mention the thievery, drunkenness, reviling, and swindling that went on in the temples as the Corinthians worshiped their idols. They loved their bodies and worked out in the gymnasiums in the nude, which was part of the Hellenistic lifestyle they held on to even though the Romans ruled politically.

They loved the wisdom of men, embraced the current philosophies, and to a degree honored their traditional gods, even though they were amused somewhat by the ancient tales of their adventures. Everyone needed some sort of god, and there were all sorts to choose from.

According to Greek mythology, many of these gods had lived lives much like those who followed them, except of course for their divine power.

When the church at Corinth was born by the Spirit from above, God did not move them away but left them in that culture. And though they were no longer powerless to live victoriously, not all who professed Christ were living as they should. As I shared earlier, they didn't go on to maturity. It was easier, more convenient to let someone else feed them and to follow that person like immature little puppies, licking the hand of whoever paid them attention, delighting their palates with delicious morsels. So the puppies gathered around their favorites with their tongues hanging out, tails wagging. Or were their tails being wagged by someone?

Not all the teachers liked Paul. Many doubted whether he was a genuine apostle. Had God sent His best to them—or was this a straggler coming on his own? Maybe they shouldn't have opened their hearts, their arms so wide? Was he really worthy of their love, their support?

This is the background of those in Corinth whom Paul was called to minister to.

As you read through 2 Corinthians 6:1–7:2, retire to a place where you can be alone, quiet. Ask God to take His precious Word and cleanse you, Beloved, so that you might perfect holiness in His sight.

As you read, follow these guidelines:

- Listen carefully to Paul's concern. Watch the words he uses.
- Note what he instructs them to do and why.
- Color every pronoun that refers to Paul, including usages of *we* and *us*.
- Mark in color every reference to the Corinthians.
- When you finish, look at what you marked and note here what you learned about each.

— D A Y   T W O —

Our society has lost its conscience. Have you ever wondered why? I believe it's because we as believers have lost our conscience, and in losing our conscience we have discredited Christianity. Very rarely do people ever apologize or try to excuse themselves because of their wrong behavior. Instead we're quick to accept another's sin because it justifies ours. It gives us an excuse: "After all, we're all human. All sinners."

Where is that constraining, controlling love that reins in our emotions, desires, passions, dreams, and ambitions, holding them tight in a determination that we will not—no matter what—discredit the ministry of reconciliation to which God has called us?

Paul was greatly concerned for some in Corinth. They were missing their opportunity of service. They were going to suffer loss needlessly at the judgment seat of Christ. They were permitting the flesh to have its way. They were careless in the company that they kept, and consequently they were "going under," so to speak. God's grace was there—totally sufficient to carry them through any situation—but they weren't appropriating it.

Isn't this the same in our day? My heart grieves every time I hear of some Christian recording artist or other public Christian figure being caught in sin, walking out of her marriage, marrying someone else who oftentimes left his mate also. It grieves me when anyone who calls himself a Christian does this, but it's worse to me when it's a public figure in Christendom. Whether the person is a genuine child of God or not, the world can make no distinction if they only know the title we carry. When they see "us" doing what they do, living as they live, then Christianity is discredited. There is no righteousness (living according to what God says is right), no cross bearing, no death to self that distinguishes us from them. We become just another religion and the brunt of their jokes and the jibes of comedians, newscasters, and talk show hosts.

And so people turn to television programs and the authors they promote—attempting to get in touch with their inner self, the spirit, the power that lies within—so they can satisfy a void that only God can fill.

Fulfilling these "spiritual" needs seems to be their only recourse—because, after all, what difference did their "Christianity" make?

Corinth needed the gospel. The door was wide open, the population transient. If those coming through that isthmus could experience the light of the knowledge of God in the face of Jesus Christ and be reconciled to God, they could take that light with them wherever they went.

Thus Paul urged the Corinthians not to receive the grace of God in vain. To receive it in vain—in emptiness, as if it were nothing—was to miss its power to sustain us through any and every situation of life we face. How this will come home to us in our last week of study on this topic!

Now is the time, not later. At the acceptable time, God listened to us. He saw our distress—the distress sin always brings. He heard our cries and He moved in salvation. He, almighty God, helped us! So now is the time to live, to appropriate His all-sufficient grace, "for He says, 'At the acceptable time I listened to you, and on the day of salvation I helped you.' Behold, now is 'the acceptable time,' behold, now is 'the day of salvation'—giving no cause for offense in anything, so that the ministry will not be discredited, but in everything commending ourselves as servants of God" (2 Corinthians 6:2-4).

The world has covered itself unconscionably with its cloak of sin and not even blushed, because we, by our willful, self-centered, nonsacrificing lifestyles, have discredited Christianity. And in doing so we've put obstacles in the way of others, deceiving them in respect to that straight, narrow way and that small gate that leads to eternal life. Instead they chose the broad way, thinking they're fine, when in reality they're groping through the darkness and headed to the precipice of hellfire and eternal damnation.

And what will you do? What will I do? How will we live so that we do not discredit the ministry?

Paul says that in every aspect of our lives, in every single thing we do, in every way that we respond, we're to give no cause for offense in anything but are to commend ourselves as servants of God. The Greek word for "offense" in this passage is *proskope*. It means a cause of stumbling, an occasion for another person to sin because of the way we behave. Because we're so human, we often excuse or accuse one another based on our behavior rather than on the written Word of God. This is why Paul, in writing to the Romans, described the reprobate mind-set and its consequential behavior in such detail:

> And just as they did not see fit to acknowledge God any longer, God gave them over to a depraved mind, to do those things which are not proper, being filled with all unrighteousness, wickedness, greed, evil; full of envy, murder, strife, deceit, malice; they are gossips, slanderers, haters of God, insolent, arrogant, boastful, inventors of evil, disobedient to parents, without understanding, untrustworthy, unloving, unmerciful; and, although they know the ordinance of God, that those who practice such things are worthy of death, they not only do the same, but also give hearty approval to those who practice them. (Romans 1:28-32)

Sinners always want company. That's why they delight when any ministry of the Lord is discredited—unless, of course, the Spirit of God is wooing them to salvation. Then there's a heartache, a painful disillusionment.

Let's look at how Paul and his faithful companions commended themselves as servants and ministers of God. And as we do, may we know the cry of a heart that says, "Search me, O God, and know my heart; try me and know my anxious thoughts; and see if there be any hurtful way in me."[2]

> *O Father, Father, as we read, bear witness to our hearts that this is Your Word, Your example, Your mirror for us to look in, so that we might see any way in which we are blemished, spotted by wrong thinking or wrong doctrine, and that we might wash it away with the water of Your Word.*

The first way Paul says we commend ourselves is in endurance. Listen to verse 4:

...in everything commending ourselves as servants of God, in much endurance, in afflictions, in hardships, in distresses. (2 Corinthians 6:4)

Endurance. Much endurance. To endure means to stay under pressure, to stay with it, stick to it, to not quit but instead to persevere. Our society is fragmented, families torn apart, relationships shattered, because we don't stay together under the pressure of unhappy times. Now please know that I'm not saying if someone in your family is physically abusing you that you should continue to allow them to behave that way. I even hesitate to bring this up, but having a live talk radio show, Jan Silvious and I realize that many who are being abused would read these words in this way.

Paul is talking about enduring when it's easier for you, more pleasing to you, to just walk away. I think the most obvious example in this epistle is Paul's continuing endurance with the church in Corinth that is not only causing him so much pain but also demanding so much time, so much care. In 7:3 he would assure them, "You are in our hearts to die together and to live together."

A servant of God doesn't walk away from afflictions, as you've already seen. Neither do servants of God remove themselves from hardships. Hardships are necessities, the difficulties of life that come our way, difficulties we can't righteously escape. They fall to us as our natural lot in life and become a platform, an arena to appropriate and display the sufficiency of His grace. It might be caring for a sick loved one or an elderly parent, or living with a difficult mate, or bearing graciously with some physical infirmity.

When Fanny Crosby was only an infant, a doctor carelessly applied a wrong medication that caused her to go blind. She would live ninety-five years and become known all over Christendom for the hymns of praise she composed, because of her willingness to endure hardships "as a good soldier of Christ Jesus."[3]

As a child with a strong sense of God and His calling upon her young heart, Fanny determined that she would commend herself as a servant of

God by submitting to the hardship brought about by her blindness. This is what she wrote when only eight years old:

> Oh what a happy child I am;
> Although I cannot see,
> I am determined that in this world
> Contented I will be.
> How many blessings I enjoy
> That other people don't;
> To sigh and weep because I'm blind
> I cannot and I won't.

Our distresses are never to be allowed to discredit our ministry. The word for "distresses" here is *stenochoria,* which means "narrowness of room." It can also be translated "calamity, anguish, distress." It is that which confines us, crowds us—that from which we long to escape, to run from, because it brings anguish, but we cannot, because we commend ourselves and His grace in situations like this.

Oh, Beloved, is this where you find yourself: afflicted, in hardship, in distress? Then read on and see if it is as bad, as difficult for you as it was for Paul:

> ...in beatings, in imprisonments, in tumults, in labors, in sleeplessness, in hunger... (6:5)

As we read on in 2 Corinthians we'll understand to an even greater degree Paul's physical sufferings for the gospel, the stripes he bore in his body; brand-marks of his Covenant Partner, the Lord Jesus Christ, as he faithfully carried on His work. The Bible tells of three of Paul's imprisonments, and the writings of Clement of Rome—a contemporary of Paul—tell of seven different imprisonments that Paul endured. Do you realize that people are incarcerated in prisons all over this world because they refuse to discredit the ministry of Jesus Christ? One of our dear workers in Chechnya was imprisoned and beheaded for his faith, and his wife did not know of his death until she saw his severed head on display in the marketplace.

Disorder is difficult to handle. That's what tumults are: situations that bring disorder, cause confusion. I know that when I get into situations like this I have to watch myself carefully so I don't react improperly, impatiently, hastily, and make a decision or do something that would discredit the ministry or me, His servant.

From these difficulties Paul turns next to the ordinary labors he's involved in as he goes about the task to which God has called him: presenting the gospel to both Jews and Gentiles. Paul was not lazy, not a slacker. In fact, he worked so hard that he didn't always get the rest he needed, nor the food. I don't believe he is proclaiming that going without sleep and food is virtuous or exemplary; rather Paul was acknowledging what he was willing to do to avoid discrediting his ministry. Don't forget that this man made tents on the side to support the work so he wouldn't be a burden on any of the churches.

For years I thought it wasn't spiritual to sleep, and I would sometimes drive my body mercilessly. However, the more I've read the stories of great saints, the more God has made me aware of the fact that we cannot abuse our bodies without paying a price, even though we're doing it for the kingdom. There are natural laws; we live in bodies of flesh that have limitations, that need sleep and proper nourishment in order to operate at their maximum. Many of these saints died young, their bodies worn out from neglect, from stress, from too many extended periods of fasting, from too many meetings, from too many hours on a horse. Pushing, pushing, and allowing no time for recovery.

I remember how my body had a difficult time healing from a second foot operation because I was on an extended fast. I believe God would have us balance our lives and not think we aren't expendable because we're about His business. There can be a very subtle sense of pride connected there, what I would call a presumptuous sin because we think we can get away with misusing our bodies because of who we are or what we are doing. I want to remember that I'm not in a hundred-yard dash but a marathon, so I can finish as strongly as He enables me.

When I watch Jesus in the gospels, I see that He spent nights in prayer, but I also know that there wasn't a frenzy about His life. I love what He said in John 17:4, as He talked with His Father on behalf of His disciples and on behalf of those who would later believe on His name: "I glorified You on the earth, having accomplished the work which You have given Me to do." This is my prayer—to finish the work *He* gives me, not the labors I myself take on for whatever reason.

Paul continues in 2 Corinthians 6:6:

> …in purity, in knowledge, in patience, in kindness, in the Holy Spirit, in genuine love…

We can discredit "the ministry" of living for Christ not only by failing in the difficult situations, but also by our responses, our reactions, our handling of people. We can discredit it in our own personal life, causing others to stumble.

Licentious living—living without moral restraints—is a natural consequence of not honoring God as God and not keeping His commands. We become like those whom we worship, those to whom we bow down and give homage. The gods of Paul's day, the Greek and Roman gods, were anything but moral.

This is the society Paul moved in, traveled in—without the companionship of a wife. Yet he determined to be pure. He was ever aware of the fact that his body was the temple of the Holy Spirit and that he could not take the members of that temple and join them to a harlot. He knew well that the mind was the battleground, and that he was to bring every thought captive to the obedience of Jesus Christ. Immorality—impurity in any form—was rooted first in the mind, then transplanted to the body.

Paul would commend himself in knowledge. He was informed. He knew what was going on, what people believed and thought. He was in tune with the world around him and yet not swayed by it. He could communicate. Watch him in Athens as he observes the people he wants to reach with the gospel, listen to him on Mar's Hill as he quotes their poets, observe him in Colossae as he challenges them to be careful of the philosophy of men. Christianity does not consign us to an intellectual vacuum. I want to learn, to continue to grow, to understand. There's so much I want to learn, but first and foremost I must know the word of truth, as Paul says in the next verse.

But I must not get ahead of the text. Paul also commended himself, exhibited himself as a servant of God by his patience with people, his kindness to them in the Holy Spirit, which of course would be with the fruit of the Spirit,[4] the character of the Spirit being seen in his life. His love for people and for God was genuine. It's so important that those who are in public ministry stay accessible to the people they minister to. I can never picture Paul "doing his thing" and then walking off the platform, never to be seen again until his next time to speak. I know that he was an imitator of Christ, and Jesus was always accessible, unless it was time for Him to be alone with His Father or alone with His disciples.

Listen again to Paul:

>...in the word of truth, in the power of God; by the weapons of righteousness for the right hand and the left...(6:7)

Paul never discredited the ministry by ignoring or distorting the Word of God. He preached no pet doctrines of his own devising; he did not twist the Scriptures to accomplish his purposes. He proclaimed the gospel in season and out of season, never compromising its message and never using it to tickle the ears. He proclaimed the gospel with sound doctrine, using it to reprove and rebuke, and he did so always with long-suffering—with kindness—in a way that would exhort his hearers, challenging them to pursue and persist. When he gave the gospel, it went forth not in word only but also in power—the power of the Holy Spirit. And they saw what kind of a man he was, because he lived righteously before them. His only weapons were not carnal; he didn't fight that way. It wasn't *his* battle, it wasn't *his* victory; it was the Lord's. It was always in righteousness. He would live by it, die for it. He was like a two-gun cowboy, the same weapons in both hands. Blow off the smoke—they work fine!

...by glory and dishonor, by evil report and good report; regarded as deceivers and yet true; as unknown yet well-known...(6:8-9)

It's one thing to serve God in the work of ministry when glory comes your way, when everyone says what a fine job you did, when you're well known, hailed, honored, respected. But it's another to continue when you're doing what God has called you to do but people dishonor you, bring evil reports about you, and call you a deceiver when that is anything but true—and when nobody knows or cares who you are. To continue when you, like Jesus, are despised and rejected, accused of having a demon, or belonging to the devil. When you persevere during times like these and when you can handle the plaudits, admiration, and honors of men—when it goes either way and you stand firm commending yourself as a servant of God—then the ministry will not be discredited. God rewards His faithful, and in time He will certainly vindicate them in the eyes of their enemies. Ours is to stand firm in His all-sufficient grace.

...as dying yet behold, we live... (6:9)

These can become deathlike situations—death to self, crucified with Christ. Nevertheless you live, yet not you but Christ in you.[5] And in His living, while death works in you, you show yourself to be a servant of your Lord. For no servant is greater than his Lord, it is simply enough to be like Him.[6]

...as punished yet not put to death... (6:9)

And when you fail—for we all do; we slip a gear and end up in carnal reverse—God will punish. The word is better translated "discipline." He disciplines, as Hebrews 12 tells us, because we're His legitimate children, and what good father is there who doesn't discipline his children for their benefit? Yet we do not stubbornly sin so that He has to take us home prematurely. We do not sin so that He has to put us to death, so that the ministry is no longer discredited.

...as sorrowful yet always rejoicing, as poor yet making many rich, as having nothing yet possessing all things. (6:10)

Weeping endures for the night, but joy comes in the morning.[7] No matter the sorrow we can always rejoice, for the sorrow is temporal. This too shall pass. Someday the tears will be wiped away. So for now, what do we do? We go with Him outside the camp, bearing His reproach and offering Him the sacrifice of praise, the fruit of our lives. Counting all things as joy because our Sovereign God has it all under control.[8]

The riches we might gain will be for others. It matters not that we're poor; the money is there to share with those who have less. Every gift we have comes down from the Father above,[9] and the gifts are ours so that we may genuinely bless those in need by giving them more than words. Although we have not the possessions, the heirlooms of the generations—the houses, lands, and stocks that others have—it matters not. We are heirs of God and joint-heirs of Jesus Christ.[10] And if we do have such riches, they're held with an open hand, for we won't allow them to possess us.

We belong to One: Jesus Christ. We live for One: Jesus Christ. Our passion is to commend ourselves as His faithful servants, enduring no matter the cost, allowing our lives to exhibit the high calling of a servant of God.

Oh, Beloved, how are you doing? Are there any changes you need to make? Any new attitudes you need to develop, any new disciplines you need to institute? If so, write them down so you have them before you. Then ask God to show you how to make these changes. Seize the day while it is yet day.

— D A Y   T H R E E —

When relationships get rough—when we become unhappy, disillusioned, disappointed, or hurt—the first thing we have a tendency to do is quit communicating. The second thing is to withhold affection. It's the way we punish, making sure the person knows he or she failed us.

This is what the Corinthians did to Paul. But Paul would not react in kind.

> Our mouth has spoken freely to you, O Corinthians, our heart is opened wide. You are not restrained by us, but you are restrained in your own affections. (6:11-12)

Paul's conscience was clear. He wasn't the one withdrawing; it was the Corinthians. When he wrote that his mouth was "open to them," which is the literal translation, he meant that he was still writing, still communicating. And his heart was as open as his mouth. Their wrong behavior couldn't quell his love, because it was God's love flowing through Paul—unconditional, never-ceasing love. Paul's behavior was not the cause of the restraint, and he would not own the blame.

How critical this is, for so often people wrongly control others by their communication or lack of it. Or by withholding their affections every time someone displeases them. As servants of God we cannot allow others to control us this way, not even members of our family or our mates. We're to be controlled only by God; we cannot serve two masters. No one can. That's why Jesus made it clear that if we're going to follow Him, all other relationships must seem as hatred in comparison to our love and allegiance to Him. Listen to what He said to the multitudes about following Him, becoming His disciple: "If anyone comes to Me, and does not hate his own father and mother and wife and children and brothers and sisters, yes, and even his own life, he cannot be My disciple."[11]

When the Judaizers—those who taught that, although you could be saved by grace, you still had to live under the Law—came into Galatia on the heels of Paul's ministry, bringing another "gospel," Paul had to deal with the situation immediately. He couldn't court their favor just for the sake of their approval or blessing. He explained it this way: "For am I now seeking the favor of men, or of God? Or am I striving to please men? If I were still trying to please men, I would not be a bond-servant of Christ."[12]

Paul cannot compromise for the sake of the Corinthians' affections or their communication, for to do so would encourage them in their wrong behavior. It's so important to keep this in mind when we're in a quandary as to how we're going to handle a difficult relationship. Healthy relationships are not manipulated. They're based on honesty and integrity.

So Paul must bring them face to face, as children, with what they must do:

Now in a like exchange—I speak as to children—open wide to us also. (6:13)

The problem for the Corinthians was the company they were keeping. They had opened their arms wide to the wrong people. This is what so often happens. We forget that the company we keep is so very important. In his first letter Paul had written this warning to the Corinthians: "Do not be deceived: 'Bad company corrupts good morals.'"[13]

I want you to read his warning for yourself, because it's also for you and me. It's a very important warning that, if not heeded, can take you to the depths of sin and despair that you never dreamed you would find yourself in.

Read this warning in 2 Corinthians 6:14-18. You can find it in the back of this book or you can read it printed out below. Mark every occurrence of the word *temple,* and note what you learn about the temple. Paul uses this term so often with the Corinthians. Watch also for the contrasts Paul lays out before them.

2 CORINTHIANS 6:14-18

[14] Do not be bound together with unbelievers; for what partnership have righteousness and lawlessness, or what fellowship has light with darkness?

15 Or what harmony has Christ with Belial, or what has a believer in common with an unbeliever?

16 Or what agreement has the temple of God with idols? For we are the temple of the living God; just as God said, "I will dwell in them and walk among them; and I will be their God, and they shall be My people.

17 "Therefore, come out from their midst and be separate," says the Lord. "And do not touch what is unclean; and I will welcome you.

18 "And I will be a father to you, and you shall be sons and daughters to Me," says the Lord Almighty.

Now list below the contrasts that Paul lays before the Corinthians in this passage.

THE CONTRASTS

_____ *VERSUS* _____

It's one thing to be in the world; it's another to be in it but not of it. You've probably heard the expression before. This is what we need to understand. What are our boundaries with unbelievers?

As we look at what Paul wrote, we first need to understand that these are not verses that remove us from the world around us, shutting out communication, dialogue, or even friendships with nonbelievers. God isn't telling us to run to our ecclesiastical sanctuaries and isolate ourselves from the world.

Remember that Jesus sent His disciples into the world to make disciples of all nations.[14] You can't make disciples if you aren't going to be with people, befriend them, and share their grief and joy as well as the gospel. We have a ministry of reconciliation, and reconciliation reunites rather than separates.

When Jesus prayed for His disciples on the way to Gethsemane, He asked the Father in their presence not to remove them from the world but to keep them from the Evil One. This is what He prayed:

> I am no longer in the world; and yet they themselves are in the world, and I come to You. Holy Father, keep them in Your name, the name which You have given Me, that they may be one even as We are. While I was with them, I was keeping them in Your name which You have given Me; and I guarded them and not one of them perished but the son of perdition, so that the Scripture would be fulfilled....
>
> I do not ask You to take them out of the world, but to keep them from the evil one. They are not of the world, even as I am not of the world. Sanctify them in the truth; Your word is truth. As You sent Me into the world, I also have sent them into the world.[15]

Jesus' concern is similar, I believe, to Paul's. Obviously the world needs us because it needs Jesus. Jesus is gone, no longer bodily with us, so we stand in the world in Christ's stead, in His place, urging people—as Paul said in 2 Corinthians 5:20—to be reconciled to God. Yet in this quest for the souls of men there will always be conflict. The enemy is not going to wave the white flag of surrender. Going down, he's going to take everyone with him he can.

Thus we're warned of the danger of yokes—believers and unbelievers harnessed together in a yoke, in a partnership. A yoke was a wooden instrument that went around the necks of two animals, harnessing them together for a task. To harness a believer with an unbeliever is dangerous, because you're trying to harness "opposites," and it doesn't work. God gave Israel that picture a long time ago in the Law: "You shall not plow with an ox and a donkey together."[16] In other words, you don't put two different kinds of animals together in a wooden yoke to plow a field. They cannot do the task together. Look at the difference in size, temperament, and strength between an ox and a donkey, let alone what they're best used for. The ox is to plow, the donkey to ride!

Righteousness and lawlessness have a totally different set of moral codes. Light and darkness cannot exist together—light is either present or it's not. Can there be harmony between a true God—Christ—and an idol, Belial? What do believers have in common with unbelievers? One believes that Jesus is the Christ, the other doesn't. And because of this they have different fathers. If you don't believe Jesus is the Christ, then you are of your father, the devil, who is a liar, a murderer, a deceiver.[17] Jesus is the opposite. He is the truth. He is the giver of life.[18] He does not deceive; rather, He came to set us free from our deception. The believer is a brand-new creature *in* Christ Jesus.

Can there be an agreement, a partnership between God's temple and idols, when God says idols are nothing but the work of man's hands that cannot speak, hear, or move? The idol is nothing, but as Paul told the Corinthians, behind the idol you'll find a demon.[19] Are we to be in partnership with something that has demons connected with it? Of course not! We are the temple of the living God!

Consequently there must be a separation. This is what sanctification is all about. This is what God graphically drew for Israel through the Law so they would get the picture, not only with an ox and a donkey but in many other ways. God's people were to be holy...separated from the unclean...*in* the world but not *of* it. We're to go, we're to take the message, we're to urge the lost to be reconciled to God, but we're not to partner with them. God shares His glory with no man, no idol—no compromise. And that's what this is all about. Paul is saying that because of who you are, because of who is in you, there can be no compromise. Such a compromise would be to compromise God. So if God is your Father, then invite the world to "visit" *His* home—to hang around *you*, for you are where He dwells and you obey the rules of the house—so they can get to know the Father of the house. Who knows? They may want to move in permanently under His authority and love!

Finally, when you're bound together in a yoke with someone who doesn't hold your same values and beliefs, you're so locked into that relationship that you can no longer act independently. You're harnessed to another who will eventually want to go in a direction you can't follow and still honor God. What are you going to do then? Who's going to win? Or whose neck will be broken in the process?

You may know what I mean from your own tragic experience. I hope you don't, Beloved, but you may have thought you could break this principle laid out in God's holy Word and somehow escape the inevitable conflict. Now you know you can't.

So what should you do? Why don't we talk about that tomorrow, and just close out this day by talking to God, reviewing what we've learned and shared and where we are in respect to all we've seen.

By the way, *you are loved.* It's just in my heart to tell you!

— D A Y   F O U R —

Promises! Promises! Always more promises...and they never come true. That may be so in your relationships with others, but believe me, precious one, it will never be true in your relationship with God. It can't be. As Paul wrote earlier. "For as many as are the promises of God, in Him they are yes; therefore also through Him is our Amen to the glory of God through us" (2 Corinthians 1:20).

When God makes a promise, all we have to do is say "Amen"—"so be it"—and take Him at His word. This is what the Corinthians were to do.

Out of respect for God, they were to respond to the condition set forth in the promise. They were to come out from the midst of those whom they were thinking of "yoking" with, and they were to cleanse themselves. Purging, purifying themselves from all defilement of the flesh and spirit that had occurred, they were to perfect holiness to bring it to maturity, to complete their course. In other words, they were to leave the yoke behind and pursue holiness instead of partnerships with people in juxtaposition to God.

But what if you yoked yourself in marriage to an unbeliever? Are you to walk away? No, Beloved—even if you entered into it willfully, knowing that you were going against God, marriage is a covenant, and God expects that covenant to stand. You are to stay with your unbeliever. There should be no separation—unless the unbeliever leaves of his or her own free will. It may be difficult for you, but according to 1 Corinthians 7, God says the unbelieving mate is "sanctified" by his or her union with you. It doesn't mean that staying married to you saves them; rather, God is saying that, because you're His, your mate is blessed by his or her union with you. Interesting, isn't it? Also, keeping your marriage intact, although it's to an unbeliever, protects your children, sets them aside for God.[20]

However, if there's any other kind of yoke you took upon yourself, then you would be very wise to get out of it if you can, even if it seems costly. Eventually, unless your partner comes to know God, it will lead to two different paths. The harmony, the fellowship, the agreement will end, because you're trying to belong to two different worlds, two different gods, the Sovereign God and the god of this world. Just remember, dear friend, when it comes to a path, a direction, a conviction that's contrary to God and His Word, you cannot compromise your relationship with God under any circumstances. God set you apart for Himself, and He must have the preeminence in your life.

Having said all this, Paul's digression is over. In 2 Corinthians 7:2 he now returns to what happened when he finally found Titus and the comfort he received.

Once again return to the text and observe 2 Corinthians 7 for yourself. Read through chapter 7 very carefully for there are some valuable insights on godly sorrow versus worldly sorrow that you need to see. Watch also the emotions Paul shares with the Corinthians as well as the emotions of the Corinthians themselves

As you read the text, mark every reference to sorrow or being made sorrowful and the following words and phrases: *affliction, comfort, I wrote,* and *repentance.*

When you finish, list on the next page what you have learned about the two different kinds of sorrow and where they lead. It will be so enlightening, especially when dealing with someone who's saying he's sorry! This will help you understand what they're really sorry about.

_____ S O R R O W   _____ S O R R O W

This will take some time, so that's all we'll do today.

– D A Y   F I V E –

Have you ever held someone in your arms who was totally broken by their sin? Their body racked with sobbing, hands trembling, groping for a tissue, wiping the tears from swollen eyes. As you hold them—saying nothing, weeping with them and for them—your heart aches for their bitterness of soul. Yet deep inside there's peace, an inward smile in your soul, because although the sin was terrible, the consequences devastating, the shame excruciating, you know it's going to be all right. Their sorrow is a godly sorrow that has led to repentance.

There's confidence. You know the sin will not be repeated because it's been dealt with as God would have it dealt with. It's over. Gone. Not to be repeated.

Weeping may endure for many long dark nights, but there will come a morning when the chill of winter's soul will be past and spring will blossom in resurrection life…and summer will follow spring.

Paul smiled. Paul probably laughed. Did he grab Titus and hug him? Did he wipe his eyes and let out a deep breath? Did he fall into a chair, weak with joy? Or maybe he bowed his head and said, "Thank You, Father. Thank You."

We don't know what form his overflowing joy took, how the tension rolled off his small frame. We just know he was relieved. Wonderfully relieved and comforted. The conflicts within, the fears without, ebbed away with the tide of this good news from Titus.

I wonder how many times Titus recounted to Paul his visit with the Corinthians, how many times Titus told him of their longing for him, their mourning over the schism, their zeal for him as a person. In the midst of all the pressures there in Macedonia, hearing Titus's account of their hearts prompted Paul to rejoice even more.

He had probably died a thousand deaths over the letter he had sent. He knew he needed to say what he said—or did he? One moment he regretted it, another moment he knew it was his duty. But to cause sorrow to those he loved—even though it was legitimate—was hard. Especially when he were unsure of their love.

But the letter had done its work, and Paul's regrets over sending it were now gone. The letter had produced a sorrow that was according to the will of God.

That, Beloved, is why you can smile deep inside when a loved one, a friend, a Christian brother or sister, is filled with a godly sorrow. You know they learned from it, and in the light of eternity that's what matters. Their heart made contact with God's heart on the issue, and now they beat as one.

As I write this, I'm reminded of a day when our son David was still in high school, and he and his dad were watching a fascinating television program on the heart. As I tripped past the family room on the way to the kitchen, I paused to watch. The image on the screen was a view through a microscope of muscle tissue from two different hearts. The cadence of the beat of each of the heart tissues was different. Then, very gently, the technician took a delicate instrument and slid one heart muscle next to the other. The minute they touched, they began to beat in unison.

A godly sorrow slides your heart toward God's, and once they touch, there is repentance. The Greek word for "repentance" is *metanoia*—a change, a reversal of a decision. Repentance is a change of mind, a change of heart that consequently brings a change of behavior.

As we watch Paul in all this, we can see valuable precepts in dealing with people who have been brought to a godly sorrow. Did you notice how Paul writes back after hearing this good news? First, he asks that they make room in their hearts for him, assuring them that he had done nothing that condemned his conscience. Listen to his words: "We wronged no one, we corrupted no one, we took advantage of no one" (2 Corinthians 7:2).

Then Paul lets them know that he is not there to condemn. He's not going to aggravate their pain; he's on their team. They're forever in his heart to die together, to live together.

This is the way I feel tonight. My oldest son, Tommy, called me, and we talked for some time about things of the Lord and family. He was once my beloved "enemy," but then came a day of godly sorrow and he was born into the kingdom. The pain of his sin, the consequences of his not listening, not believing, not obeying, had been great, but he learned and I know he won't go there again. My joy overflows. He's in my heart to die together and to live together. He's always been there, and he knows it. And that's what's so important—the security of unconditional love.

It's so good for offenders to know that despite the sin, despite the pain, they bring you joy. I always love it when I know I've brought someone joy. My spirits are lifted, and my heart is warmed. One who has sinned so greatly needs to know that his life is good for something else than bringing pain.

Offenders also need reassurance that you've seen their heart, that you believe them. They don't need to hear you take a wait-and-see attitude. I'd rather believe them than send them spiraling into deeper shame and bitterness by my hesitancy to acknowledge that they're genuinely broken. I cannot look on their heart. I am not God. I am not their judge. Sin has judged them, and they've reaped the awful consequences. I am not there to cause further pain but to comfort with the comfort I myself received from God when I failed. Paul lets them know that he believes their longing, their mourning, their zeal (7:7).

Then Paul lets them know that his intention in dealing with their situation was not to cause more sorrow for them, but to see them come to a godly sorrow that would bring repentance—a repentance that would never be regretted. A worldly sorrow would not do, for it doesn't deal thoroughly with the sin. It only writhes in anguish over the consequences.

A worldly sorrow doesn't bring salvation from the situation because it doesn't bring repentance. You're simply sorry you got caught and were exposed and inconvenienced by the situation. You were embarrassed. You suffered some uncomfortable consequences. But you weren't broken by your sin; you weren't grieved at what you had done to God and to others. Therefore, in all probability, you'll do it again.

The sorrow of the world does not bring life and salvation from the sin; rather, it brings death. And when lust has conceived, it gives birth to sin, and when sin is accomplished, it brings forth death.[21]

Godly sorrow breaks sin's power. And you can know when godly sorrow has really happened because of what follows. Listen again:

> For behold what earnestness this very thing, this godly sorrow, has produced in you: what vindication of yourselves, what indignation, what fear, what longing, what zeal, what avenging of wrong! In everything you demonstrated yourselves to be innocent in the matter. (7:11)

Did you see the list of things that happened as a result of their godly sorrow? It produced something *in* them.

First, they vindicated themselves. The word for vindicate is *apologia*. They were ready to answer for what they had done. No covering up, no skirting their sin and not naming it for what it was. They cleared themselves, as God tells us to clear our sins in 1 John 1:9. We're to confess them, call them what they are, acknowledge them. Then God can forgive us and cleanse us from all unrighteousness, because He knows our heart has touched His on the issue. You've agreed with God that what He calls sin, you call sin.

Second, their godly sorrow brought indignation. The word is *aganaktesis*. The verb *aganakteo* comes from *agan*, "much," and *achomai*, "to grieve." It's a word that carries the connotation of anger coming from displeasure. Doesn't sin make you angry? It does me. I feel an anger born out of grief over sin's triumph and its spoils.

And what else did godly sorrow evoke? Fear. The word used for "fear" is *phobos,* which means "to be afraid, to have fear, alarm." How we need more of that today! There's no fear of God before our eyes—and it's the fear of God that causes us to depart from evil. Godly sorrow drives you from sin; that's why it leads to salvation. The use of salvation by Paul is not meant to say that they finally became children of God, but rather that the salvation they experienced was deliverance from the power sin had over their lives.

With this godly sorrow we see three other manifestations that seem part of a threefold cord, testifying of the genuineness of their grief: a longing, a zeal, and an avenging of wrong. Once your heart touches God's on the issue of your sin, there's a longing to be right before Him and before everyone else, a zealous earnestness to do all you can to correct it and a commitment to totally avenge the wrong that was done.

These are things that bring a smile deep down inside, even though you weep with those who weep, for you know that their repentance is real.

Now, having affirmed all that, Paul wants them to know why he wrote them as he did. He did not write merely for the sake of the offender nor for the sake of the one who was offended, but that they might see the importance of following his instructions, of doing what was right in the sight of God as he pointed out. He hoped that deep down inside they might realize how much they truly appreciated him for who he was and for what he faithfully stood for. That's why the letter was written—and it worked. This was Paul's comfort. What he intended to happen, happened.

And not only that, but through all this, Titus loves them even more. The way the Corinthians received Titus—the respect, the trembling—showed Titus their hearts were right with God and with God's servant, Paul, who so faithfully brought them the message of reconciliation. A reconciliation that first makes us right with God and then enables us to put things right with others.

O Father, use what we've just learned to help us discern
the difference between worldly sorrow and godly sorrow

*in our own lives. Help us to see the fruit of godly sorrow
so we won't be deceived and fall right back into sin. Give
us a heart for You that would rather be denied its deepest
desires than hurt You or bring shame to Your name.*

*May we embrace any rebuke, any reproach, that's
going to be used to purify our hearts and our lives and
bring us to godly sorrow that will lead to our salvation
from that sin.*

*You know where our hearts have been quickened in
this week's study. Now may we not forget what we learned;
may we rather put it into practice immediately so that
truth becomes ours—the very fabric of our being.*

*We ask this in the name of our Savior and King—
the Lord Jesus Christ.*

Amen. So be it!

MEMORY VERSE

For the sorrow that is according to the will of God produces a repentance without regret, leading to salvation,
but the sorrow of the world produces death.

2 CORINTHIANS 7:10

SMALL-GROUP DISCUSSION QUESTIONS

1. What does *endurance* mean? Give an example either from your own
   life or the life of someone you've seen make it through distressful
   times.
2. What is the "word of truth" in 2 Corinthians 6:7? How can you be
   sure that when you speak for God, you're speaking the truth?
3. Why had the Corinthians withdrawn from Paul? And what is Paul's
   instruction regarding this?
4. Why does God leave us in this evil world, and how can we keep from
   comprising?

5. What are our boundaries with unbelievers? Discuss the contrast you saw in 2 Corinthians 6:14-18.

6. What is the instruction in 2 Corinthians 6:17? What does this mean in practical terms?

7. What is the difference between "godly sorrow" (2 Corinthians 7:11) and the "sorrow of the world" (7:10)?

8. What is the result of godly sorrow?

9. What does *repentance* mean? And how does it relate to our "perfecting holiness in the fear of God" (7:1)?

APPLICATION:

10. How can you be careful to give no cause for offense in your actions and in your responses to others? How can they see the reality of Christ in you?

11. Have you determined to endure when faced with "a narrowness of room" that seems to press you in? What does this determination mean for you?

12. Have you made it your goal to be like Christ? Are you diligent to keep yourself pure, to be a faithful servant of God? In doing this, what do you need to say no to?

13. How can you give assurance and encouragement to someone who has repented of sin? How can you keep from communicating to them a wait-and-see attitude through your words and actions?

------

1. From *The New Inductive Study Bible* (Eugene, Oreg.: Harvest House, 2000), 1794.
2. Psalm 139:23-24.
3. 2 Timothy 2:3.
4. Galatians 5:22-23.
5. Galatians 2:20.
6. John 13:16; Matthew 10:24-25.
7. Psalm 30:5.
8. Hebrews 13:13,15; James 1:2-3.
9. James 1:17.
10. Romans 8:17, KJV.

11. Luke 14:26.
12. Galatians 1:10.
13. 1 Corinthians 15:33.
14. Matthew 28:19.
15. John 17:11-12,15-18.
16. Deuteronomy 22:10.
17. John 8:23-44.
18. John 5:21.
19. 1 Corinthians 10:19-20; Deuteronomy 32:17.
20. 1 Corinthians 7:14.
21. James 1:15.

UNDERSTANDING THE MINISTRY OF GIVING

– D A Y   O N E –

I was scared. I had to admit it. I knew the Scriptures and the promises of God's provision. I'd read enough wonderful biographies, such as *Hudson Taylor's Spiritual Secret*, to know example after example of how God provided the needs of His children in delightful ways—although many times only at the last minute.

I knew how George Mueller supported the orphans through prayer alone. I remember the time those children sat down for breakfast at a table without one bit of food on it. Then, led in childlike faith, they joined Brother Mueller in thanking their heavenly Father for the food He was about to provide.

I remembered my tears, my prayers of gratitude, when I read how God provided. A milk truck broke down right outside the orphanage. The driver came banging on the door, asking if the orphanage could use his milk for surely it would spoil before the truck could be fixed. And then another knock on the door. God had awakened a baker in the middle of the night and sent him to his bakery to bake bread for the orphanage. That day God put milk and freshly baked bread on the table.

I remembered, but I was still scared. How would God provide? No one knew.

I remembered how Jack and I—newly married—and my two sons from a previous marriage, left for Mexico as missionaries to live in a twenty-eight-foot trailer. My confidence before all was great: "Faithful is he that calleth you, who also will do it."[1] Although our support as independent missionaries was meager, we were confident in our God and His promise to "supply all your need according to his riches in glory by Christ Jesus."[2]

I remembered these things, but still I was scared. For the first time we had no money whatsoever, and we needed desperately to pay for medicine. The doctors believed I had a light case of typhoid fever, and as a family we all had to take a course of medicine that would cost thirty dollars. Thirty dollars was so much money to us. And if we didn't begin the course soon, I could possibly become a carrier of the germ.

I could sense Jack's tension also. He was a seasoned missionary, having traveled with Pocket Testament League throughout Africa and South America. He had his own stories of God's provision in times of need. But now, it wasn't just Jack. It was Kay and Tommy and Mark...and Ebony, our dog.

There was food in the cupboard, but it was the middle of the month of December. My illness had cost us the last of our cash. And no support check would come until January.

We prayed. But still there was no relief. We could make it; it wasn't that we didn't have shelter, food, or clothing. We just didn't have money for the medicine, and it was hard to watch my husband struggle with it all.

I had to be alone, and the only place that could happen was in our tiny bathroom. So I grabbed my Bible, put the toilet seat down, and locked the door. Then, taking my Bible in hand, I opened up to Psalm 34, which I hoped and prayed God was laying on my heart. I began to read, pausing almost with each verse to cast myself on God in prayer.

> I will bless the LORD at all times;
> His praise shall continually be in my mouth.

> *O Father, I* will, *I will bless You at all times. Your praise*
> will *be in my mouth. Help me, Father, help me...*

> My soul will make its boast in the LORD;
> The humble will hear it and rejoice.

O magnify the LORD with me,
And let us exalt His name together.

I sought the LORD, and He answered me,
and delivered me from all my fears.

*Father, I am afraid. I'm sorry, but I am afraid, and I need
Your help. Lord, You know we must have that money for the
medicine. All I need is a word from You, an assurance—*

They looked to Him and were radiant,
And their faces will never be ashamed.
This poor man cried, and the LORD heard him,
and saved him out of all his troubles.

*Father, I am, I am looking to You. I am crying to You, and I
trust that You are hearing me, that You are going to deliver
us...*

The angel of the LORD encamps around those who fear
    Him,
And rescues them.
O taste and see that the LORD is good;
How blessed is the man who takes refuge in Him!
O fear the LORD, you His saints;
For to those who fear Him there is no want.

*I fear You, Lord. I trust You. You are God, and there is
nothing too hard for You...*

Then it came—*my* word from the Lord!

The young lions do lack and suffer hunger;
But they who seek the LORD shall not be in want of any good
    thing.[3]

The dam broke. Tears of joy filled my eyes. I closed the Bible. "That's it, Lord! That's it. Thank You, thank You, thank You…"

I was confident. It would be all right. Instantly the verse was memorized, indelibly written on my heart by the Spirit of the Lord.

I was bounding out of the bathroom. "Jack! JACK! Sweetheart! It's going to be okay. Listen to what the Lord just gave me!"

There was no change in our situation, no visible evidence of the fact that God was going to send the money. I didn't know from where or when or how, but I knew that when we needed the medicine we would have it. I was convinced, for did He not say, "They that seek the LORD shall not be in want of any good thing"?

I had the promises of God, the testimonies of others, but now I had my very own verse. And no one—no one—could convince me otherwise.

On the day we had to buy the medicine, the doorbell rang and I opened it up to a tall skinny man standing before me in a brown uniform. For a moment, I panicked. We went in and out of the country every six months on our tourist visa. Had they found out that we were living there as missionaries?

The man thrust something into my hand with a few words of Spanish that I didn't understand.

But I did understand what I read.

It was a money telegram for fifty dollars. FIFTY DOLLARS! Not thirty but fifty. Not only did we have the money for the medicine, but the boys would have something for Christmas. Yes, the young lions may lack and suffer hunger, but those who love the Lord would not lack any good thing. Our delight knew no bounds.

A couple from the church we attended before leaving for Mexico had bred some dogs and sold one of the puppies for fifty dollars—and the Lord had laid it on their hearts to send it to us. This dear couple didn't have money like that. Fifty dollars was quite a bit of money in the late 1960s. But they did have a puppy, and what they had they gave.

How we have loved to tell that story of God's provision and the process He took us through.

What joy! What giving of thanks! What prayers of thanksgiving were

made for this dear couple and their gracious ministry to us. To us, it was a
gift of sacrifice. They gave out of their poverty.

There have been many others who have done the same, and that's
where we're going next. What does a heart for God look like when it
comes to sharing our resources with others in need? There are such wonderful truths for us in these next two chapters of 2 Corinthians that will
help you so much, I believe, in your quest for a heart like God's. What a
privilege it is to share these with you! Such a deep privilege. Thank you,
Beloved, for allowing me this opportunity as one called of God to be a
teacher of His Word. Thank you so very much.

"Now…"

That's the way Paul begins the second segment of his letter to the
Corinthians.

He has written of his affliction,

his anguish over the severe letter he had to write,

his torment in waiting for news from Titus,

his joy in hearing of their godly sorrow

and of their earnest care and love for him.

Now. Now there were two other matters Paul needed to address. The
hardest would be dealing with false apostles. It would come last. Before
the "hard stuff," there was the matter of something the church in Corinth
had begun to do and now needed to complete.

How would Paul approach them about this matter? How would he
bring up the subject of the collection that he had mentioned in 1 Corinthians 16:1, the collection for the suffering saints in Jerusalem?

Like I did today, Paul began by sharing his experience, one that
touched him deeply and which he believed would inspire the Corinthians
to complete what they began.

Read through 2 Corinthians 8 today.

- Mark in some distinctive color or way every reference to *this gracious work*—the ministry of giving. Watch for pronouns and synonyms that refer to giving. You don't want to miss a one of them.
- Mark every phrase relating to time so that you don't miss the
  sequence of events.

- Look for the word *readiness* and mark it.
- Mark the word *affliction* as you've done previously.
- Mark *love* and *heart*—a red heart will do fine!

When you finish, go back through the text and see what you can observe from marking these words. You may want to list below what you learn from marking *this gracious work* and the synonyms that go with it.

Finally, ask our Father what He would have you learn about His heart—and yours—from these next two chapters in 2 Corinthians.

– D A Y   T W O –

We're inherently selfish, aren't we? It's so easy to see. We see in our children how early it starts. From the moment of their birth, in their helplessness, everything has to be provided for them. They cannot feed themselves or care for themselves. They're totally dependent upon another for everything. If they don't get what they want, they cry. When they get it, they coo! And when we can't figure out what it is that our children want, they scream!

This is the way life begins—with *me,* centered around *me.* And what is maturity? It's learning that there are *others* besides me. It's learning to care for others, to meet their needs—or as the proverbial Golden Rule goes, it's doing unto others what you would have them do unto you.

And what is maturity after you meet Christ? Or maybe I should ask *what should it be* after you meet Christ? After God removes your heart of stone and gives you a heart of flesh?[4]

To me, giving takes on a whole new glorious dimension once you become a new creature in Christ Jesus. And nowhere is that better seen and understood than in 2 Corinthians 8 and 9.

When you observed the text yesterday and marked every reference to *this gracious work,* did you also mark in the same way the phrase "the grace of God which has been given" in verse 1?

Let's look at this passage again. Watch how Paul equates "the grace of God which has been given" with what he says in verse 6 below, as he tells how he urged Titus to complete in them "this gracious work *as well*"? In verse 7, Paul goes on to urge the Corinthians to "abound in this gracious work." Mark or circle these three things below in verses 1, 6, and 7.

▶ 2 CORINTHIANS 8:1-7

1 Now, brethren, we wish to make known to you the grace of God which has been given in the churches of Macedonia,

2 that in a great ordeal of affliction their abundance of joy and their deep poverty overflowed in the wealth of their liberality.

3 For I testify that according to their ability, and beyond their ability, they gave of their own accord,

4 begging us with much urging for the favor of participation in the support of the saints,

5 and this, not as we had expected, but they first gave themselves to the Lord and to us by the will of God.

6 So we urged Titus that as he had previously made a beginning, so he would also complete in you this gracious work as well.

7 But just as you abound in everything, in faith and utterance and knowledge and in all earnestness and in the love we inspired in you, see that you abound in this gracious work also.

Have you ever seen that giving is a ministry? A work of grace? Something that happens because of the grace of God that's bestowed upon us through the New Covenant?

I don't know about you, but this is an exciting insight to me. When I become God's child and grow more and more into His likeness, the focus of my life turns more and more away from me toward God and then to others. It's not so much that God has to teach me how to share, as we teach our children in their selfish immaturity. Instead, because the Father has given me a new heart, it's just natural to share. Life takes on different values as more and more we see the world for what it is—temporal. And we understand that people are eternal—so we want to invest in them. We want to help them as we have been helped of God. Our hearts are softened.

Someone has said, "Show me how a person spends his money and I'll tell you what their relationship with God is like." It's an interesting statement, isn't it? How true do you think it is?

As Paul brings up this subject, he begins by sharing with the Corinthians how the Macedonian Christians were spending money they really didn't have to spare. Philippi, Thessalonica, and Berea were all cities in Macedonia, where the churches were suffering greatly because of persecution from the Jews. In fact, the warfare was so great in Thessalonica that Paul wondered if the believers had stood firm or if his labor there had been in vain.

Once again, when he could stand it no longer—even as it was with Corinth but for a different reason—Paul had to send one of his coworkers to Macedonia to find out what was happening.

As you read the following passage, mark all references to affliction and see what you learn from this passage. Also mark the word *tempter.* I always draw a red pitchfork over every reference to the devil or his demons.

▶ 1 THESSALONIANS 3:1-8

¹ Therefore when we could endure it no longer, we thought it best to be left behind at Athens alone,

2 and we sent Timothy, our brother and God's fellow worker in the gospel of Christ, to strengthen and encourage you as to your faith,

3 so that no one would be disturbed by these afflictions; for you yourselves know that we have been destined for this.

4 For indeed when we were with you, we kept telling you in advance that we were going to suffer affliction; and so it came to pass, as you know.

5 For this reason, when I could endure it no longer, I also sent to find out about your faith, for fear that the tempter might have tempted you, and our labor would be in vain.

6 But now that Timothy has come to us from you, and has brought us good news of your faith and love, and that you always think kindly of us, longing to see us just as we also long to see you,

7 for this reason, brethren, in all our distress and affliction we were comforted about you through your faith;

8 for now we really live, if you stand firm in the Lord.

This is one example of the deep affliction endured by the churches in Macedonia that Paul was probably referring to. From what Paul wrote to the church at Corinth, we know that the Corinthians' problem was not suffering for the gospel but rather their acting like insufferable children in many arenas of their lives.

And how were the believers in Macedonia enduring? I love Paul's description: "In a great ordeal of affliction their abundance of joy and their deep poverty overflowed in the wealth of their liberality" (2 Corinthians 8:2).

The suffering they were experiencing, their deep poverty, filled them with joy! So much so that when they heard about the collection Paul was taking up, they had to help. They begged to help! Do you suppose, Beloved, that the more we suffer, the more we're weaned from the things of this life? I think it's obvious that the answer is yes. Suffering helps us see what's really important.

Times of prosperity and ease are dangerous for the church, because we forget our need for God. We forget life is to be lived in total dependence upon Him no matter what our circumstances—poor, rich, or in between.

Just two years ago, I sat in our Romanian training center with some brothers from Macedonia who work with Precept Ministries International. Tears welled up in my eyes as I shook my head in amazement. Inwardly I cried, *Father, O Father, how privileged I am to be here, to be in the presence of men like these.*

Almost two thousand years after Paul wrote 2 Corinthians, I was sitting with dear brothers in Macedonia who, like their predecessors, were in deep poverty themselves. They, too, were scraping together from their meager supplies all they could to send to the suffering believers in Chechnya. People whose lives were totally disrupted and whose economy was set back decades because the forces of NATO had bombed their country in an attempt to drive strongman Slobodan Milosevic from power in neighboring Yugoslavia.

Could I sit there, hearing what they were doing, and not do what I could? what Precept Ministries International could? Of course not.

And the Corinthians should not have been able to do any differently! That, I believe, is why Paul brings up in this way the subject of giving. The Corinthians needed motivation because they never completed what they started. They began a collection but then forgot about it. Or was it maybe that their own needs or desires began to take precedence, so they slacked off? Titus had just returned from there. The Corinthians had not begged him to tell Paul of their love and obedience nor had they asked him to take what they had already collected and get it to those in need as quickly as possible.

Maybe they thought, "Why send money to Jerusalem when we can use it here?" I don't know, but if this is what they thought, then I see how typical it is of many here in America, this nation that lives in such plenty in comparison to the rest of the world.

Sometimes my heart breaks as I look at the abundance of all that we have just in the way of Bibles in our nation. We have more kinds, styles, versions, editions, and translations than we need or can use. Yet publishers continue to produce and publish more and different versions, when so much of the world is in such desperate need just for one good translation in their language. That's why Precept Ministries International takes every penny we get for selling the *New Inductive Study Bible* and pours it into translating and printing Bibles in other languages.

When I see the faces of the people—their joy, their tears, their gratitude, how they treasure receiving such lovely Bibles that enable them to study God's Word inductively on their own—I think, *O Father, it's worth every sacrifice we make.*

We desperately need a media building at Precept Ministries. It's critical for our future because everything in the old building is in bad shape. The new building could have been built and equipped more than once with the monies we used instead for the various printings of the *New Inductive Study Bible* into Romanian, Russian, Chinese, Korean, and other languages. This Bible knows no denominational boundaries, because it doesn't have interpretive study notes in it. Because of that, we have an open and effectual door of ministry beyond our dreams. But we couldn't build our building while saying no to people who want to discover truth for themselves. We could not stand to have them see and desire a Bible like mine in their language and not do everything we could to see that they have it. To them it's worth more than going to Bible school or seminary.

And yet the cry comes for more and more, in other languages, in greater quantities.

Paul needed help for the suffering saints in Jerusalem. The Jews in Jerusalem were double-taxed by Rome and Israel. A famine had hit hard. The Jews who believed on Jesus Christ had no sympathy or help from their countrymen. They were considered traitors. Thus Paul had written once before to the church at Corinth with the following instruction (with which we need to familiarize ourselves):

> Now concerning the collection for the saints, as I directed the churches of Galatia, so do you also. On the first day of every week each one of you is to put aside and save, as he may prosper, so that no collections be made when I come. When I arrive, whomever you may approve, I will send them with letters to carry your gift to Jerusalem.[5]

Just so you don't miss what's being said here, list the specifics of Paul's instructions below.

The Macedonians gave out of their poverty, but Paul asked the Corinthians to simply give according to their ability. The Macedonians begged "with much urging for the favor of participation in the support of the saints" (2 Corinthians 8:4). The Corinthians knew the need before the Macedonians did. They knew what to do and how to do it. Paul's instructions were clear, but still they hadn't done it.

So Paul had to write and say, "But now finish doing it also, so that just as there was the readiness to desire it, so there may be also the completion of it by your ability" (2 Corinthians 8:11).

O precious child of God, has the Lord laid it upon your heart to help another, to share your resources with something that's on God's heart for the furtherance of His kingdom? Have you done it? Did you carry through?

What should you do? Talk to your Father.

— D A Y   T H R E E —

What puts giving in its proper perspective and keeps it pure in its motives—making it a gracious work in the sight of God?

For don't you know some…

who give only to get?

who want everything that's free from a church or ministry
but have no intention of contributing to that work at all?

who give because they believe it will give them greater
favor with God?

We know that the poverty-smitten Macedonians in their giving had pure motives, honorable ones—not because they gave out of their poverty, but because they "first gave themselves to the Lord and to us by the will of God" (2 Corinthians 8:5).

If you belong to God, then all belongs to Him. You hold everything in an open hand, knowing that every good and perfect gift you possess is from the Father above in whom there is no variableness or shadow of turning.[6] God never changes. There are no hidden shadows with God. He's totally trustworthy. He is Father. The cattle on a thousand hills are His.[7] The land, the sea, and all that is in them are His. Nothing is too difficult for Him. And through His Son, the Lord Jesus Christ, He promised to supply all our needs according to His riches in glory through Christ Jesus, our Lord.[8]

Knowing all that, how could you help but give yourself to the Lord before you gave anything else to another? For it's in the giving of yourself to God that you're able to give to others. You tap into His eternal resources, His "unemptyable" warehouses, to coin a word.

Paul never approached the Macedonians to give. How could he when they were in such need themselves? Yet to his delight they gave themselves to the Lord and to Paul, and going beyond their own ability, they gave of their own accord. They gave because they had a heart for God.

Don't you think, Beloved, that it would be good for us to examine our motives when we give so that we don't miss His best? I find that it helps to pray something like this:

> *Father, everything I am, everything I have, is Yours. I exist because of You and for You. Now Father, I have heard of a need, seen a need. What would You have me to do? Lay it upon my heart, Father, and I will do it.*

I think it's as simple as that: understanding that giving is a ministry. A ministry to which we're all called in one degree or another. A ministry that proves our love: our love of God, our love of the family of God, and our love for the world that He loves and wants to reach. Thus Paul urges the Corinthians to "show them the proof of your love and of our reason for boasting about you" (2 Corinthians 8:24).

When Paul in verse 8 encourages the Corinthians to prove the sincerity of their love—"proving through the earnestness of others the sincerity of your love also"—he reminds them of Another's ministry of giving: "For you know the grace of our Lord Jesus Christ, that though He was rich, yet for your sake He became poor, that you through His poverty might become rich" (8:9).

The Macedonians gave out of their poverty; our precious Lord gave out of His riches.

> The One who spoke and brought the world into existence by
> the power of His word,
> who was of purer eyes than to behold iniquity,
> who walked the ivory palaces in glory,
> who knew no limitations of time and space,
> who heard only continuous praise in the corridors of
> heaven,
> who reigned in sovereignty and lived in perfect harmony
> with His Father—
> this One became poor for us,
> humbling Himself,
> making Himself of no reputation,
> confining Himself to the womb of a woman,
> becoming flesh and blood,
> living in subjection to earthly parents,
> taking upon Himself the form of a
> servant.
> He had no place to lay His head, no home of His own.
> He borrowed a boat, a donkey, an upper room.

He rescued a coin from the mouth of a fish to pay

His taxes.

And

He used a young lad's lunch to feed a multitude.

He was despised and rejected of men,

reviled and accused of having a demon,

of being of Beelzebub's kingdom.

He became sin for us—forsaken of the Father.

And because He loved us in all our poverty of spirit, soul,

mind, and body,

He willingly became poor

so that through His poverty

we might become rich.

This is the grace of the Lord Jesus Christ, your model of the gracious work, the ministry to which you've been called: the ministry of giving.

Worship Him!

— D A Y   F O U R —

The Macedonians gave out of their poverty; Jesus gave out of His riches; the Corinthians were to give out of their ability. And they were to desire to do it. Giving should be a desire—a desire to use our abilities, our resources to help the people of God and to assist in the work of God.

In this next portion of 2 Corinthians 8, mark the occurrences of the words *desire* and *ability.*

◗ 2 CORINTHIANS 8:10-12

10 I give my opinion in this matter, for this is to your advantage, who were

the first to begin a year ago not only to do this, but also to desire to do it.

11 But now finish doing it also, so that just as there was the readiness to

desire it, so there may be also the completion of it by your ability.

12 For if the readiness is present, it is acceptable according to what a person has, not according to what he does not have.

All they needed was a readiness—a predisposition to do it, an eagerness. If the predisposition to give is there, then "it is acceptable according to what a person has, not according to what he does not have" (8:12). Just because we can't give a lot or all that is needed doesn't mean that we aren't to give. We give as we can, and when we do that or more, Jesus is pleased.

Do you remember this lesson that Jesus taught?

And He sat down opposite the treasury, and began observing how the people were putting money into the treasury; and many rich people were putting in large sums. A poor widow came and put in two small copper coins, which amount to a cent. Calling His disciples to Him, He said to them, "Truly I say to you, this poor widow put in more than all the contributors to the treasury; for they all put in out of their surplus, but she, out of her poverty, put in all she owned, all she had to live on."[9]

Do you give simply out of your surplus, my friend? Maybe you tithe, and you call it done? You've done what God requires, you've met the mean standard, and you're finished?

No! No, Beloved. That's not the way it's to be.

Do you realize that nowhere in the New Testament does God tell the church to tithe? Tithing, except as a practice of the Pharisees, is never mentioned in any message on giving in the New Testament. That was the Law—the way God supplied the Levites and the temple. We're in a new era, that of grace. Giving is a ministry—a ministry of grace.

Let's look at a few principles from the text regarding giving, in addition to what we've already seen.

First, we give according to what we have. According to what our Sovereign God has given us.

Second, God doesn't expect us to bring ease to others through our giving while bringing greater pressure on ourselves, so that we have a difficult time making it. Paul makes that clear as he urges the Corinthians to finish what they began in respect to giving. He reassures them that "this is not for the ease of others and for your affliction, but by way of equality" (8:13).

And what about the Macedonians and the widow at the temple? They gave beyond their ability! Correct. They went beyond what was required, and it was commended—but not required.

The third principle we see in this passage is that we should give to help bring about equality within the body of Christ. Not an equality where everyone lives on the same socioeconomic level, but an equality so that no brother or sister ever lacks—ever has a genuine need that goes unmet—while others have a surplus, an abundance.

Let's look at the text again so I don't lose you in all this. I want to make sure that you see what the Scriptures say. Circle or underline the word *equality*.

▶ 2 CORINTHIANS 8:12-15

12 For if the readiness is present, it is acceptable according to what a person has, not according to what he does not have.

13 For this is not for the ease of others and for your affliction, but by way of equality—

14 at this present time your abundance being a supply for their need, so that their abundance also may become a supply for your need, that there may be equality;

15 as it is written, "He who gathered much did not have too much, and he who gathered little had no lack."

In God's order, if there's equality, then one party doesn't suffer helping the other.

This, to me, is so clearly seen in a covenant relationship. When two people enter into covenant, they become responsible to their covenant partner, for through covenant two become one. My resources become available to my covenant partner should they be needed, and it's the same with him or her. Therefore my abundance is there so I can meet my partner's need. When and if I have a need, then my covenant partner's abundance is there for me.

To illustrate this—and it's so beautiful—Paul reminds them of the gathering of manna every morning. There was enough to go around. No one went hungry even if one gathered less or more than was needed.

And who is to handle the administration of all this—the collection of the funds and the transport and safe delivery of the funds? This is an important question. And while it isn't raised in the text as a question per se, Paul gives us some important precepts by detailing the way it will be handled.

It will be administered very cautiously, with total integrity by men of integrity. Men who, according to verse 22, have been "tested and found diligent in many things"—not just money!

Whenever people talk of "dangers" in the ministry, it's in three basic areas: morals, money, and accountability. Paul has taken every precaution necessary so that no one should "discredit" the Corinthians in their administration of this generous gift. He wants what is honorable not only in the sight of God, but also in the sight of men. If you cover those two bases, no one will strike out.

– D A Y   F I V E –

Has your heart been stirred, dear one, as mine has, to want to excel more and more in this awesome ministry? Have you seen the heart of God in it all? Has your heart touched His?

Paul has yet more to say on the subject, not only to the Corinthians but to us as well, for whom this was also written. And since I don't want you to miss any of these God-breathed words, read through 2 Corinthians 9. Once again, mark every reference to the ministry of giving. Also mark the word *readiness.*

Watch also for how we're to give, what God does in response, and what happens when we live according to these precepts.

When you've done this, write your insights below.

One of Paul's purposes in writing this letter known as 2 Corinthians was to let the Corinthian believers know that Titus was coming to Corinth again—this time with the other brothers—so that the church at Corinth would be fully prepared for carrying out this important and bountiful gift for the saints in Jerusalem.

What they do, the way they handle this, is so important to them and to Paul, because Paul has boasted about them not only to the Macedonians but also to those in Achaia, just north of Greece, and they have been stirred up by the Corinthians in this very important ministry to the saints.

As Paul brings all this to a close, we can uncover a number of principles on giving that I believe will be invaluable to those of us who want a heart like God's. I've listed ten things that I think we need to see. You may want to categorize them differently, which is fine. It isn't the number but rather the principles themselves that we don't want to miss. So be patient with me if we differ a little.

The first thing I want us to see is the principle of sowing and reaping: "Now this I say, he who sows sparingly will also reap sparingly, and he who sows bountifully will also reap bountifully" (2 Corinthians 9:6). You reap what you give when you give. I believe the reaping comes in many forms, as we'll see, but it's according to what you sow. It's a principle every farmer understands. You cannot reap what you do not sow. You determine the benefits by your generosity or your lack of it.

As I share this though, I cannot help but tremble as I have heard so many television preachers use this principle to motivate people to give for the wrong reason. That so grieves me. Our motive in giving should never be material gain, and yet that's what so many televangelists promote. Although I am on Christian television, I have to admit that I am sickened by what I see a lot of people believing. That's why I so desperately want to teach people to study God's Word for themselves so they can "discern good and evil"[10] in any doctrine they hear taught.

My heart broke as I heard a preacher who delivered a well-researched message about tithing from the Old Testament and then, of all things, told the people that if they drove a wreck of a car they shouldn't be parking it in the church parking lot. It was a slam against God, he said; God's children don't have to drive cars like that because they're God's kids!

Immediately my mind raced to the godly saints in the other countries I've visited, where I ride in their aging, dilapidated cars every time we go to minister with our Euro-Asian ministry directors, Mia and Costel Oglice. Many of these dear people, who suffer great material deprivation for the sake of the gospel, could live in the United States at a much higher economic level without all the hardships they now endure. But they don't because they're called to teach people in their country how to study God's Word inductively.

The second thing we need to see is in verse 7: Giving is never an obligation; rather, it's a matter of the heart. What you've purposed in your heart. This is why, when we present a need at Precept Ministries International, we always ask people to pray and give only as they believe God is directing. Just because there's a need doesn't mean that they're to meet it. How can we as individuals begin to cover all the needs? We can't. But God can and He will. We simply need to understand what He would have us do. When I give according to what I have purposed in my heart, then it won't be grudgingly or under compulsion. Rather it will be with a cheerful heart. And cheerful it ought to be, that we, like the Macedonians, might be allowed to participate in so great a ministry. O dear one, do you see? Do you see what a joyous ministry this is?

Third, we need to understand that when we give as directed—knowingly, generously, cheerfully—God will meet us, supplying what we need in order to give. Incredible, isn't it?

In the text below, circle or underline the words *sufficiency, abundance, enriched,* and *liberality* as you read.

⏵ 2 CORINTHIANS 9:8-12

8 And God is able to make all grace abound to you, so that always having all sufficiency in everything, you may have an abundance for every good deed;

9 as it is written, "He scattered abroad, He gave to the poor, His righteousness endures forever."

10 Now He who supplies seed to the sower and bread for food will supply and multiply your seed for sowing and increase the harvest of your righteousness;

11 you will be enriched in everything for all liberality, which through us is producing thanksgiving to God.

12 For the ministry of this service is not only fully supplying the needs of the saints, but is also overflowing through many thanksgivings to God.

As I read this, having just finished writing five *Precept Upon Precept* inductive study courses on the Torah, or Pentateuch, as some call Genesis through Deuteronomy, I am reminded of God's promise in Leviticus 25 in respect to a rest for the land every seven years. Of course their concern would be, "But God, if we do that, what will we eat?" Anticipating their objections, God answered before they could ask!

But if you say, "What are we going to eat on the seventh year if we do not sow or gather in our crops?" then I will so order My blessing for you in the sixth year that it will bring forth the crop for three years. When you are sowing the eighth year, you can still eat old things from the crop, eating the old until the ninth year when its crop comes in.[11]

God can order blessings anytime He wants to because He is God, and this is what He's doing in 2 Corinthians 9:8-12. A blessing to those who give as He gave and would have them give.

The fourth thing that I saw in verse 10 is that God will also increase our righteousness. Isn't that interesting that when we give, it brings greater righteousness in our lives? I think this could be because giving is so much a part of the heart of God. He so loved that He *gave*. Awesome, isn't it!

Verse 11 gives me a fifth insight: Giving enriches the giver, for God says, "You will be enriched in everything for all liberality." What I seem to see is that when I give, God enriches me, enabling me to have more to give. I am not sure that this is something hard and fast, but it seems that when I understand how I can be a channel for God in supporting His work, then more can simply flow through me because I'm not going to stop the flow. In other words, when I have more, I'm not going to keep it for myself. Rather, I see it as more to give.

Sixth, we see that "the ministry of this service" (verse 12) of giving fully supplies the needs of the saints. We are the means God uses to answer their prayers, to meet the needs of our colaborers with God. God doesn't grow money on trees or rain cash from heaven or have tornadoes rip through banks and send the money flying through the air. He works through people.

And what does this bring? In verses 11 and 12 we discover a seventh insight: Giving brings thanksgiving to God. It brings praise because a need has been met, a prayer answered. And although God works through people, it is *God* at work, and we know it. How exciting to think that through this ministry you can motivate people to be grateful to God! That your obedience and stewardship bring Him praise!

The eighth thing I noticed is that my giving brings God glory because it proves the reality of my faith. "God got a hold of my billfold!" as some would say. This ministry (don't you love how God calls it a "ministry" over and over?) of giving is an act of obedience that bears witness to my confession of the gospel and causes people to glorify God. Now that's something to meditate on!

Let me write out the verse for you, so you can see it again and digest its truth:

> Because of the proof given by this ministry, they will glorify God for your obedience to your confession of the gospel of Christ and for the liberality of your contribution to them and to all. (9:13)

The ninth thing is so neat: When you give, people pray for you. They're grateful, they see, hear, or experience your giving, and it causes them to pray for you. What a blessing it is to be prayed for by others! I know I would fall in a heap if people didn't help me through their prayers, as Paul mentions in 2 Corinthians 1:11.

Finally, for a perfect ten: Bonds are formed between the giver and the receiver. You may never see the recipients of your gift face to face, but just know this: They "yearn for you because of the surpassing grace of God in you" (9:14).

Well, Beloved, that's it. What more is there to tell about giving but to look heavenward and say with Paul…

"Thanks be to God for His indescribable gift!" (verse 15)

When He gave us Jesus Christ, He gave us all, in giving us *His* all.

MEMORY VERSE

And God is able to make all grace abound to you, so that always having all sufficiency in everything, you may have an abundance for every good deed.

2 CORINTHIANS 9:8

SMALL-GROUP DISCUSSION QUESTIONS

1. What was this "gracious work" Paul is bringing to the attention of the Corinthian believers? Why does he bring this issue up?

2. In what ways is our financial giving a ministry and a work of grace? For whose benefit have we received this ministry?

3. How does the way a person spends his money show his relationship to God?

4. In what ways were the Thessalonian believers (in Macedonia) an example for the Corinthian believers? What contrasts do you see between these two groups of believers?

5. How is Jesus Christ the supreme example of the ministry of giving?

6. How much are we to give?

7. Why was Paul letting the Corinthian believers know that Titus was coming?

8. As you briefly discuss each principle on giving from 2 Corinthians 9, think about these questions: What can keep us from giving under compulsion or grudgingly? What can we know for sure about God if we are giving as He says to give? What does our giving prove about us?

APPLICATION:

9. What is really important in your life? Does the way you give show you have a heart for God?

10. Have you faithfully followed up with your decisions to give financially?

11. To what degree are you a cheerful giver? To what degree do you give out of obligation?

12. Does your giving lead to praise and thanksgiving? As you give, what can you especially be thankful for?

------

1. 1 Thessalonians 5:24, KJV.
2. Philippians 4:19, KJV.
3. Psalm 34:1-10.

4. Ezekiel 36:26.
5. 1 Corinthians 16:1-3.
6. James 1:17, KJV.
7. Psalm 50:10.
8. Philippians 4:19.
9. Mark 12:41-44.
10. Hebrews 5:14.
11. Leviticus 25:20-22.

CONFRONTING THE ENEMY

– D A Y   O N E –

Warfare is never welcome, but as long as Satan remains the prince of this world we can know that the work of the kingdom will never go forward unopposed. We would love to ignore the conflict, to live as peaceably as possible, even if it means placating the enemy a little, but we can't. There can be no peaceful coexistence. "What harmony has Christ with Belial?" (2 Corinthians 6:15). None whatsoever.

The enemy must be identified, exposed, and dealt with. If he isn't, he'll soon have established a stronghold that will be hard—and costly—to bring down. History testifies to this, as we study the biographies of malevolent dictators and learn how they came to power and subsequently destroyed hundreds of thousands, even millions, in their diabolical, egocentric quest for power.

War is war, and humanly speaking, victory rises or falls on the discernment and military prowess of those who lead us. Neville Chamberlain returned to England deceived, convinced that Adolf Hitler was not an enemy of England, that he could be trusted. Consequently Britain was drawn into a war and suffered great casualties that could have been avoided had Chamberlain not been taken in by Hitler's lies.

The Corinthians were being taken in by the emissaries of Satan. It was warfare, and although they didn't recognize it as such, Paul did. He could not, would not stand by idly and allow the enemy to gain a greater stronghold in their lives.

Thus we begin the third segment of his letter to the Corinthians. The tone and tenor quickly change. The shepherd has spotted the wolves, savage wolves that have come in among them, not sparing the flock. It's time to awaken the Corinthians, for the enemy has infiltrated the troops and they haven't recognized it.

The destructive subterfuge of these "wolves" was directed against Paul. If they could discredit him, drive him from his God-ordained position, cut him off the Corinthians, then they could devour the flock.

Paul knew this, and it could not go on, it could not continue. And I am so thankful that he recognized it, for in Paul's defense of himself we're going to gain invaluable insights into this warfare, which in turn will keep us from being taken in by the enemy. Even more so, in the process we'll learn things about Paul that aren't shared any other place in the Word of God, things that will inspire us to faithfully persevere as true servants of our living God.

To truly appreciate and better understand all that God would have us learn, you must get into this passage for yourself. Therefore, I have an assignment for you today that may seem a little long, but it's one you need to do for your own good and your growth.

First I want you to read through 2 Corinthians 10:1-10. As you read, mark any reference to *war* or *warfare*. You might want to use a symbol like this:

● 2 CORINTHIANS 10:1-10

1 Now I, Paul, myself urge you by the meekness and gentleness of

Christ—I who am meek when face to face with you, but bold toward you

when absent!

2 I ask that when I am present I need not be bold with the confidence

with which I propose to be courageous against some, who regard us as if we

walked according to the flesh.

3 For though we walk in the flesh, we do not war according to the flesh,

4 for the weapons of our warfare are not of the flesh, but divinely powerful for the destruction of fortresses.

5 We are destroying speculations and every lofty thing raised up against the knowledge of God, and we are taking every thought captive to the obedience of Christ,

6 and we are ready to punish all disobedience, whenever your obedience is complete.

7 You are looking at things as they are outwardly. If anyone is confident in himself that he is Christ's, let him consider this again within himself, that just as he is Christ's, so also are we.

8 For even if I boast somewhat further about our authority, which the Lord gave for building you up and not for destroying you, I will not be put to shame,

9 for I do not wish to seem as if I would terrify you by my letters.

10 For they say, "His letters are weighty and strong, but his personal presence is unimpressive and his speech contemptible."

Now read through 2 Corinthians 10 and 11. It might help you to read it aloud. However you read, mark every reference to those first mentioned in 10:10 and referred to as "they." As you continue, you're going to need to mark a number of synonymous terms used for "they." For instance in 10:11, you would mark *such a person* the same way as *they* in verse 10. In verse 12 you would mark *some of those, they,* and *themselves.*

Paul is going to refer intermittently to these people while interspersing other things about himself in the text, so you'll find out more about them in chapter 11.

When you finish reading and marking these chapters, list below everything you have learned about "they," and their identity will become clear.

Who was Paul's warfare with? With men who had disguised themselves as "apostles of Christ" (11:13). And whom did they serve? They served Satan (11:14-15). Do you think there are people around like this today, or was this only true in Paul's time?

Unfortunately it wasn't just a problem of Paul's time. It's a problem we will have until our Lord returns and puts all things in subjection under the feet of almighty God.[1] That is why this study is so needed. We don't need to be taken captive. If we are, it will be our own fault.

– D A Y   T W O –

How do you approach someone who has been deceived by the enemy or possibly taken captive? Watch Paul and you'll see a very valuable example. It begins with his opening words in this section, as he broaches this tense situation.

Now I, Paul, myself urge you by the meekness and gentleness of Christ—I who am meek when face to face with you, but bold toward you when absent! (10:1)

Paul doesn't rant, rave, attack, or belittle them for their blindness, their stupidity. He doesn't yell, scream, use harsh words. Strong, yes! Harsh, no.

Rather, Paul comes in the character of Jesus, as a shepherd would move among his lambs. Lambs are easily frightened; they need quiet, peace. Paul comes in the confidence of quietness, moving forward in Jesus' yoke; he has learned of Him, just as his Lord had said:

Take My yoke upon you and learn from Me, for I am gentle and humble in heart, and you will find rest for your souls.[2]

These words Jesus used to describe Himself—"gentle and humble of heart"—indicate mildness, humility, a suitableness, taking a low road versus a high hand.

This is what I want to learn, what I want to move into—into the gentleness of Jesus, into the strength of meekness that simply "is" without having to prove myself to anyone. Jesus didn't have to flaunt Himself or prove Himself to anyone. Jesus simply *was* Himself.

Although Paul's detractors accused Paul of being meek with people when he was with them in person, they pointed out that he was bold when absent (10:1). Paul wouldn't let their accusation turn him from walking as Christ walked. We aren't to be manipulated by the strategies of men, deterred by their behavior from Christ's character or ruled by the conduct or accusations of others. If we're going to win in warfare, we must hold a steady course. Not man's. Not the path the flesh would take. But the way Christ would take.

Paul did not walk according to the flesh. Let's look at his words again. As you do, mark every reference to the flesh.

◑ 2 CORINTHIANS 10:1-4

1 Now I, Paul, myself urge you by the meekness and gentleness of Christ—I who am meek when face to face with you, but bold toward you when absent!

2 I ask that when I am present I need not be bold with the confidence with which I propose to be courageous against some, who regard us as if we walked according to the flesh.

3 For though we walk in the flesh, we do not war according to the flesh,

⁴ for the weapons of our warfare are not of the flesh, but divinely powerful for the destruction of fortresses.

Although Paul walks "in the flesh"—a fleshly body, as we all do—he does not walk "according to the flesh," that is, under the dominion of the flesh. Nor does he war "according to the flesh." You never win in spiritual warfare when you use fleshly weapons, because it's a spiritual battle. Paul had taught that to the church at Ephesus:

> Our struggle is not against flesh and blood, but against the rulers, against the powers, against the world forces of this darkness, against the spiritual forces of wickedness in the heavenly places. Therefore, take up the full armor of God, so that you will be able to resist in the evil day, and having done everything, to stand firm.³

The armor of God is truth, righteousness, peace with God, faith, salvation—and the sword of the Spirit, which is the Word of God. Having all this, standing in all this then we "pray at all times…on the alert with all perseverance and petition for all the saints."⁴

These are the divinely powerful weaponry that destroy the fortresses, the strongholds of the enemy.⁵ And what is this fortress, this stronghold that Paul says needs to be destroyed? I think it's explained in 2 Corinthians 10:5.

> We are destroying speculations and every lofty thing raised up against the knowledge of God, and we are taking every thought captive to the obedience of Christ.

The battleground in spiritual warfare is the *mind*. This is where the enemy is going to send his flaming missiles, because the mind is the epicenter of the body. "For as [a man] thinks within himself, so he is."⁶ This is why God tells us, "Watch over your heart [mind] with all diligence, for from it flow the springs of life."⁷

The word for "speculations" in 10:5 is *logismos* and speaks of computations, imaginations, reasonings that in and of themselves are not wrong. They become fortresses that need to be destroyed only when they go against truth. These speculations were "raised up against the knowledge of God." What the false apostles were saying about Paul was not true. They were lying through their teeth and were not to be believed and embraced. If they were, they would become the devil's stronghold.

How thankful we should be for this insight. Let's bring this biblical precept into our world, our society. Stop and consider all the things our society considers acceptable that God says is sin: adultery, homosexuality, abortion, etc. The issue in these things is not a matter of personal opinion or preference; rather it's whether a person is going to embrace truth or become captive to a lie. Truth is truth. A lie is a lie. And lies destroy if they are not themselves destroyed. Look at our society and you'll see it for yourself.

But let's move on. "Every lofty thing" is a translation of the phrase *pan hypsoma*. *Hypsoma* is an elevated place or thing, figuratively a barrier. It refers to "any human act or attitude that forms an obstacle to the emancipating knowledge of God contained in the gospel of Christ crucified and therefore keeps men in oppressive bondage to sin."[8] As I think about this, I'm reminded of these words from Paul to the Romans:

> For the wrath of God is revealed from heaven against all ungodliness and unrighteousness of men who suppress the truth in unrighteousness.[9]

God's wrath comes on men who, through their unGodlike lifestyles, suppress the truth of how God created man to be and who consequently become an obstacle to others. It's the same with "every lofty thing." When men become proponents of things that are in direct opposition to God's Word, they're seeking to put people into bondage through believing a lie. It's a warfare for our minds—and once they have the mind, the body will follow in tow, living out what is embraced in the heart.

So in this battle, in this warfare, what is to be my strategy? First, I must get truth. Everything that's against truth must be blown up, wiped out, destroyed. The "belief" may be "lofty," relevant to today with all its philosophies, psychologies, and popular reasoning and rationalization, but if it goes against the knowledge of God, which is the Word of Truth, then it must be destroyed with absolutely no consideration of whose it is or where it came from.

David Franks, a dear friend of ours, is an Israeli and the owner of the tour agency we work with in Israel. He just sent Jack and me an e-mail that keeps coming to my mind as I think about the destruction of these strongholds:

> On Friday evening 05 January 2001, a small black bag (a men's "sissy bag") was blown up by the Israeli Security Forces on the main road outside the King David Hotel.
>
> This bag it turns out contained 1 Wallet with some cash and credit cards etc, 1 hard spectacle case with optical sunglasses inside, various aspirin, "Juice Plus" vitamins, a daily pocket diary, various pens and a Casio Boss with over 1200 telephone numbers stored inside. Plus other odds & ends.
>
> Everything was blown to smithereens. The bag, may its memory be blessed, was owned by yours truly—David Frank.
>
> What actually happened was that I had returned from a long day out with another group, got out of their car carrying three huge bags of peanuts, a newspaper and my "sissy bag." I went to my car parked outside the King David, but did not have a hand free to take out the car keys, so placed the peanuts and the sissy bag on the wall outside the YMCA opposite the King David, opened the car, threw my newspaper inside and drove home.
>
> The rest is history. The street outside the King David was closed off, people were not allowed out of the hotel, and the bomb squad blew up the bag.

Israeli security takes absolutely no chances. If any bag anywhere is left alone, it's set for destruction. This is why I feel far safer in Israel than I feel in the United States. There is constant, well-thought-out vigilance against anything that can harm their people and their security.

Paul was the same way; anything that was against the truth had to be "taken out," in other words, destroyed. If it isn't taken out, then it can take you out! And that's what was going to happen if Paul didn't confront this situation head-on—but in the meekness and gentleness of Christ.

So what is our strategy in this warfare?

First, you must know truth so you can examine everything in its light. Remember Satan's kingdom is one of darkness. Jesus said that men prefer darkness because their deeds are evil. That's why people don't come to the light. They don't want to be seen for what they really are.[10] Truth liberates: "You will know the truth, and the truth will make you free."[11] Lies bring bondage. Turn over the lie, and a snake will slither out from under it! You'll find the devil lurking behind every lie, because Satan is the father of lies.

Second, you must resolve that you're going to take "every thought captive to the obedience of Christ" (2 Corinthians 10:5). In other words, if what you think, hear, believe, *or* feel doesn't line up with the knowledge of God, then it has to go. You determine: If it isn't truth, you will not, cannot receive it or let it influence who you are and what you do. You are *not* going to walk in darkness.

Paul illustrates this for us beautifully. He is not going to let the comments, criticisms, evaluations of those false apostles defeat him, discourage him, or destroy his "self-image." He will not buy into their lies!

Third, once your obedience is complete—once you do what God tells you to do, what truth commands—there's to be a punishment of "all disobedience, whenever your obedience is complete" (10:6). You are to confront the lie.

Let me explain it this way: You're in the midst of warfare. Your eyes are open, you see truth, and you realize that you've embraced a lie. So you determine to believe God and let go of that lie. You do it. Then what? Then you deal with the offenders, the perpetrators of the lie. You confront. You don't allow the lie, the deception to continue. You don't want it to destroy others, do you? Of course not.

Look at how Paul models this in the rest of chapters 10 and 11 as he exposes these false apostles for what they are.

First, he lets the Corinthians see their tactics in 10:10-13. Then in 11:13-14, Paul makes it clear whom they serve—none other than Satan!

Oh, Beloved, can you see how important it is that you guard your every thought, that you know truth, and that you walk in it? The battle for your mind and consequently your emotions rages and will continue to rage until you finally arrive in heaven. That's why you must saturate yourself in the Word of God. Remember, it's truth that takes down the devil's strongholds, brick by brick, until it's nothing but a piece of rubble.

Why don't you bring today's lesson to a fitting close by sitting quietly before God and asking Him to reveal to you any lies that you've embraced? As God shows you these, write them down. Then next to the lie, write down what the truth is. If you can't find a truth to go against the lie, then ask God to reveal it to you in His Word. He will in His time. When He does, make sure you record it.

Once the lies have been exposed and the "fortress" is brought down with truth by bringing it up against the knowledge of God, then ask God if there is any disobedience to be dealt with. Does the source of the lie need to be confronted? If so, do it. If not, rest and just cling to the truth, tighten that belt of truth.

— D A Y   T H R E E —

Who sets the standard of how you should conduct yourself? How do you measure up to our culture's standards, socially, intellectually, physically, culturally, sociologically? Once you settle these questions with the right answers, you'll find yourself gloriously free from having to have the approbation of others by meeting their standards rather than God's.

Although the Corinthians were on Paul's heart and he desired their love and affection, he would not allow them or any man to set his standards. Paul didn't have to commend himself to anyone. He knew that he met the standard of Jesus Christ and had His approval.

The Jews who had come all the way from Israel to Corinth, claiming to be apostles of equal stature with Paul, were out to discredit him. They agreed that the letters Paul wrote were weighty and strong, but according to them, his words belied what he was really like.

Like many today, the Corinthians—undoubtedly influenced by the deceitful workers who had come to Corinth—judged Paul according to his physical appearance and the way he presented himself publicly. They measured Paul against the standard of their day, of their times. "You are looking at things as they are outwardly," he says in 10:7, which means they were looking at what was right was in front of their faces.

Paul's detractors were quick to point out a number of ways that Paul failed to meet the standard. First, he wasn't as authoritative as an apostle ought to be; he didn't come down hard enough. Yet Paul tried to explain that the authority the Lord had bestowed upon him was for building up, not destroying (10:8). People who have to live under tight authority seldom mature. They don't have to take responsibility for their decisions, as there are none to make. They're all made for them. Paul wouldn't do that. Jesus led His sheep; He didn't drive them.

While Paul's letters were "weighty and strong" (10:10), his personal appearance certainly wasn't like the way he sounded on paper. That was their complaint. But Paul wouldn't let them get away with such judging. Paul was what he was, whether on paper or in person.

And then there was the statement that not only was Paul "unimpressive" in person but his speech was "contemptible" (10:10). Shouldn't an apostle, a messenger sent out from God, have the ability to express himself better, more eloquently? Was this the kind of man they wanted for an apostle?

Paul would agree that he was unskilled in speech, but the fact that he didn't reach their standard didn't defeat him. He was secure in who he was and had a sober assessment of himself. He may have been unskilled in speech, but he wasn't ignorant (11:6), and if the Corinthians would be objective, they would admit it.

The false apostles apparently even accused Paul of overextending himself—going where he shouldn't be going (10:14). Paul had to remind the Corinthians that he was the one who came to them first. He wasn't like these false apostles who simply came in and capitalized on the labors of others, never doing anything themselves but simply riding on the popular tides of others' ministries. Finding out what "worked," what pleased the people, what tickled their ears, what kind of leadership they wanted—and then giving them what they wanted.

What were these false apostles doing? You saw this earlier when you made your list about these men, and we just mentioned it, but it bears repeating: They were looking at things outwardly (10:7). They were measuring themselves by themselves (10:12). They *set* the standard. They *became* the standard.

The problem was that they fell far short of God's standard and either didn't know this or didn't care. They had what they wanted: the attention they commanded from the Corinthians. They had their financial support; they weren't working to support themselves, as Paul did. They exercised authority and got away with it. And some of the people believed they were apostles just like Paul (11:12,20-22). The Corinthians needed to stop and take a closer look, not at Paul, for they had his example, but at the standards of the false apostles and their deeds.

And we need to do the same. Not everyone who proclaims the name of Christ, who casts out demons, who does miracles, or who prophesies is from God. Jesus made this very clear:

So then, you will know them by their fruits.

Not everyone who says to Me, "Lord, Lord," will enter the kingdom of heaven, but he who does the will of My Father who is in heaven will enter. Many will say to Me on that day, "Lord, Lord, did we not prophesy in Your name, and in Your name cast out demons, and in Your name perform many miracles?" And then I will declare to them, "I never knew you; depart from Me, you who practice lawlessness."[12]

The standard of the "many" referred to by Jesus was not God's standard. These thought they were headed for heaven, but they were deceived. They had judged by the wrong standard.

Stop for a moment and think about the standards of our day. Who sets them? Who determines what is right? Moral? Correct? Socially acceptable? Just? Fair? How we should dress, think, act, behave?

Let me challenge you to sit in front of your television for a couple of hours and listen with an analytical ear to what's being said. Listen to the talk shows, the interviews, the news commentaries, the political analysts, the sitcoms. Check out what the comedians are joking about. Look at the celebrities and musicians—the way they dress, the way they perform, what they believe, what they endorse and promote. What values, morals, and philosophies are being proposed? What political and moral agendas are emphasized? Ignored? Questioned? Opposed? Ridiculed? Listen to someone's speech, then listen to the analysis of it. Did the analysts really hear what was said? Do they repeat what was said, or do they distort it—even subtly?

Jot down what you see and what you hear. And as you do, bring each thing up against the standard of God's Word. What are the differences, the discrepancies? Or are there any?

Then take a good look at yourself. Where do you want to be? What do you admire? What do you want to imitate? What is your dream? Your desire? What gives you your sense of worth?

Where are you in this world? In the flow of our culture? Who sets the standard for you? Whose standard do you come closer to? How does that feel? Does it alarm you at all? Why?

Is there any danger, Beloved, that possibly you've been "led astray from the simplicity and purity of devotion to Christ" (11:3)?

That was Paul's concern for the Christians at Corinth. Would it also be his concern for you today?

Once again, spend time with the Lord. How would you answer these questions? Record your responses below.

— D A Y F O U R —

There was a jealousy in Paul's heart for the Corinthians—a godly jealousy. He was the one who had introduced them to their heavenly bridegroom. Now his one passion was to present them to Him as a pure virgin. Unblemished. Untainted.

His parental concern was great. The Corinthians, like so many today in "Christian circles," were being seduced away from Christ, lured into the devil's bed. And they didn't even know it.

What happened in Corinth is happening today, and you need to see it for yourself. Therefore, before we go further, read 2 Corinthians 11:1-15 and mark every reference to the serpent of old, Satan. As I've mentioned earlier, I use a red pitchfork as my symbol. When I wrote my book on warfare—*Lord, Is It Warfare? Teach Me to Stand*—I marked every reference in the Bible to the devil, his demons, and evil spirits in this manner. It was most enlightening.

When you finish, list below everything you have learned about the serpent from this text. Then we'll look at some other scriptures that will help us better understand his tactics.

The serpent's tactics haven't changed. As I said on Day Two, Satan's target is our mind—what we believe and the way we think. Paul was concerned that "as the serpent deceived Eve by his craftiness, your minds will be led astray from the simplicity and purity of devotion to Christ" (11:3).

The identity of the serpent is made clear in the Word of God. The first book of the Bible, Genesis, refers to Satan as the serpent; the last, Revelation, nails his identity, as it gives us a glimpse into the future when he's finally cast out of heaven to earth. As you read this passage, put the pitchfork where it needs to go.

▶ REVELATION 12:9

9 And the great dragon was thrown down, the serpent of old who is called the devil and Satan, who deceives the whole world; he was thrown down to the earth, and his angels were thrown down with him.

Now list what you learn from Revelation 12:9 about the devil.

How did this serpent deceive Eve? What was his m.o.?

The first thing he did was to cause her to question the veracity of God's Word. Let's read the account from Genesis. As you do, underline exactly what the devil says, and then there are some things I want to share with you. Just remember as you read this that these are the devil's first recorded words, and nothing about him has changed since then.

▶ GENESIS 3:1-5

1 Now the serpent was more crafty than any beast of the field which the LORD God had made. And he said to the woman, "Indeed, has God said, 'You shall not eat from any tree of the garden'?"

2 The woman said to the serpent, "From the fruit of the trees of the garden we may eat;

3 but from the fruit of the tree which is in the middle of the garden, God has said, 'You shall not eat from it or touch it, or you will die.'"

4 The serpent said to the woman, "You surely will not die!

5 "For God knows that in the day you eat from it your eyes will be opened, and you will be like God, knowing good and evil."

Now read the passage again, and this time, number the main points of what the serpent says. If you want to, list them below.

The first thing the enemy does is to question God's Word. "Has God really said?" Are you sure this is God's Word? Are you sure this is what God Himself really said? You can hear his hiss: *That's just your interpretation…*

Nothing has changed, has it?

The next thing the serpent does is deny what God said. "You surely will not die!" Oh yes, she would die!—and he knew it. But he didn't want her to know it. Satan wanted this woman for his own pleasure. What did it matter what would happen to her? She was his avenue to the world.

All the serpent had to do was convince her of one more thing: God really didn't care about her. God was holding out on her. God didn't want her best, so she better cut the cord and go for it herself.

Hardly a breath was taken before the rest of the lie shot from his mouth like a poison dart. Listen again to him:

For God knows that in the day you eat from it your eyes will be opened, and you will be like God, knowing good and evil.

You can be like God! You can know good and evil yourself! You don't need anyone dictating to you, telling you what's right and wrong, what's good or bad for you. Forget God! Besides, He's a God of love; He's not going to turn you away! Forget absolutes. You decide what is good and what is evil.

O precious one, can you see it? Do you see how seduced we are as a nation? We're sleeping with the enemy, and we don't know how perverted and twisted he is. He has lured us into his bed in order to murder us.

Listen to what Jesus says about the devil. As you do, mark him with a pitchfork:

▶ JOHN 8:44

44 "You are of your father the devil, and you want to do the desires of

your father. He was a murderer from the beginning, and does not stand in

the truth because there is no truth in him. Whenever he speaks a lie, he

speaks from his own nature, for he is a liar and the father of lies.

Now what did you learn about him from this scripture? List it below.

Did you notice that the devil "was a murderer *from the beginning*"? "From the beginning" tells us that when the serpent approached the woman, he did it with the intention of causing her death. And how did he murder her? With a lie.

He led her away from the simplicity and purity of devotion. He robbed her of the virginity of her mind. He caused her to doubt the Word of God, the love of God, the goodness of God, the judgment of God.

Have you been there? Have you questioned the veracity of the Bible? Have you questioned His love? His goodness? His care? His judgment?

Quit it—NOW.

It's a lie. It's a lie meant to seduce you and destroy you. It is *not* true. Bring that thought captive immediately. Resist the devil. Command him to leave you alone. Overcome him.

You can, if you're a true child of God. You do it by the blood of the Lamb and the Word of God.[13] Do as Jesus did; say to him, "Go, Satan! For it is written…"[14] Then stand firm in the whole armor of God.[15]

This is what the Corinthians were missing. They didn't realize it was warfare. They hadn't cinched the belt of truth tightly around their waist. It was as if they were lounging in their pajamas and threw wide open the doors and windows to their minds and allowed every wind of doctrine to blow through. If someone came and preached "another Jesus," it was no problem. If they received a "different spirit" than what Paul presented or someone wanted to preach a "different gospel," it was perfectly fine to them (11:4).

The Corinthians were being seduced from the simplicity and purity of devotion to Christ. So Paul spread the facts on the table so they could take a good look at them.

Paul wasn't at all inferior to the most eminent apostles (11:5). They needed to quit judging him, because he didn't take any financial support from them while he was with them, but instead preached the gospel to them without charge. He had already explained that he knew that he had the right to ask (1 Corinthians 9:12), but he wasn't going to exercise it for them or for the ministry he would have in Achaia (2 Corinthians 11:10), no matter how great his physical need was.

In everything Paul kept himself from being a burden to the Co-rinthians, and even though he loved the Corinthians, he was *not* going to change. He wanted to cut off every opportunity of these deceitful workers who were trying to seduce the people Paul had betrothed to Jesus Christ. Like their father the devil, they had disguised themselves as servants of righteousness so they wouldn't be seen for what they knew they were—false apostles. But their end would be according to their deeds. Paul knew that if you watch a person's deeds long enough, you'll see who his father is.

— D A Y   F I V E —

Sometimes the enemy will slither into our mind with all sorts of doubts. Because he's a deceiver, a destroyer, a murderer, this is to be expected. It's part of his strategy. He doesn't want us to believe on Jesus Christ, but once we do, the question becomes...

How can he torment us?

Make our life difficult?

Hinder our ministry?

Frustrate us or bring us to a standstill?

Make us think we're cut off from our Source of

power?

One of the ways—and note, Beloved, that I say *one,* because that's all I'll touch on—is to cause us to question our relationship with God. To make us doubt our salvation.

I remember a time when I was a brand-new Christian, maybe not even two months old in the family of God. My husband, Tom, whom I had divorced, was still living. He hadn't yet committed suicide. I had two precious sons, Tommy and Mark, and we lived in Baltimore where I worked on a research team at Johns Hopkins Hospital. I was a nurse by profession, but through a set of circumstances, I ended up in this very interesting job.

One of my duties—for which I certainly wasn't qualified (but God knew my future, and He was preparing me as His workmanship)—was typing up research papers for one of the doctors. One error and I had to start over again! In our age of computers it's hard to understand just how tedious and difficult this can be, especially for someone who'd had only one semester of typing in high school. (And that was because Daddy felt that someday I would need it!) Oh, the sovereignty of our God!

Anyway, I was sitting in the office struggling with typing this research paper when all of a sudden I thought, *This isn't real. All this about God isn't real.*

I couldn't believe it! Where did that thought come from? How could I, now that I was saved, think something like that? My thoughts scrambled in my mind. *That is blasphemy! Surely I couldn't be saved and have thoughts like that!*

I was devastated. I felt like a betrayer. Unclean. That evening, with my head hung in shame, I confessed my awful thoughts to a dear and, fortunately, mature brother. I remember his gentle laugh as he said, "Oh, Kay, that's warfare," then went on to explain some of the battle tactics of the enemy.

Since that time there have been several instances in my walk with the Lord when the question has come into my mind as to whether I was really saved. But not being ignorant of Satan's m.o., I recognized where the thought came from and knew how to deal with it. You always confront lies with truth. The greatest way I know that I am saved is by my changed life. But another is because of my perseverance through the rough and trying times of walking with Christ. In both these areas I can confidently *boast* to the enemy of my salvation.

To those of us who know the value God places on humility, boasting seems like a pretentious action that no one would want to admit to or some egotistical display that causes others to have disgust or embarrassment for the person who's doing it.

Paul, however, uses the word far differently in this letter to the Corinthians. Since it's used about twenty-three times in this epistle, I believe we need to take a closer look at the word and how he uses it. It's going to be so worthwhile, because as we do so we're going to take a look at one of the evidences that proves the genuineness of our salvation.

The word for boast is *kauchaomai.* It means to boast or vaunt, either in a good sense or bad sense, depending on the context in which it's used. It has also been translated "glory," "joy," and "rejoice." It's different from another word, *megalaucheo,* which comes from two different words— *megala,* "great things," and *aucheo,* "to lift up the neck"—with a meaning that's closer to the sense of the word as you and I usually think of it. Something no one ought to do, a self-centered bragging.

Read through 2 Corinthians 10:8–11:33 and mark any form of the word *boast* as you did in chapter 2. Do it in some bright color combination so you don't miss it. When you finish, so that you have more than a colorful page in your book, list below what you learn from marking this word in these chapters.

BOASTING

What do we learn from Paul's use of boasting in these two chapters?

The *first* insight comes from 10:8. When Paul "boasted" of his authority, it was obvious he wasn't bragging. If he had been, you would have seen self-promotion, indignation, rigid authority that bucked no questioning. Rather, Paul accepted the authority that came with his apostleship and exercised it accordingly—building up rather than destroying.

Second, Paul did not boast beyond his measure (10:13-16). He didn't move or exercise his authority as an apostle where God hadn't sent him. An apostle is one sent forth from another as a delegate, with a message, as a representative. Paul hadn't overextended himself in going to Corinth; he was simply obedient to the call to come to Macedonia and help them. It was the Spirit of God who constantly propelled him farther southwest through Achaia and finally and logically to Corinth, though dogged persecutors followed him, biting at his heels. Paul would not bring the gospel "again" where others had labored; rather, he hoped through the Corinthians to enlarge the borders of the gospel through the Corinthians' faithfulness in their ministry of reconciliation (10:15-16).

Third, nothing would deter Paul from boasting—exulting—in his determination to deliver the gospel without charge (11:7-12). Paul was firmly convinced before God that this was what he was called to do. It wasn't necessary. He could legitimately receive their support, but that wasn't the way it was going to be while he was with them, even though he loved the Corinthians and they might have preferred it otherwise (11:10-11).

This boasting would cut off the wrong boasting of those who aspired to be in Paul's place of authority: the false apostles, deceitful workers who disguised themselves as apostles of Christ (11:13).

Their boasting was illegitimate; Paul's was not.

Finally, Paul knew that boasting could take place in only one sphere and have God's blessing, and that was "in the Lord" (10:17). Paul was quite familiar with God's words through Jeremiah the prophet:

> Thus says the LORD, "Let not a wise man boast of his wisdom, and let not the mighty man boast of his might, let not a rich man boast of his riches; but let him who boasts boast of this, that he understands and knows Me, that I am the LORD who exercises lovingkindness, justice, and righteousness on earth; for I delight in these things," declares the LORD.[16]

Paul could boast for he knew his God and understood His parameters (boundaries). But now Paul is about to "play the fool" and do some other boasting, yet not without purpose and not in a sinful way. Paul is going to boast according to the flesh (11:18).

Love and a godly jealousy for the Corinthians—not the Lord—compel him to indulge in this kind of boasting. And the Corinthians will have to bear with him even as they have borne (yet not rightly so) with the foolish. When any among the false apostles enslaved them, devoured them, took advantage of them, exalted himself, or—of all things—hit them in the face,[17] they bore it. So they can bear with him in this!

How thankful I am that Paul was moved to boast according to the flesh, for in his boasting we get a glimpse into the depth of Paul's light afflictions. And, oh, how our own afflictions pale in comparison! What Paul is about to share helps us realize that no matter what comes our way, we can make it. We can have a heart for God that will not fail or faint in the day of adversity. We can "run with footmen and...compete with horses."[18]

Let's watch Paul run his God-ordained course. Go get a cup of coffee or tea or hot chocolate—something warm that nourishes and quiets you. Then find a place all alone, where you can close the door on distractions, and thoughtfully read 2 Corinthians 11:22-33.

Let the words wash over your soul. Go with Paul on this journey of affliction. Feel the lash of the whip, the cold abrasiveness of the chains about your ankles, the dampness and darkness of a prison cell. Reel with the monstrous waves as they sweep you into the cold inky sea. Cling to a piece of wood and cry to heaven above to keep you from going down to the depths.

Walk with caution in the darkness of the night, jumping at the sound of footsteps seeking to overtake you, to rob you of your possessions and beat you to the ground in merciless greed. Feel the stinging bite of bold-face confrontation and brazen contradiction from your opposers. Take hold of your stomach growling in hunger, steady yourself as you rise weak from a lack of food.

Work late...and long...and on and on...until you turn your head and realize it's dawn already. Feel the incessant pressure of the ministry. Weep over those who gave into sin. Cry out to God for those in affliction, praying that they'll remain faithful, proving the genuineness of their faith.

Then come back and we'll talk just a little bit more about how understanding all this can be used to quickly quell the accusations of the enemy when he wants you to doubt your salvation.

Don't you want to bow before God and tell Him you want a heart for Him just like Paul's? Oh, to be that faithful...that strong in faith...that committed to being His ambassador!

These were Paul's momentary light afflictions that he referred to earlier in this letter (4:17). Afflictions he was assured were producing for him, and for those who suffered with him, an *eternal* weight of glory far beyond all comparison! Paul knew eternity was on the other side of suffering. When a person passes through the fires of affliction, suffering, and persecution, their endurance becomes the evidence of their salvation. This is why Paul could boast—exult—in the sight of God as he did.

Later he would write the church at Rome, telling them how they could exult in tribulation and have a "hope that did not disappoint." As you read this passage, mark the words *exult* and *hope*.

▶ ROMANS 5:3-5

3 And not only this, but we also exult in our tribulations, knowing that tribulation brings about perseverance;

4 and perseverance, proven character; and proven character, hope;

5 and hope does not disappoint, because the love of God has been poured out within our hearts through the Holy Spirit who was given to us.

This is so neat. The word here for "exult"—*kauchaomai*—is the same word translated "boast" in 2 Corinthians 10 and 11. Tribulations are a cause of boasting because of what they prove, the hope they bring. Watch the progression:

tribulation…

perseverance…

proven character…

hope.

We boast in tribulation not because of the grief or pain or hardship it brings, but because of the fruit it produces. In God's children, tribulation produces perseverance. The word for "perseverance" is *hupomeno: hupo,* meaning "under," and *meno,* "to abide, to remain there." According to James 1:4, the result of this endurance is that we are "perfect and complete, lacking in nothing." "Perfect" means mature. The process of suffering causes us to mature, to become more like our Lord. Thus, proven character, or *dokime*—character that has been put to the test and passed!

The fact that we don't run away, don't go back to our old ways, don't wither in our faith and fall away, shows what we're made of. We're made of genuine stuff. We know that we know we are His because we made it through the testing of our faith—and faith is not faith until it's tested! Thus we have a hope that does not disappoint. When we're absent from the body, we know with a bold confidence that we'll be at home with our Lord.

Can you hear the organ, the choir, and the words of that old hymn? "Blessed assurance, Jesus is mine! Oh, what a foretaste of glory divine! Heir of salvation, purchase of God, born of His Spirit, washed in His blood!"

Once you pass through a great trial, precious one—a difficult test of your faith—you'll understand how it's possible to say with great confidence, "Be gone, Satan! Because not only is it written, but I have been put to the test through my trials and I have endured. My salvation is genuine!"

MEMORY VERSES

For though we walk in the flesh, we do not war according to the flesh, for the weapons of our warfare are not of the flesh, but divinely powerful for the destruction of fortresses. We are destroying speculations and every lofty thing raised up against the knowledge of God, and we are taking every thought captive to the obedience of Christ.

2 CORINTHIANS 10:3-5

SMALL-GROUP DISCUSSION QUESTIONS

1. According to this week's Scripture passages, who was Paul in conflict with? And how are they described?
2. How did Paul approach the Corinthians about this deception from the enemy?

3. Why is it important to understand that "we do not war according to the flesh" (2 Corinthians 10:3)?

4. Where does the enemy attach? Why?

5. What must we do to keep from being deceived by what is false?

6. How was Paul able to keep from being defeated by his enemies? Will this strategy work for us as well?

7. What were the "false apostles" like whom Paul described in 2 Corinthians 11:13? In what form do we see such "false apostles" today?

8. What did you learn about Satan from Revelation 12:9?

9. According to Genesis 3:1-5, how did Satan deceive Eve? How does he continue to deceive today?

10. When Paul speaks of "boasting," what is he boasting about? How did he boast?

APPLICATION:

11. What do you need to do when you find yourself in warfare with the enemy?

12. Is it easier for you to believe a lie or the truth? How can you be careful to guard your mind against falsehood? How sure are you that what you believe is really what God has said in His Word?

13. What do you need to do to keep from being led away from "the simplicity and purity of devotion to Christ" (2 Corinthians 11:3)?

14. How quick are you to judge others by their outward appearance?

15. In what ways have you found yourself in war with the enemy? How can you prove by your actions that you believe God's Word is more powerful than the father of lies?

---

1. 1 Corinthians 15:27.
2. Matthew 11:29.
3. Ephesians 6:12-13.
4. Ephesians 6:18.
5. The whole subject of spiritual warfare is studied and explained thoroughly in my book *Lord, Is It Warfare? Teach Me to Stand.*

6. Proverbs 23:7.
7. Proverbs 4:23.
8. *Expositors Bible Commentary* (Grand Rapids, Mich.: Zondervan, 1976), Volume 10, 380.
9. Romans 1:18.
10. John 3:19-21.
11. John 8:32.
12. Matthew 7:20-23.
13. Revelation 12:11.
14. Matthew 4:10.
15. Ephesians 6:10-17.
16. Jeremiah 9:23-24.
17. Some believe that this was what happened to Paul—that he was slapped in the face by the offender he had forgiven (2 Corinthians 2:10).
18. Jeremiah 12:5.

THE POWER
OF WEAKNESS

— D A Y   O N E —

Weakness is often such a source of shame and embarrassment. I'm sure you may have dealt with it yourself. You look at your inadequacies, your weaknesses, and you say, "I can't," "I don't have it." "Not me; it will never happen." "There's no way!" When we do that, do you think we may be limiting God?

Weaknesses were something the apostle Paul would literally boast in. In fact, in the insults, distresses, persecutions, and difficulties Paul experienced, he came to know the incredible power of weakness, because his weakness threw him to his knees.

Paul is not yet finished with this boasting. Driven by his zeal to protect and defend those whom he loves and whom he so greatly desires to present to Christ as a pure virgin, Paul now says, "If I have to boast, I will boast of what pertains to my weakness" (11:30).

It sounds so contradictory, doesn't it? When we think about boasting, we usually focus on our strengths and analyze how they can best be used in our quest for whatever. But to look at our weaknesses seems ludicrous. Really defeating! Certainly contrary to what the world would tell us to do.

And this, Beloved, is where we become so aware of the difference between the wisdom of the world and the wisdom of God. The Corinthians, like all Greeks, were enamored not only with rhetoric but with wisdom. A subject Paul dealt with immediately in 1 Corinthians 1 when he pointed out that at Christ's greatest point of weakness on the cross, "the weakness of God is stronger than men" (verse 25).

On the heels of that wonderful, glorious truth, Paul reminds them of their calling. As you read this passage, mark every occurrence of the words *chosen* and *boast.* There are key things we need to see so we can have God's perspective on the power of weakness and why we can boast in it.

I think you're going to be so blessed, my friend, and that just thrills my heart. I wonder if you realize how precious you are to God?

▶ 1 CORINTHIANS 1:26-31

26 For consider your calling, brethren, that there were not many wise according to the flesh, not many mighty, not many noble;

27 but God has chosen the foolish things of the world to shame the wise, and God has chosen the weak things of the world to shame the things which are strong,

28 and the base things of the world and the despised God has chosen, the things that are not, so that He may nullify the things that are,

29 so that no man may boast before God.

30 But by His doing you are in Christ Jesus, who became to us wisdom from God, and righteousness and sanctification, and redemption,

31 so that, just as it is written, "Let him who boasts, boast in the LORD."

List below the things God chooses.

Now, according to the text, why has God chosen people like this? Observe the verses carefully and be thorough in your answer.

Finally, let's reason from the text. According to what God says, does it really matter who God chooses? Why or why not?

Do you realize, Beloved, that these truths belong to you? These are precepts for your life today, right where you're living. If you're a person who feels so inadequate, so totally "nothing" in comparison to others with their talents, abilities, and gifts, have you begun to catch an inkling of what God wants you to know about yourself?

Now what do you learn about boasting from 1 Corinthians 1:26-31?

Understanding these truths helped Paul overcome what he deemed his deficiencies and timidity in the great task to which God had called him. Listen as he continues:

▶ 1 CORINTHIANS 2:1-5

1 And when I came to you, brethren, I did not come with superiority of speech or of wisdom, proclaiming to you the testimony of God.

2 For I determined to know nothing among you except Jesus Christ, and Him crucified.

3 I was with you in weakness and in fear and in much trembling,

⁴ and my message and my preaching were not in persuasive words of wisdom, but in demonstration of the Spirit and of power,

⁵ so that your faith would not rest on the wisdom of men, but on the power of God.

Why don't you go back and mark the words *weakness* and *power* in these verses.

Now what do you learn about Paul from these verses?

Does it surprise you? It did me the first time I ever read it. I could never imagine the mighty Paul ever being afraid, weak, or trembling. There are so many, many times that I feel this way as I stand to speak before different groups, especially when God has given me a "tough" message to deliver, one that convicts of sin and calls us to holiness. Or one that directly goes against a "popular" doctrine. There have been a few times when I thought, *Father, I think I'm going to have a heart attack.*

Do you know what touches me most about Paul in this passage? His willingness to walk into a situation like that and not depend upon anything else but the power of God. To not bring a message that he knows would wow or move the crowd or tickle their ears, but instead to totally rely on the Lord, giving people not what they want, expect, or would be impressed with, but what they truly need—the truth about Jesus Christ and His death, burial, and resurrection. Paul's concern was not what they thought about him, but that they know Jesus Christ and the salvation He brings to all who believe in Him.

Paul knew that it was vain to boast in man, and we don't need to, either in ourselves or in others. Our significance is not in who we are but in Whose we are and in what we have because we belong to Him. "So then let no one boast in men. For all things belong to you, whether Paul or Apollos or Cephas or the world or life or death or things present or things to come; all things belong to you, and you belong to Christ; and Christ belongs to God."[1]

This is why, precious one, you can boast in your weaknesses.

– D A Y   T W O –

The man's story was sensational. People flocked to hear him. Churches were packed. Invitations came from all over. Popular writers and speakers promoted him. "You have to hear this man. You won't believe what happened to him."

What had happened to him? The man said that he had been caught up to heaven. Mouths hung open in awe as he described what he saw and how it all came to pass. When I heard he had said, "When I got to heaven, God and I just pulled up a chair and had a good talk," I didn't know where this man thought he had been. I just knew it wasn't heaven. No one pulls up a chair and has a good talk with God. Rather, according to the Word of God, those in His presence—the whole heavenly host with the twenty-four elders—fall prostrate before His throne in worship.[2]

There was another brother who was greatly troubled over the spirit of this man and the sensation he was creating. As he prayed, he felt impressed of the Lord to confront him. The confrontation was difficult. When he challenged the man on the validity of his experience, he told him he believed God was going to take him home because what he was doing was so dishonoring to Him. The man died unexpectedly a very short time later.

As I heard this story, I couldn't help but wonder if the man who went about telling of his "heavenly" experience had ever carefully observed the story of Paul's account. Maybe it would have kept him from the chastening hand of the Lord.

Let's look at Paul's account of "boasting in his weaknesses" in 2 Corinthians 11:30–12:10. Read it though once and color code every reference to Paul. Then read it through a second time. Mark any reference to boasting, weaknesses, Satan, and power. Also mark time phrases with a clock like this: ⏰

And—you guessed it! Make a list of what you have learned about Paul, boasting, and weakness.

PAUL   BOASTING   WEAKNESS

When Paul begins to boast in his weaknesses, the first thing he does is tell us of an incident that took place early in his ministry—that of being lowered in a basket through a window in the wall (probably one the city walls) so no one would detect his escape from Damascus. Listen to this account again:

> The God and Father of the Lord Jesus, He who is blessed forever, knows that I am not lying. In Damascus the ethnarch under Aretas the king was guarding the city of the Damascenes in order to seize me, and I was let down in a basket through a window in the wall, and so escaped his hands. (11:31-33)

As you read this account, remember Paul is using it as an illustration of weakness. Why this event? I think it's because Paul was totally power-less in the situation, totally humbled. He cannot flee on foot or disguise himself and slip through the city gate; rather, he must be folded into a basket and lowered by a rope through a window in a city wall. If nothing else, it reminded him of just how small he was!

From this incident Paul takes us to another event that had happened fourteen years prior to his writing this, an event he shares no place else in any of his preserved writings. Listen again to this amazing account:

I know a man in Christ who fourteen years ago—whether in the body I do not know, or out of the body I do not know, God knows—such a man was caught up to the third heaven. And I know how such a man—whether in the body or apart from the body I do not know, God knows—was caught up into Paradise and heard inexpressible words, which a man is not permitted to speak. On behalf of such a man I will boast; but on my own behalf I will not boast, except in regard to my weaknesses. For if I do wish to boast I will not be foolish, for I will be speaking the truth; but I refrain from this, so that no one will credit me with more than he sees in me or hears from me. (12:2-6)

Isn't it interesting how Paul almost detaches himself from "this man" who had such a supernatural revelation, even though the man is Paul himself? I believe it's because the event only serves as the necessary backdrop for the weakness he will boast in. In telling this incident Paul is adamant that no one, absolutely no one, would credit him in any way for what happened.

Now stop and think about that, dear friend. Could a person actually have the experience Paul had and not talk about it, share it, use it as a press release to draw people to hear the gospel?

Come hear THE apostle who *entered into the third heaven* as he shares what NO one on earth has EVER seen!

Don't miss this incredibly uplifting evening that will take you beyond the sun, the stars, and the galaxies…and into heaven itself, right to the very throne of God!

Hear this amazing story from the very lips of the man who stepped into heaven and returned to tell us about it!

Gain insights into God and His kingdom that have never been revealed before—not even in Scripture! *This is a faith-building evening that you cannot miss* if you want to let others know of the promise of heaven and the certainty of hell. Bring the lost! Compel them to come! If nothing else has convinced them to believe on the Lord Jesus Christ, *this will do the trick!*

Tonight can be their night to have their sins washed away.

Be on time, because there's not just one revelation to be shared but MANY that *you must hear* in order to be a more effective and powerful ambassador for Jesus Christ!

This may seem ludicrous, but believe me, in our American culture it isn't far-fetched.

As with the man I told you about, surely there would be a packed house and multitudes who would be greatly impressed and influenced, and many even who would come to Jesus Christ. But is this the way God carries on the work of His kingdom? By giving men revelations, visions, great powers of healing, in order to draw and save the lost? Or does He do it as He did in Corinth with the simple, clear proclamation of the Lord Jesus Christ and Him crucified, buried, and raised from the dead?

As you saw the first day of this week's study—and as you've seen ever since the first week we began our study together—God carries on the work of His kingdom and does it through the proclamation of the gospel. That's why Paul wrote to the church at Rome that he was not ashamed of the gospel of Jesus Christ because it was *the power* of God unto salvation to everyone who believed. Not a vision, not a revelation, not an experience, but the message, whether they were Jews or Gentiles.[3]

Paul stayed detached from his experience because he didn't want anyone to "credit me with more than he sees in me or hears from me" (12:6). Do you catch Paul's caution, his humility, his desire for the glory of only One—God and God alone?

Although Paul tells very little of his experience, it did happen. It was not a delusion, a dream, a deception. He was there. *How* he was there, in the body or out of the body, he doesn't know, but he was there. And he "heard inexpressible words, which a man is not permitted to speak." Those words—and Paul assures us the revelations were beyond greatness—were never told. They weren't meant to be shared, no matter how great or convincing they were. Men had the Word of God; it was enough.

As I write this, I wonder how many people you know in "Christendom" who think God's Word is *not* enough? Who don't want to hear someone exegete* the Word of God to them, opening the Bible and explaining the text with integrity in the fear of God? But instead they're constantly looking for, delighting in, getting spiritually high on some new message, some new prophecy, some new miracle, some new experience, some new "revelation," some new "the Lord just told me and showed me that I should share it with you so you would know." I can still hear one television evangelist's voice as I write these words.

My heart grieves, my spirit groans as I watch programs like this and see the sheep that follow such people, holding them in awe, convinced that these are men or women of God because of their revelations and the power they have to do these things—things they believe to be manifestations of the power of the Spirit of God.

But why does Paul even relate this event if he isn't going to share what he saw, what he heard? Because his point in sharing this experience is not the experience but what came from it—a "thorn" delivered by Satan that would keep Paul from ever exalting himself. A thorn God would never take away. A thorn that experientially, day by day, reminded Paul that God's power was perfected in weakness. It seems incongruous, doesn't it, that an event of such spiritual magnitude would reduce someone to persistent humility? Total dependence is the divine reason for every thorn in our flesh.

Oh, Beloved, at this point has His Word struck a nerve? Is God speaking to your heart in respect to something you asked Him to take away or change in your life, and He's never done it? Maybe as you beseeched Him in prayer, you presented your request with such logic, such sound reasoning, such fervent pleading, such faith that you thought surely this time God would hear you and understand and answer.

Maybe your autistic child would be healed, and you would be freed for greater ministry, even released as a family to take the gospel across the oceans to the neediest of people.

---

* Basically when a person exegetes a portion of the Word of God, he or she moves through the text of Scripture systematically, explaining its meaning.

Maybe you would miraculously be healed of your own disease, your blindness, your deafness, your paralysis, your "sentence of death"—whatever form it takes—so you could serve the Lord in strength and health.

Maybe God would convert or remove your adversaries so you wouldn't find yourself always having to deal with their criticism, their opposition, and would be able to forget their incessant attacks and focus on His Word and His work without distraction.

Maybe you could make the millions you were always sure you would make and give a great portion of it to God's work.

Maybe your unsaved mate would get saved—or die prematurely, releasing you to a life of unopposed, unthwarted devotion to Him.

Maybe your child would call you, ask your forgiveness, and say that more than anything else she wanted to be reconciled, to have a relationship centered on the Lord so you could think about the things of the Lord instead of living in emotional and mental torture over a past you could never change.

Maybe… *You fill it in, dear one…*

I don't want to guess your "maybe," but I do want you to know without a shadow of doubt that if God doesn't move the way you beg Him to move, it will turn out to be an untold blessing to you and to others if you'll learn to boast in your weakness, for it will etch you in His likeness.

And how do you do that? That's for tomorrow, precious one. Today is for resting in His all-sufficient grace, for meditating on these truths.

— D A Y   T H R E E —

When we think of grace, we have a tendency to associate it only with salvation. Either we forget or don't realize that grace is the ever-present commodity of God's unmerited favor that we're to live in. Grace is everything Jesus Christ is and has, all made available to us through no merit of our own.

Grace can never be earned, bought, or won; it can only be appropriated by faith, believing God says what He means and means what He says. Romans 5 tells us that having been justified by faith, we have "obtained our introduction by faith into this grace in which we stand" (verse 2). As Paul writes this under divine inspiration, he puts this verb *stand* in the perfect tense—a past completed action with a present or continuous result. In other words, once we're God's children, we forever stand in His all-sufficient, lavish, extravagant grace that out-abounds our every circumstance or need. Awesome, isn't it! Really incomprehensible, yet attainable just for the believing!

And it's our weaknesses that help us realize how attainable this grace is!

Like Jesus, Paul asked the Father three times to remove the instrument of pain and death, and the Lord said, "No." Why? Because it was necessary. Yet both Jesus and Paul found God's grace sufficient to sustain them. In the Garden of Gethsemane—a name which means "olive press"—Jesus was pressed out beyond measure, in such agony of spirit over what lay before Him that He sweat great drops of blood so profuse that they dropped from His brow to the ground. "Father, if it is possible, let this cup pass from Me; yet not as I will, but as You will" (Matthew 26:39).

Of course, anything is possible for God. But to remove Jesus' cup of suffering and death would mean that His mission would fail. Man would remain lost. Can you sense Jesus' humanity? I'm sure this is why this intimate time with His Father was preserved for us in the Gospels. We need to know and understand that we aren't alone in our suffering or in our service for our Lord, service that at times seems as if it will cost us our very lives. Life is dear. We want to hang on to it with as much ease, peace, and joy as possible. And yet, as we've already seen, "death works in us, but life in you" (2 Corinthians 4:12). With every plea that was uttered by Jesus for the removal of the cup, there followed, "Your will be done."

And His Father's will was done. And Jesus was sustained through it all! "For indeed," Paul says, "He was crucified because of weakness, yet He lives because of the power of God" (13:4).

He lives because of the power of God. That, Beloved, is the way we, as followers of Christ, are to live.

Three times Paul went to God to ask Him to take away the thorn in his flesh. It was an unrelenting messenger of Satan permitted by God. I use the term "unrelenting" because the verb *buffet,* as it appears in the *King James Version* of 2 Corinthians 12:7, is in the present tense, which means continuous or habitual action. The word "buffet" is *kolaphizo,* which comes from *kolaphos,* "a fist." Thus the word means "to rap or strike a blow with the fist, with clenched hands." The word is used in Matthew 26:67 when, after being arrested in Gethsemane, Jesus is examined by the high priest at the house of Caiaphas. Once the illogically gathered counsel pronounced their vindictive verdict—"He deserves death!" —they spat in His face and beat Him with their fists *(kolaphizo)* while others slapped Him. It's one thing to experience pain and know that soon it will be over. It's another thing to live with it. Paul had to live with this thorn that continually, incessantly pounded at his flesh.

As I write this, I think of my brother, Jack, who lives in incessant pain from shingles. When we're together, which is rarely, since he lives so far away, I'll catch the grimace on his face as he's intermittently attacked by the pain.

As physical as Paul's thorn was, as debilitating and wearing as Satan could make it—for we know that his power is limited, and we're promised that it's never more than we can bear[4]—God would not give the word for Satan to retreat. We have no idea of any conversation between God and Satan in respect to Paul and his thorn, such as that recorded for us in Job 1 regarding the faithfulness of God's servant Job; we only know that Satan was allowed to touch Paul, even as he was allowed to touch Job. In Paul's instance, I believe it's wise to note that there's no rebuking of the devil, no commanding him to be gone, to take his thorn and go home. Rather Paul only pleads with God, for he knows God is the Sovereign One. As He said through the prophet Isaiah: "There is no one besides Me. I am the LORD, and there is no other, the One forming light and creating darkness, causing well-being and creating calamity; I am the LORD who does all these."[5]

If God is the One who does all these things, then He is the One we're to talk to—and there's nothing wrong with asking God to take away our thorn. And Paul does this, until God tells him after his third request—and listen carefully, Beloved, for these are apples of pure gold—"My grace is sufficient for you, for power is perfected in weakness" (12:9).

Look at his statement very carefully and write out what you learn about power here. What is this statement synonymous with?

Let's read on in the text for a moment:

Most gladly, therefore, I will rather boast about my weaknesses, so that the power of Christ may dwell in me. Therefore I am well content with weaknesses, with insults, with distresses, with persecutions, with difficulties, for Christ's sake; for when I am weak, then I am strong. (12:9-10)

Paul is strong when he is weak because he's dependent upon, cast upon, God's grace. God isn't taking away the thorn, but there's power to deal with it, because grace *is* power. And this power, this grace, "dwells" in him. "Dwells" here means "to tabernacle." It means that God throws up a tent of power in Paul and never takes it down. "Dwells" is in the present tense to indicate that it's something continuous, never stopping. O precious one, do you see it? Let me say it again: Grace *is* power; power that is *yours*.

Do you see the surpassing greatness of this truth that's revealed to us because God did *not* deliver Paul? Because He did *not* answer Paul's prayer the way Paul wanted him to answer? Forever and ever it is written, never to pass away, for it is the Word of God: *My grace is sufficient for you.*

For every child of God who wonders if he or she can continue in their great weakness, there is God's promise and testimony: "My grace is sufficient for you. My power (grace!) is perfected in weakness." And what does this bring? Contentedness! Blessed contentedness! Do you know how so many people are so discontented? Nothing can please them, make them happy, assuage the bitterness, wipe away the gloom, the sorrow, the disappointment, the grief, the pessimism.

All Paul needed was to hear God's final answer, and he did: "And He has said to me." "Has said" is in the perfect tense—a past completed action with a present and continuous result. And what was that answer? "My grace is sufficient for you." Grace is *all* you need—and you've got it! You *can* handle it as more than a conqueror!

Thus comes Paul's "therefore"—a term of conclusion. We're about to see the way Paul is going to respond to God's answer. Watch carefully, Beloved, for in this you see Paul's heart for God: "Therefore I am well content." Paul was saying, "If this is what God wants, if this is what is best for me, and He gives me His grace to handle it, then I am *well* content!"

We don't know what Paul's thorn was; he didn't record it. We can speculate, as many have done—perhaps wondering if he suffered from a terrible eye disease that was repulsive to look at, provoked people out of love to want to give them his eyes,[6] and also caused him to write in such large letters[7]—but that's all we can do. God has left it open, blank. I believe it's for your sake and mine, so that we can understand that whatever we bear in our weakness for Christ's sake brings us grace's strength.

Therefore, gaining God's divine perspective, Paul determines to be well content...

> with weaknesses...
> with insults...
> with distresses...
> with persecutions...
> with difficulties....

That pretty much covers it, doesn't it?

Assess your weaknesses, precious one, and see them as strengths, for this is where you will lean on your Lord in greatest dependency. This is what will cause you to remember Him, turn to Him, and appropriate His all-sufficient grace. And it is all-sufficient. To worry that it won't be enough is as ridiculous as a little bird fretting that it will run out of sky to soar in, or a worm that it will run out of earth to burrow in, or a little fish that it will drink the oceans dry.

At the same time you assess your weaknesses, beware of your strengths, lest in your success you forget to rely on God and you try to handle something in your own frail humanity. As I share this with you, I am reminded of two things Agur asked of God in the book of Proverbs:

> Two things I asked of You,
> Do not refuse me before I die:
> Keep deception and lies far from me,
> Give me neither poverty nor riches;
> Feed me with the food that is my portion,
> That I not be full and deny You and say, "Who is the LORD?"
> Or that I not be in want and steal,
> And profane the name of my God.[8]

This wise man wanted to be ever dependent on the Lord, and he knew that when things were easy—plentiful and satisfying—that he might forget God, or in his need he might not seek God. Thus his caution and his prayer.

Let's pause for a moment, my friend, and think about this. When do you pray the most? Remember God the most?

Power is the downfall of many a person, even in Christian circles, unfortunately. Somehow we get the mistaken idea that because we are God's and because what we're doing is so valuable to the kingdom of God, we can push His boundaries and get away with it. You can't, Beloved. I can't. No child of God can, because our Father is a holy God. Pride is tattooed all over Satan, and God will not have His children looking like or imitating His archenemy.

We must be ever so vigilant in our strengths, for it's when we're strong and successful that we're the most vulnerable.

Think of King Uzziah. As you read the following text, mark any reference to strength and to pride. Also watch for any time phrases and mark them with a clock.

❿ 2 CHRONICLES 26:3-5,14-16

3 Uzziah was sixteen years old when he became king, and he reigned fifty-two years in Jerusalem; and his mother's name was Jechiliah of Jerusalem.

4 He did right in the sight of the LORD according to all that his father Amaziah had done.

5 He continued to seek God in the days of Zechariah, who had understanding through the vision of God; and as long as he sought the LORD, God prospered him....

14 Moreover, Uzziah prepared for all the army shields, spears, helmets, body armor, bows and sling stones.

15 In Jerusalem he made engines of war invented by skillful men to be on the towers and on the corners for the purpose of shooting arrows and great stones. Hence his fame spread afar, for he was marvelously helped until he was strong.

16 But when he became strong, his heart was so proud that he acted corruptly, and he was unfaithful to the LORD his God, for he entered the temple of the LORD to burn incense on the altar of incense.

God struck Uzziah with leprosy. For the rest of his life, he was cut off from the house of the Lord. God resists the proud. This young king who started well could have ended well, if only he had realized where his strength came from and continued to live in habitual dependence upon his God.

Uzziah could have learned a good lesson from his predecessor, King Asa, if he had studied his life. When Asa began his reign, he walked in total dependence upon God, doing what was right in the sight of the Lord. When Zerah the Ethiopian came out against him with an army of a million men and three hundred chariots, Asa knew he was beaten unless God intervened. His army was half that size and devoid of iron chariots. Listen to his prayer, whipping against the wind in the valley of Zephathah at Mareshah, as he stands before an army that consumes the landscape with its presence and turns his opened eyes heavenward.

▶ 2 CHRONICLES 14:11

Then Asa called to the LORD his God and said, "LORD, there is no one besides You to help in the battle between the powerful and those who have no strength; so help us, O LORD our God, for we trust in You, and in Your name have come against this multitude. O LORD, You are our God; let not man prevail against You."

Doesn't your heart stir at such faith! How pleasing it was to God to hear Asa pray such a prayer. Asa believed that God was sovereign and that God would help him. Did you notice the words that indicated strength and weakness? If not, read his prayer again and mark them. Then notice his total faith.

Asa has assessed the enemy's army and his own. Compared to the Ethiopians, Judah had no strength; they were weak. The enemy was powerful. "So help us," Asa prayed.

Nothing could have made Asa any stronger—for in his utter weakness he ran to the one and only true source of power—God.

And God moved! God answered! Asa knew the sweet taste of victory through faith, the power of grace.

And God was kind, ever so watchful over his servant. He sent His Spirit to Azariah, the son of Oded, so that Asa might not get caught up in prideful glory of the victory.

And he went out to meet Asa and said to him, "Listen to me, Asa, and all Judah and Benjamin: the LORD is with you when you are with Him. And if you seek Him, He will let you find Him; but if you forsake Him, He will forsake you."[9]

In other words, "Continue to depend on Me. I am here; seek Me. Don't try to do anything without Me. I am God; you are man. You need Me. Whatever you do, don't forget that."

God's words gave Asa courage. He moved forward, doing what any good king would do, ridding the land of idols, restoring the altars of the Lord, and calling people to enter into a covenant to seek the Lord God of their fathers with all their heart and soul. And if anyone refused they were to be put to death "small or great, man or woman."[10]

And then it happened. It was the thirty-sixth year of his reign. Asa made an alliance with the king of Aram, Ben-hadad, to go to war against his enemy. He never consulted God. Instead of relying on his God, Asa formed an alliance. Asa forgot the words of Azariah and turned from his all-sufficient source of power to the arm of flesh. He didn't remember the truth about his situation:

> The king is not saved by a mighty army;
> A warrior is not delivered by great strength.
> A horse is a false hope for victory;
> Nor does it deliver anyone by its great strength.
> Behold, the eye of the LORD is on those who fear Him,
> On those who hope for His lovingkindness,
> To deliver their soul from death
> And to keep them alive in famine.[11]

In this battle, Asa apparently thought he didn't need God. It was a done victory; he had the king of Aram. So God let his enemy escape out of his hand. Then He sent Hanani the seer with the following message. As you read it, mark any words that have to do with strength or weakness:

◗ 2 CHRONICLES 16:7-9

⁷ At that time Hanani the seer came to Asa king of Judah and said to him, "Because you have relied on the king of Aram and have not relied on the LORD your God, therefore the army of the king of Aram has escaped out of your hand.

⁸ "Were not the Ethiopians and the Lubim an immense army with very many chariots and horsemen? Yet because you relied on the LORD, He delivered them into your hand.

⁹ "For the eyes of the LORD move to and fro throughout the earth that He may strongly support those whose heart is completely His. You have acted foolishly in this. Indeed, from now on you will surely have wars."

Asa heard God's words, but they only made him angry. Wasn't he the king? How dare a seer reproach him?

God waited almost three years. Nothing changed; Asa never repented. And so God sent him a thorn in the flesh—a disease in his feet. But even then, Asa hardened his heart. He refused to seek God, to even ask God to heal him. "His disease was severe; yet even in his disease he did not seek the LORD, but the physicians."¹²

The physicians couldn't cure him, nor could they give him the grace he needed to endure.

Oh, Beloved, God is looking for hearts that are fully His, totally dependent on Him, relying on nothing but His power. Hearts that are humbled by thorns and made strong in His grace.

And how do you keep your heart like this? You must guard your time of quiet, of being alone in His presence, reading and meditating on His Word and then talking with Him about all the issues of life. I cannot stress this enough. When you get in a hurry, when you're so pressured, so stressed out, so preoccupied by the affairs of daily living that you cannot have leisure in His presence and in His Word, then you're in grave danger of ending up as Uzziah did or as Asa did.

The Lord's eyes are running to and fro across the earth, looking for a heart that is fully His. When He sees you meditating on His Word, taking time to commune with Him in prayer—He stops. He has found what He's looking for: a heart that's fully His.

Oh, precious one, do His eyes rest on you?

— DAY FOUR —

Paul's boasting has ended. His purpose is accomplished. And his purpose, he wants them to understand, has not been to defend himself; rather, it's much higher than that.

Let's look at it, because I don't want you to miss how Paul lived out his faith on the highest of planes. Read through 2 Corinthians 12:11–13:4. As you do, color each reference to Paul, including the plural pronoun *we*, and color each reference to the Corinthians as you've done before. Watch the "I—you." Then, when you finish, list below what you have learned from marking these references.

Also mark any reference to time with a clock as usual. And mark the words *love, sin, repent,* and *weakness* in their various expressions.

PAUL   THE CORINTHIANS

As I read of Paul's need to confront the church at Corinth in respect to the way the people are dishonoring him, I think of the abuse inflicted on many pastors by their congregations. The Corinthians, instead of recognizing and respecting Paul's gifts and calling from God (12:11-12), questioned him and took sides with those who came against him. They were quick to listen to others, but not to Paul. In fact, they listened with an open spirit to heretical teaching that outsiders brought in, but they questioned Paul's doctrine (11:4). And this is the way so many today treat their pastors. I wonder if people involved in things like this realize that their carnality is on display.

Listen carefully: If you're into pastor bashing, then you're sinning against God, and I would suggest that there are some, if not maybe many, areas in your life where you're failing to walk as God would have you walk. I can assure you that you're not in an intimate relationship with God. If you were, you would immediately stop judging your pastor and fall on your face and beg God's forgiveness for treating one of His servants this way.

If a pastor sins or lives in a high-handed, authoritative, prideful way, then he's to be disciplined by the leaders of the church according to the principles laid out in the passage printed out here. As you read it, don't miss the positive side of how we're to honor those who rule well. Also you'll note that there's a plurality of leaders in the church—more than one elder (overseer, pastor-teacher). When you come to any reference to the elders, mark it in a distinctive way. Watch the pronouns. Also mark every reference to sin.

● 1 TIMOTHY 5:17-21

17 The elders who rule well are to be considered worthy of double honor, especially those who work hard at preaching and teaching.

18 For the Scripture says, "You shall not muzzle the ox while he is threshing," and "The laborer is worthy of his wages."

19 Do not receive an accusation against an elder except on the basis of two or three witnesses.

20 Those who continue in sin, rebuke in the presence of all, so that the rest also will be fearful of sinning.

²¹ I solemnly charge you in the presence of God and of Christ Jesus and of His chosen angels, to maintain these principles without bias, doing nothing in a spirit of partiality.

Why don't you take a moment, Beloved, and list exactly what's to be done when there's an accusation or complaint against a pastor, an elder. Number the steps according to their proper sequence. It will help you remember it better, especially if you read it aloud when you finish.

There's another passage given by our Lord during His earthly ministry before church order was officially instituted. Let's take a look at it. It's probably a passage you're familiar with. Jesus said:

If your brother sins, go and show him his fault in private; if he listens to you, you have won your brother. But if he does not listen to you, take one or two more with you, so that by the mouth of two or three witnesses every fact may be confirmed. If he refuses to listen to them, tell it to the church; and if he refuses to listen even to the church, let him be to you as a Gentile and a tax collector.¹³

In other words separate yourself from him, even as Paul told the Corinthians to do with the so-called brother who was sleeping with his father's wife (1 Corinthians 5).

Jesus continues:

Truly I say to you, whatever you bind on earth shall have been bound in heaven; and whatever you loose on earth shall have been loosed in heaven.

Again I say to you, that if two of you agree on earth about anything that they may ask, it shall be done for them by My Father who is in heaven. For where two or three have gathered together in My name, I am there in their midst.[14]

How often we quote that last sentence out of context, claiming it as a promise of answered prayer when it doesn't carry that meaning at all. The setting of that verse is the discipline of a brother or sister in sin and our Savior's accompanying assurance that when the church deals with it properly (two or three proper witnesses gathered in His name), they have His assurance that God is there in full support of their action. We see the same "two or three" in 1 Timothy 5:19 and 2 Corinthians 13:1, where Paul says every fact is to be confirmed by the testimony of two or three witnesses.

Well, we've talked about the discipline of a pastor; now let's turn to the authority that accompanies biblical leadership. Whenever authority is exercised, you'll be able to discern whether it is godly authority or not by its purpose and the way in which it is done.

For the second time, Paul affirms that his apostolic authority is legitimate and that the Corinthians should have recognized and commended him. Though Paul was a nobody, in no aspect was he inferior to the eminent apostles, and he's going to carry out his responsibilities regardless of the personal cost. Yet his authority, even if it has to be carried out in severity, will be carried out God's way—for building and not destroying (2 Corinthians 10:8; 12:19; 13:10). This will be the proof "of the Christ who speaks in me" (13:3).

Never forget that whenever godly authority is exercised, the purpose is the long-term spiritual health of the sinner or the sinning factions. Paul has already shown this to be true in his exhortation to the Corinthians in respect to forgiving the man who sinned, so that Satan would not take advantage of them (2:4-11).

It's love that compels Paul to do this. Any time known sin is allowed to continue in a church fellowship or among Christians who are friends, you're opening the door to the enemy. Sin gives Satan his power.

On the other hand, repentance (having a change of mind about your sin) and confession (naming the sin for what it is) breaks the sin's power, because the inevitable result will be forsaking the sin, turning from it. It's then that the blood of Jesus Christ keeps on cleansing us from all unrighteousness.[15]

Paul was about to make his third trip to Corinth (12:14). When he arrived, he did not want to find strife, jealousy, angry tempers, disputes, slanders, gossip, arrogance, and disturbances. Who would? And who could let it continue among those who name the name of Christ and are suppose to be temples of the living God? Paul's fear was that when he arrived, he would once again be humbled in tears over those who had sinned in the past and had not repented of their impurity, immorality, and sensuality.

Can you sense his love? A love that's involved? Remember how he said, "Who is weak without my being weak? Who is led into sin without my intense concern?" (11:29).

Paul loves them so much that he would "gladly spend and be expended for [their] souls" (12:15).

Jesus said, "Greater love has no one than this, that one lay down his life for his friends."[16]

But what of the Corinthians? Had Paul not clearly explained in 1 Corinthians 13 the importance of love and the nothingness of any spiritual gift or service without love? Had they missed his point? Forgotten what he said? Disregarded it? His question was, "If I love you more, am I to be loved less?" (2 Corinthians 12:15). It seems the more he expressed and demonstrated his love, the more they withdrew theirs. And oftimes this is the way it can be in a church. The pastor loves and loves, but it's never enough. A sinning, carnal congregation will never be satisfied.

Oh, how Paul longed that the Corinthians would be what he wished and that he could be what they wished! It would all depend on how they dealt with the "sin in the camp."

– D A Y   F I V E –

There was "sin in the camp" in the Corinthian church. Whenever there's sin, you need to stop and test yourself and "see if you are in the faith"

(2 Corinthians 13:5). "Examine yourselves!" Paul says. "Or do you not recognize this about yourselves, that Jesus Christ is in you—unless indeed you fail the test?" (13:5).

It was obvious that Paul and Titus didn't fail the test, but it wasn't obvious that all in Corinth would pass. Why? Because of sin. It is a Christian's relationship to sin and the way that he or she walks that helps you discern whether or not you have only religion or a true relationship.

A religion is something you perform, rituals that you go through in worship of a higher being. A relationship is Christ in you—the Father, the Son, and the Spirit taking up their abode within. Jesus said, "If anyone loves Me, he will keep My word; and My Father will love him, and We will come to him and make Our abode with him."[17] That takes care of the Father and the Son. Second Corinthians 1:22 assures us that God "sealed us and gave us the Spirit in our hearts."

When God is in us, sin cannot habitually reign over us. In John's first epistle, which was written that we might know that we have eternal life (5:13), John says:

▶ 1 JOHN 3:7-10

7 Little children, make sure no one deceives you; the one who practices righteousness is righteous, just as He is righteous;

8 the one who practices sin is of the devil; for the devil has sinned from the beginning. The Son of God appeared for this purpose, to destroy the works of the devil.

9 No one who is born of God practices sin, because His seed abides in him; and he cannot sin, because he is born of God.

10 By this the children of God and the children of the devil are obvious: anyone who does not practice righteousness is not of God, nor the one who does not love his brother.

The reason we need to test ourselves in respect to our relationship with God is that we can be deceived. Did you see John's concern? "Make sure no one deceives you." Unfortunately there can be many well-meaning but biblically illiterate people who want to assure us that we're saved, even though we don't act or live the way real believers do. They're sure we're saved because we asked Jesus to come into our heart, because we prayed the sinner's prayer. However, no place does the Word of God tell us that this is how we know. When you have time, you ought to read through 1 John and simply follow the instructions in the *New Inductive Study Bible* and fill in the chart that's included there. Then you'll see for yourself and know that you know the identifying marks of true Christianity.

We aren't going to go through 1 John at this time, but I do want us to see some important principles in the passage you just read. In fact, read it again and mark the following words and phrases: *sin, righteousness, the devil, born of God,* and *love.* As you read, this will help you realize that every time you see the verb *sin* in these verses, it's used in the present tense, which indicates "continual or habitual action."

When you finish reading and marking the text, list below what you have learned about the children of God and the children of the devil.

THE CHILDREN OF GOD   THE CHILDREN OF THE DEVIL

Now, Beloved, I know you realize that what you've just read and analyzed yourself through careful observation is truth. It stands. It cannot be altered. "We can do nothing against the truth, but only for the truth" (2 Corinthians 13:8). What God has said needs no fancy interpretation. No theological scholars need explain the text. God has spoken to us in a perspicuous way. *Perspicuous* means "plain to the understanding, especially because of the clarity and precision of the presentation." Therefore if what others believe or have taught or experienced doesn't agree with God's Word, you must know they're wrong; they've been deceived.

John's concern was also Paul's. Paul had already challenged the Corinthians and warned them about being deceived. Read the following passage from 1 Corinthians and mark any reference to deception. Mark the word *unrighteous* as you did *righteous* in 1 John, but put a slash (/) through it to indicate the negative.

▶ 1 CORINTHIANS 6:8-11

8 On the contrary, you yourselves wrong and defraud. You do this even to your brethren.

9 Or do you not know that the unrighteous will not inherit the kingdom of God? Do not be deceived; neither fornicators, nor idolaters, nor adulterers, nor effeminate, nor homosexuals,

10 nor thieves, nor the covetous, nor drunkards, nor revilers, nor swindlers, will inherit the kingdom of God.

11 Such were some of you; but you were washed, but you were sanctified, but you were justified in the name of the Lord Jesus Christ and in the Spirit of our God.

List below what you have learned from this text about the Corinthians.

WHAT THEY WERE   WHAT THEY ARE

What correlation do you see between this passage and the one you observed earlier from 1 John?

Now of course we must pause and reflect on what we've seen. We must do as Paul tells us to do: examine ourselves to see if Jesus Christ is really in us. Take time to do that. When you finish, write down how you know.

If Jesus is not in you, but you want Him to be, then I believe you're probably ready, having spent this much time in the Word of God. The soil of your heart had been duly prepared and the seed sown and watered these past eight weeks. Now is the time for the harvest, the increase, the yield of righteousness to be brought in.

Dear friend, it's as simple as believing in your heart that Jesus is the Christ, God in the flesh, the One who knew no sin but was made sin for you. Thank Him. Tell Him you believe. Then make your confession. Confess Jesus Christ as your Lord, your God, for with the mouth confession is made unto salvation.[18] If you did this—if you became His child at any point in this study—how I would love to know it! To rejoice with you and over you. Just drop me a note, tell me what happened, and write "personal" on the envelope. (And by the way, you would address your sister simply as "Kay.")

As we're bringing our study to a close, Paul is bringing his letter to a close. He has told the church at Corinth that he's coming a third time. When he comes, he doesn't want to be humiliated because they haven't dealt with the sin. Nor does he desire to deal with them in severity; he will do it if necessary, but he would rather see the Christ who "was crucified because of weakness" be mighty in them. Christ's power is there, but they must appropriate it. Power over sin, power to live righteously bear witness to the fact that "Jesus Christ is in you" (13:4-5).

Paul has said what needs to be said. He has poured out his heart, shared his anguish and joy, told them of the collection they need to take. Then finally, saving the hardest until last, he has dealt with the "false apostles" who have come in among them, seeking to cut off the sheep from their God-ordained earthly shepherd and devour the flock.

And what is Paul's prayer, his final work of exhortation? Read through 2 Corinthians 13:5-14. Mark key words that you've marked previously if you see them in the text, words like *weak, love, comfort, grace*. Also watch for any reference to his writing and another phrase that he's going to use twice.

After you've read and marked these final verses in 2 Corinthians, let me ask you: What is Paul's concern? What does he say twice? What does he pray? It's what I pray for you, Beloved—"that you be made complete." The word for "complete" is interesting here, for instead of using a word for maturity *(teleios)* he uses *katartizo,* a word that means "to complete thoroughly, in the sense of repair or adjust or restore."

This is the reason Paul is writing these things. He wants to build, he wants to restore, mend, and adjust what needs to be adjusted. And isn't that one of the primary works of the Word of God? The Word is not only doctrine—that which we learn, embrace, and teach—it's also that which reproves us, corrects us, and instructs us in righteousness, so that you and I can be prepared for every good work of life.[19]

Oh, precious, precious one, I thank you from the depths of my heart for allowing me this privilege of sharing God's Word with you. Thank you for your desire to have a heart for God and for disciplining yourself to attain this wonderful prize of His high calling in Christ Jesus—Christlikeness—for it is in our Savior, and in Paul, that we see the anatomy of a heart for God.

May we heed Paul's words in 1 Corinthians 11:1: "Be imitators of me, just as I also am of Christ."

The grace of the Lord Jesus Christ,
and the love of God,
and the fellowship of the Holy Spirit,
be with you, precious one.

MEMORY VERSES

And He has said to me, "My grace is sufficient for you, for power is perfected in weakness." Most gladly, therefore, I will rather boast about my weaknesses, so that the power of Christ may dwell in me. Therefore I am well content with weaknesses, with insults, with distresses, with persecutions, with difficulties, for Christ's sake; for when I am weak, then I am strong.

2 CORINTHIANS 12:9-10

SMALL-GROUP DISCUSSION QUESTIONS

1. What did you learn about Paul from 1 Corinthians 2:1-5? What was it that made his message to the Corinthians so powerful?
2. What else do we learn about Paul from the incidents described in 2 Corinthians 11:30–12:10?
3. Why was Paul given a "thorn in the flesh"? How was he able to accept it?
4. How does one boast in weakness? Why is weakness necessary?
5. What do we learn about God from His answer to Paul in 2 Corinthians 12:9?
6. What do we learn about Paul from his response in 2 Corinthians 12:9-10?
7. What do we learn from the accounts of Kings Uzziah and Asa about power and weakness? Why is that when we are comfortable and at ease, we often forget God?
8. What is the correct, biblical way to discipline a church leader or any church member? What is the purpose of this discipline?
9. How can we test ourselves to see if we are "in the faith" (2 Corinthians 13:5)? What would be the proof that we are indeed "in the faith"?
10. How would you summarize the warning we find in 1 John 3:7-10 as well as 1 Corinthians 6:9-11?

11. What does Paul mean by the phrase "be made complete" (2 Corinthians 13:9,11)? How are we made complete?

12. How would you summarize Paul's purpose for writing this letter to the Corinthians?

APPLICATION:

13. Has there been a time recently where you especially realized that God's grace is sufficient for you, and that "power is perfected in weakness"? Share that experience with the group, that they, too, could be encouraged.

14. In your own life, how would you describe the process of going to God for answers, waiting for Him, and then accepting His answer as being best for you?

15. How can you best honor those in leadership in your local church?

16. Is sin a habitual way of life for you? If so, what does that say about you?

----

1. 1 Corinthians 3:21-23.
2. Isaiah 6:1-5; Revelation 4:3-11.
3. Romans 1:16.
4. 1 Corinthians 10:13.
5. Isaiah 45:6-7.
6. Galatians 4:15.
7. Galatians 6:11.
8. Proverbs 30:7-9.
9. 2 Chronicles 15:2.
10. 2 Chronicles 15:8-15.
11. Psalm 33:16-19.
12. 2 Chronicles 16:12.
13. Matthew 18:15-17.
14. Mathew 18:18-20.
15. 1 John 1:9.
16. John 15:13.
17. John 14:23.
18. Romans 10:10.
19. 2 Timothy 3:16-17.

Second Corinthians

1 Paul, an apostle of Christ Jesus by the will of God, and Timothy our brother,

To the church of God which is at Corinth with all the saints who are throughout Achaia:

2 Grace to you and peace from God our Father and the Lord Jesus Christ.

3 Blessed be the God and Father of our Lord Jesus Christ, the Father of mercies and God of all comfort,

4 who comforts us in all our affliction so that we will be able to comfort those who are in any affliction with the comfort with which we ourselves are comforted by God.

5 For just as the sufferings of Christ are ours in abundance, so also our comfort is abundant through Christ.

6 But if we are afflicted, it is for your comfort and salvation; or if we are comforted, it is for your comfort, which is effective in the patient enduring of the same sufferings which we also suffer;

7 and our hope for you is firmly grounded, knowing that as you are sharers of our sufferings, so also you are sharers of our comfort.

8 For we do not want you to be unaware, brethren, of our affliction

which came to us in Asia, that we were burdened excessively, beyond our strength, so that we despaired even of life;

9 indeed, we had the sentence of death within ourselves so that we would not trust in ourselves, but in God who raises the dead;

10 who delivered us from so great a peril of death, and will deliver us, He on whom we have set our hope. And He will yet deliver us,

11 you also joining in helping us through your prayers, so that thanks may be given by many persons on our behalf for the favor bestowed on us through the prayers of many.

12 For our proud confidence is this: the testimony of our conscience, that in holiness and godly sincerity, not in fleshly wisdom but in the grace of God, we have conducted ourselves in the world, and especially toward you.

13 For we write nothing else to you than what you read and understand, and I hope you will understand until the end;

14 just as you also partially did understand us, that we are your reason to be proud as you also are ours, in the day of our Lord Jesus.

15 In this confidence I intended at first to come to you, so that you might twice receive a blessing;

16 that is, to pass your way into Macedonia, and again from Macedonia to come to you, and by you to be helped on my journey to Judea.

17 Therefore, I was not vacillating when I intended to do this, was I? Or what I purpose, do I purpose according to the flesh, so that with me there will be yes, yes and no, no at the same time?

18 But as God is faithful, our word to you is not yes and no.

19 For the Son of God, Christ Jesus, who was preached among you by us—by me and Silvanus and Timothy—was not yes and no, but is yes in Him.

20 For as many as are the promises of God, in Him they are yes; therefore also through Him is our Amen to the glory of God through us.

21 Now He who establishes us with you in Christ and anointed us is God,

22 who also sealed us and gave us the Spirit in our hearts as a pledge.

23 But I call God as witness to my soul, that to spare you I did not come again to Corinth.

24 Not that we lord it over your faith, but are workers with you for your joy; for in your faith you are standing firm.

CHAPTER 2

1 But I determined this for my own sake, that I would not come to you in sorrow again.

2 For if I cause you sorrow, who then makes me glad but the one whom I made sorrowful?

3 This is the very thing I wrote you, so that when I came, I would not have sorrow from those who ought to make me rejoice; having confidence in you all that my joy would be the joy of you all.

4 For out of much affliction and anguish of heart I wrote to you with

many tears; not so that you would be made sorrowful, but that you might know the love which I have especially for you.

5 But if any has caused sorrow, he has caused sorrow not to me, but in some degree—in order not to say too much—to all of you.

6 Sufficient for such a one is this punishment which was inflicted by the majority,

7 so that on the contrary you should rather forgive and comfort him, otherwise such a one might be overwhelmed by excessive sorrow.

8 Wherefore I urge you to reaffirm your love for him.

9 For to this end also I wrote, so that I might put you to the test, whether you are obedient in all things.

10 But one whom you forgive anything, I forgive also; for indeed what I have forgiven, if I have forgiven anything, I did it for your sakes in the presence of Christ,

11 so that no advantage would be taken of us by Satan, for we are not ignorant of his schemes.

12 Now when I came to Troas for the gospel of Christ and when a door was opened for me in the Lord,

13 I had no rest for my spirit, not finding Titus my brother; but taking my leave of them, I went on to Macedonia.

14 But thanks be to God, who always leads us in triumph in Christ, and manifests through us the sweet aroma of the knowledge of Him in every place.

15 For we are a fragrance of Christ to God among those who are being saved and among those who are perishing;

16 to the one an aroma from death to death, to the other an aroma from life to life. And who is adequate for these things?

17 For we are not like many, peddling the word of God, but as from sincerity, but as from God, we speak in Christ in the sight of God.

CHAPTER 3

1 Are we beginning to commend ourselves again? Or do we need, as some, letters of commendation to you or from you?

2 You are our letter, written in our hearts, known and read by all men;

3 being manifested that you are a letter of Christ, cared for by us, written not with ink but with the Spirit of the living God, not on tablets of stone but on tablets of human hearts.

4 Such confidence we have through Christ toward God.

5 Not that we are adequate in ourselves to consider anything as coming from ourselves, but our adequacy is from God,

6 who also made us adequate as servants of a new covenant, not of the letter but of the Spirit; for the letter kills, but the Spirit gives life.

7 But if the ministry of death, in letters engraved on stones, came with glory, so that the sons of Israel could not look intently at the face of Moses because of the glory of his face, fading as it was,

8 how will the ministry of the Spirit fail to be even more with glory?

⁹ For if the ministry of condemnation has glory, much more does the ministry of righteousness abound in glory.

¹⁰ For indeed what had glory, in this case has no glory because of the glory that surpasses it.

¹¹ For if that which fades away was with glory, much more that which remains is in glory.

¹² Therefore having such a hope, we use great boldness in our speech,

¹³ and are not like Moses, who used to put a veil over his face so that the sons of Israel would not look intently at the end of what was fading away.

¹⁴ But their minds were hardened; for until this very day at the reading of the old covenant the same veil remains unlifted, because it is removed in Christ.

¹⁵ But to this day whenever Moses is read, a veil lies over their heart;

¹⁶ but whenever a person turns to the Lord, the veil is taken away.

¹⁷ Now the Lord is the Spirit, and where the Spirit of the Lord is, there is liberty.

¹⁸ But we all, with unveiled face, beholding as in a mirror the glory of the Lord, are being transformed into the same image from glory to glory, just as from the Lord, the Spirit.

CHAPTER 4

¹ Therefore, since we have this ministry, as we received mercy, we do not lose heart,

2 but we have renounced the things hidden because of shame, not walking in craftiness or adulterating the word of God, but by the manifestation of truth commending ourselves to every man's conscience in the sight of God.

3 And even if our gospel is veiled, it is veiled to those who are perishing,

4 in whose case the god of this world has blinded the minds of the unbelieving so that they might not see the light of the gospel of the glory of Christ, who is the image of God.

5 For we do not preach ourselves but Christ Jesus as Lord, and ourselves as your bond-servants for Jesus' sake.

6 For God, who said, "Light shall shine out of darkness," is the One who has shone in our hearts to give the Light of the knowledge of the glory of God in the face of Christ.

7 But we have this treasure in earthen vessels, so that the surpassing greatness of the power will be of God and not from ourselves;

8 we are afflicted in every way, but not crushed; perplexed, but not despairing;

9 persecuted, but not forsaken; struck down, but not destroyed;

10 always carrying about in the body the dying of Jesus, so that the life of Jesus also may be manifested in our body.

11 For we who live are constantly being delivered over to death for Jesus' sake, so that the life of Jesus also may be manifested in our mortal flesh.

12 So death works in us, but life in you.

13 But having the same spirit of faith, according to what is written, "I believed, therefore I spoke," we also believe, therefore we also speak,

14 knowing that He who raised the Lord Jesus will raise us also with Jesus and will present us with you.

15 For all things are for your sakes, so that the grace which is spreading to more and more people may cause the giving of thanks to abound to the glory of God.

16 Therefore we do not lose heart, but though our outer man is decaying, yet our inner man is being renewed day by day.

17 For momentary, light affliction is producing for us an eternal weight of glory far beyond all comparison,

18 while we look not at the things which are seen, but at the things which are not seen; for the things which are seen are temporal, but the things which are not seen are eternal.

CHAPTER 5

1 For we know that if the earthly tent which is our house is torn down, we have a building from God, a house not made with hands, eternal in the heavens.

2 For indeed in this house we groan, longing to be clothed with our dwelling from heaven,

3 inasmuch as we, having put it on, will not be found naked.

4 For indeed while we are in this tent, we groan, being burdened, because we do not want to be unclothed but to be clothed, so that what is mortal will be swallowed up by life.

5 Now He who prepared us for this very purpose is God, who gave to us the Spirit as a pledge.

6 Therefore, being always of good courage, and knowing that while we are at home in the body we are absent from the Lord—

7 for we walk by faith, not by sight—

8 we are of good courage, I say, and prefer rather to be absent from the body and to be at home with the Lord.

9 Therefore we also have as our ambition, whether at home or absent, to be pleasing to Him.

10 For we must all appear before the judgment seat of Christ, so that each one may be recompensed for his deeds in the body, according to what he has done, whether good or bad.

11 Therefore, knowing the fear of the Lord, we persuade men, but we are made manifest to God; and I hope that we are made manifest also in your consciences.

12 We are not again commending ourselves to you but are giving you an occasion to be proud of us, so that you will have an answer for those who take pride in appearance and not in heart.

13 For if we are beside ourselves, it is for God; if we are of sound mind, it is for you.

14 For the love of Christ controls us, having concluded this, that one died for all, therefore all died;

15 and He died for all, so that they who live might no longer live for themselves, but for Him who died and rose again on their behalf.

16 Therefore from now on we recognize no one according to the flesh; even though we have known Christ according to the flesh, yet now we know Him in this way no longer.

17 Therefore if anyone is in Christ, he is a new creature; the old things passed away; behold, new things have come.

18 Now all these things are from God, who reconciled us to Himself through Christ and gave us the ministry of reconciliation,

19 namely, that God was in Christ reconciling the world to Himself, not counting their trespasses against them, and He has committed to us the word of reconciliation.

20 Therefore, we are ambassadors for Christ, as though God were making an appeal through us; we beg you on behalf of Christ, be reconciled to God.

21 He made Him who knew no sin to be sin on our behalf, so that we might become the righteousness of God in Him.

CHAPTER 6

1 And working together with Him, we also urge you not to receive the grace of God in vain—

2 for He says,

"At the acceptable time I listened to you,

And on the day of salvation I helped you."

Behold, now is "the acceptable time," behold, now is "the day of salvation"—

3 giving no cause for offense in anything, so that the ministry will not be discredited,

4 but in everything commending ourselves as servants of God, in much endurance, in afflictions, in hardships, in distresses,

5 in beatings, in imprisonments, in tumults, in labors, in sleeplessness, in hunger,

6 in purity, in knowledge, in patience, in kindness, in the Holy Spirit, in genuine love,

7 in the word of truth, in the power of God; by the weapons of righteousness for the right hand and the left,

8 by glory and dishonor, by evil report and good report; regarded as deceivers and yet true;

9 as unknown yet well-known, as dying yet behold, we live; as punished yet not put to death,

10 as sorrowful yet always rejoicing, as poor yet making many rich, as having nothing yet possessing all things.

11 Our mouth has spoken freely to you, O Corinthians, our heart is opened wide.

12 You are not restrained by us, but you are restrained in your own affections.

13 Now in a like exchange—I speak as to children—open wide to us also.

14 Do not be bound together with unbelievers; for what partnership have righteousness and lawlessness, or what fellowship has light with darkness?

15 Or what harmony has Christ with Belial, or what has a believer in common with an unbeliever?

16 Or what agreement has the temple of God with idols? For we are the temple of the living God; just as God said,

"I will dwell in them and walk among them;

And I will be their God, and they shall be My people.

17 "Therefore, come out from their midst and be separate," says the Lord.

"And do not touch what is unclean;

And I will welcome you.

18 "And I will be a father to you,

And you shall be sons and daughters to Me,"

Says the Lord Almighty.

CHAPTER 7

1 Therefore, having these promises, beloved, let us cleanse ourselves from all defilement of flesh and spirit, perfecting holiness in the fear of God.

2 Make room for us in your hearts; we wronged no one, we corrupted no one, we took advantage of no one.

3 I do not speak to condemn you, for I have said before that you are in our hearts to die together and to live together.

4 Great is my confidence in you; great is my boasting on your behalf. I am filled with comfort; I am overflowing with joy in all our affliction.

5 For even when we came into Macedonia our flesh had no rest, but we were afflicted on every side: conflicts without, fears within.

6 But God, who comforts the depressed, comforted us by the coming of Titus;

7 and not only by his coming, but also by the comfort with which he was comforted in you, as he reported to us your longing, your mourning, your zeal for me; so that I rejoiced even more.

8 For though I caused you sorrow by my letter, I do not regret it; though I did regret it—for I see that that letter caused you sorrow, though only for a while—

9 I now rejoice, not that you were made sorrowful, but that you were made sorrowful to the point of repentance; for you were made sorrowful according to the will of God, so that you might not suffer loss in anything through us.

10 For the sorrow that is according to the will of God produces a repentance without regret, leading to salvation, but the sorrow of the world produces death.

11 For behold what earnestness this very thing, this godly sorrow, has produced in you: what vindication of yourselves, what indignation, what fear, what longing, what zeal, what avenging of wrong! In everything you demonstrated yourselves to be innocent in the matter.

12 So although I wrote to you, it was not for the sake of the offender nor for the sake of the one offended, but that your earnestness on our behalf might be made known to you in the sight of God.

13 For this reason we have been comforted.

And besides our comfort, we rejoiced even much more for the joy of Titus, because his spirit has been refreshed by you all.

14 For if in anything I have boasted to him about you, I was not put to shame; but as we spoke all things to you in truth, so also our boasting before Titus proved to be the truth.

15 His affection abounds all the more toward you, as he remembers the obedience of you all, how you received him with fear and trembling.

16 I rejoice that in everything I have confidence in you.

CHAPTER 8

1 Now, brethren, we wish to make known to you the grace of God which has been given in the churches of Macedonia,

2 that in a great ordeal of affliction their abundance of joy and their deep poverty overflowed in the wealth of their liberality.

3 For I testify that according to their ability, and beyond their ability, they gave of their own accord,

4 begging us with much urging for the favor of participation in the support of the saints,

5 and this, not as we had expected, but they first gave themselves to the Lord and to us by the will of God.

6 So we urged Titus that as he had previously made a beginning, so he would also complete in you this gracious work as well.

7 But just as you abound in everything, in faith and utterance and knowledge and in all earnestness and in the love we inspired in you, see that you abound in this gracious work also.

8 I am not speaking this as a command, but as proving through the earnestness of others the sincerity of your love also.

9 For you know the grace of our Lord Jesus Christ, that though He was rich, yet for your sake He became poor, so that you through His poverty might become rich.

10 I give my opinion in this matter, for this is to your advantage, who were the first to begin a year ago not only to do this, but also to desire to do it.

11 But now finish doing it also, so that just as there was the readiness to desire it, so there may be also the completion of it by your ability.

12 For if the readiness is present, it is acceptable according to what a person has, not according to what he does not have.

13 For this is not for the ease of others and for your affliction, but by way of equality—

14 at this present time your abundance being a supply for their need, so

that their abundance also may become a supply for your need, that there may be equality;

15 as it is written, "He who gathered much did not have too much, and he who gathered little had no lack."

16 But thanks be to God who puts the same earnestness on your behalf in the heart of Titus.

17 For he not only accepted our appeal, but being himself very earnest, he has gone to you of his own accord.

18 We have sent along with him the brother whose fame in the things of the gospel has spread through all the churches;

19 and not only this, but he has also been appointed by the churches to travel with us in this gracious work, which is being administered by us for the glory of the Lord Himself, and to show our readiness,

20 taking precaution so that no one will discredit us in our administration of this generous gift;

21 for we have regard for what is honorable, not only in the sight of the Lord, but also in the sight of men.

22 We have sent with them our brother, whom we have often tested and found diligent in many things, but now even more diligent because of his great confidence in you.

23 As for Titus, he is my partner and fellow worker among you; as for our brethren, they are messengers of the churches, a glory to Christ.

24 Therefore openly before the churches, show them the proof of your love and of our reason for boasting about you.

CHAPTER 9

1 For it is superfluous for me to write to you about this ministry to the saints;

2 for I know your readiness, of which I boast about you to the Macedonians, namely, that Achaia has been prepared since last year, and your zeal has stirred up most of them.

3 But I have sent the brethren, in order that our boasting about you may not be made empty in this case, so that, as I was saying, you may be prepared;

4 otherwise if any Macedonians come with me and find you unprepared, we—not to speak of you—will be put to shame by this confidence.

5 So I thought it necessary to urge the brethren that they would go on ahead to you and arrange beforehand your previously promised bountiful gift, so that the same would be ready as a bountiful gift and not affected by covetousness.

6 Now this I say, he who sows sparingly will also reap sparingly, and he who sows bountifully will also reap bountifully.

7 Each one must do just as he has purposed in his heart, not grudgingly or under compulsion, for God loves a cheerful giver.

⁸ And God is able to make all grace abound to you, so that always having all sufficiency in everything, you may have an abundance for every good deed;

⁹ as it is written,

"He scattered abroad, he gave to the poor,

His righteousness endures forever."

¹⁰ Now He who supplies seed to the sower and bread for food will supply and multiply your seed for sowing and increase the harvest of your righteousness;

¹¹ you will be enriched in everything for all liberality, which through us is producing thanksgiving to God.

¹² For the ministry of this service is not only fully supplying the needs of the saints, but is also overflowing through many thanksgivings to God.

¹³ Because of the proof given by this ministry, they will glorify God for your obedience to your confession of the gospel of Christ and for the liberality of your contribution to them and to all,

¹⁴ while they also, by prayer on your behalf, yearn for you because of the surpassing grace of God in you.

¹⁵ Thanks be to God for His indescribable gift!

CHAPTER 10

¹ Now I, Paul, myself urge you by the meekness and gentleness of Christ—I who am meek when face to face with you, but bold toward you when absent!

2 I ask that when I am present I need not be bold with the confidence with which I propose to be courageous against some, who regard us as if we walked according to the flesh.

3 For though we walk in the flesh, we do not war according to the flesh,

4 for the weapons of our warfare are not of the flesh, but divinely powerful for the destruction of fortresses.

5 We are destroying speculations and every lofty thing raised up against the knowledge of God, and we are taking every thought captive to the obedience of Christ,

6 and we are ready to punish all disobedience, whenever your obedience is complete.

7 You are looking at things as they are outwardly. If anyone is confident in himself that he is Christ's, let him consider this again within himself, that just as he is Christ's, so also are we.

8 For even if I boast somewhat further about our authority, which the Lord gave for building you up and not for destroying you, I will not be put to shame,

9 for I do not wish to seem as if I would terrify you by my letters.

10 For they say, "His letters are weighty and strong, but his personal presence is unimpressive and his speech contemptible."

11 Let such a person consider this, that what we are in word by letters when absent, such persons we are also in deed when present.

12 For we are not bold to class or compare ourselves with some of those

who commend themselves; but when they measure themselves by themselves and compare themselves with themselves, they are without understanding.

13 But we will not boast beyond our measure, but within the measure of the sphere which God apportioned to us as a measure, to reach even as far as you.

14 For we are not overextending ourselves, as if we did not reach to you, for we were the first to come even as far as you in the gospel of Christ;

15 not boasting beyond our measure, that is, in other men's labors, but with the hope that as your faith grows, we will be, within our sphere, enlarged even more by you,

16 so as to preach the gospel even to the regions beyond you, and not to boast in what has been accomplished in the sphere of another.

17 But he who boasts is to boast in the Lord.

18 For it is not he who commends himself that is approved, but he whom the Lord commends.

CHAPTER 11

1 I wish that you would bear with me in a little foolishness; but indeed you are bearing with me.

2 For I am jealous for you with a godly jealousy; for I betrothed you to one husband, so that to Christ I might present you as a pure virgin.

3 But I am afraid that, as the serpent deceived Eve by his craftiness, your minds will be led astray from the simplicity and purity of devotion to Christ.

4 For if one comes and preaches another Jesus whom we have not preached, or you receive a different spirit which you have not received, or a different gospel which you have not accepted, you bear this beautifully.

5 For I consider myself not in the least inferior to the most eminent apostles.

6 But even if I am unskilled in speech, yet I am not so in knowledge; in fact, in every way we have made this evident to you in all things.

7 Or did I commit a sin in humbling myself so that you might be exalted, because I preached the gospel of God to you without charge?

8 I robbed other churches by taking wages from them to serve you;

9 and when I was present with you and was in need, I was not a burden to anyone; for when the brethren came from Macedonia they fully supplied my need, and in everything I kept myself from being a burden to you, and will continue to do so.

10 As the truth of Christ is in me, this boasting of mine will not be stopped in the regions of Achaia.

11 Why? Because I do not love you? God knows I do!

12 But what I am doing I will continue to do, so that I may cut off opportunity from those who desire an opportunity to be regarded just as we are in the matter about which they are boasting.

13 For such men are false apostles, deceitful workers, disguising themselves as apostles of Christ.

14 No wonder, for even Satan disguises himself as an angel of light.

15 Therefore it is not surprising if his servants also disguise themselves as servants of righteousness, whose end will be according to their deeds.

16 Again I say, let no one think me foolish; but if you do, receive me even as foolish, so that I also may boast a little.

17 What I am saying, I am not saying as the Lord would, but as in foolishness, in this confidence of boasting.

18 Since many boast according to the flesh, I will boast also.

19 For you, being so wise, tolerate the foolish gladly.

20 For you tolerate it if anyone enslaves you, anyone devours you, anyone takes advantage of you, anyone exalts himself, anyone hits you in the face.

21 To my shame I must say that we have been weak by comparison.

But in whatever respect anyone else is bold—I speak in foolishness—I am just as bold myself.

22 Are they Hebrews? So am I. Are they Israelites? So am I. Are they descendants of Abraham? So am I.

23 Are they servants of Christ?—I speak as if insane—I more so; in far more labors, in far more imprisonments, beaten times without number, often in danger of death.

24 Five times I received from the Jews thirty-nine lashes.

25 Three times I was beaten with rods, once I was stoned, three times I was shipwrecked, a night and a day I have spent in the deep.

26 I have been on frequent journeys, in dangers from rivers, dangers from

robbers, dangers from my countrymen, dangers from the Gentiles, dangers in the city, dangers in the wilderness, dangers on the sea, dangers among false brethren;

27 I have been in labor and hardship, through many sleepless nights, in hunger and thirst, often without food, in cold and exposure.

28 Apart from such external things, there is the daily pressure on me of concern for all the churches.

29 Who is weak without my being weak? Who is led into sin without my intense concern?

30 If I have to boast, I will boast of what pertains to my weakness.

31 The God and Father of the Lord Jesus, He who is blessed forever, knows that I am not lying.

32 In Damascus the ethnarch under Aretas the king was guarding the city of the Damascenes in order to seize me,

33 and I was let down in a basket through a window in the wall, and so escaped his hands.

CHAPTER 12

1 Boasting is necessary, though it is not profitable; but I will go on to visions and revelations of the Lord.

2 I know a man in Christ who fourteen years ago—whether in the body I do not know, or out of the body I do not know, God knows—such a man was caught up to the third heaven.

3 And I know how such a man—whether in the body or apart from the body I do not know, God knows—

4 was caught up into Paradise and heard inexpressible words, which a man is not permitted to speak.

5 On behalf of such a man I will boast; but on my own behalf I will not boast, except in regard to my weaknesses.

6 For if I do wish to boast I will not be foolish, for I will be speaking the truth; but I refrain from this, so that no one will credit me with more than he sees in me or hears from me.

7 Because of the surpassing greatness of the revelations, for this reason, to keep me from exalting myself, there was given me a thorn in the flesh, a messenger of Satan to torment me—to keep me from exalting myself!

8 Concerning this I implored the Lord three times that it might leave me.

9 And He has said to me, "My grace is sufficient for you, for power is perfected in weakness." Most gladly, therefore, I will rather boast about my weaknesses, so that the power of Christ may dwell in me.

10 Therefore I am well content with weaknesses, with insults, with distresses, with persecutions, with difficulties, for Christ's sake; for when I am weak, then I am strong.

11 I have become foolish; you yourselves compelled me. Actually I should have been commended by you, for in no respect was I inferior to the most eminent apostles, even though I am a nobody.

12 The signs of a true apostle were performed among you with all perseverance, by signs and wonders and miracles.

13 For in what respect were you treated as inferior to the rest of the churches, except that I myself did not become a burden to you? Forgive me this wrong!

14 Here for this third time I am ready to come to you, and I will not be a burden to you; for I do not seek what is yours, but you; for children are not responsible to save up for their parents, but parents for their children.

15 I will most gladly spend and be expended for your souls. If I love you more, am I to be loved less?

16 But be that as it may, I did not burden you myself; nevertheless, crafty fellow that I am, I took you in by deceit.

17 Certainly I have not taken advantage of you through any of those whom I have sent to you, have I?

18 I urged Titus to go, and I sent the brother with him. Titus did not take any advantage of you, did he? Did we not conduct ourselves in the same spirit and walk in the same steps?

19 All this time you have been thinking that we are defending ourselves to you. Actually, it is in the sight of God that we have been speaking in Christ; and all for your upbuilding, beloved.

20 For I am afraid that perhaps when I come I may find you to be not what I wish and may be found by you to be not what you wish; that perhaps

there will be strife, jealousy, angry tempers, disputes, slanders, gossip, arrogance, disturbances;

21 I am afraid that when I come again my God may humiliate me before you, and I may mourn over many of those who have sinned in the past and not repented of the impurity, immorality and sensuality which they have practiced.

CHAPTER 13

1 This is the third time I am coming to you. Every fact is to be confirmed by the testimony of two or three witnesses.

2 I have previously said when present the second time, and though now absent I say in advance to those who have sinned in the past and to all the rest as well, that if I come again I will not spare anyone,

3 since you are seeking for proof of the Christ who speaks in me, and who is not weak toward you, but mighty in you.

4 For indeed He was crucified because of weakness, yet He lives because of the power of God. For we also are weak in Him, yet we will live with Him because of the power of God directed toward you.

5 Test yourselves to see if you are in the faith; examine yourselves! Or do you not recognize this about yourselves, that Jesus Christ is in you—unless indeed you fail the test?

6 But I trust that you will realize that we ourselves do not fail the test.

7 Now we pray to God that you do no wrong; not that we ourselves may

appear approved, but that you may do what is right, even though we may appear unapproved.

8 For we can do nothing against the truth, but only for the truth.

9 For we rejoice when we ourselves are weak but you are strong; this we also pray for, that you be made complete.

10 For this reason I am writing these things while absent, so that when present I need not use severity, in accordance with the authority which the Lord gave me for building up and not for tearing down.

11 Finally, brethren, rejoice, be made complete, be comforted, be like-minded, live in peace; and the God of love and peace will be with you.

12 Greet one another with a holy kiss.

13 All the saints greet you.

14 The grace of the Lord Jesus Christ, and the love of God, and the fellowship of the Holy Spirit, be with you all.

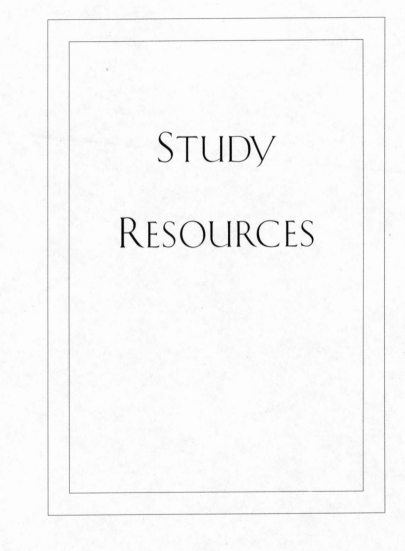

STUDY

RESOURCES

HOW TO MARK YOUR BIBLE

One of the things we at Precept Ministries International teach you to do in inductive Bible study is to find the key words in the passage you're studying and to mark them in a distinctive way. This is a very helpful and important element of the essential Bible study step known as observation—discovering exactly what the text says. So many times a Scripture passage is misinterpreted simply because the initial work of accurate observation has not been done. Remembering to mark key words will help you not to overlook this critical step.

WHAT ARE KEY WORDS?

Key words or phrases are those that are essential to the text. If they were to be removed, you would find it difficult or impossible to grasp the essence of what the passage is about. Like keys, these words "unlock" the meaning of the text. Recognizing them will help you uncover the author's intended purpose and emphasis in his message.

Key words can be nouns, descriptive words, or action words. Very often an author will repeat these words or phrases in order to emphasize his message. They may be repeated throughout an entire book—like the key words *love* and *abide,* which we see throughout the book of 1 John. Or they may be repeated throughout a shorter section of text, as with the key word *fellowship,* which is used four times in the first chapter of 1 John but not elsewhere in the book.

In the "Lord" series of Bible studies, you will often be asked to find and mark certain key words or phrases in the passage you're studying. This is a method that you will want to make a lifelong habit in your personal Bible study.

HOW TO MARK KEY WORDS

Marking key words can be done in several ways.

1. You can use different colors or a combination of colors to highlight different words. When I mark a passage, I like to choose a color that to

me best reflects the word I'm marking. I color references to God in yellow because God is light and in Him there is no darkness. I color sin brown. Any Old Testament reference to the temple is colored blue.

2. You can use a variety of symbols—simply drawing a circle around a word, underlining it, or marking it with a symbol of your own creation, such as these:

$$O \; \triangle \; \sim\sim\sim \; \text{ξ}\text{}\text{₃}$$

When I use symbols, I try to devise one that best pictures the word. For example, the key words *repent* and *repentance* in Matthew 3 might be marked with the symbol ⟿ since in Scripture this word's root meaning represents a change of mind, which often leads to a change in direction.

3. You can combine colors with symbols. For example:
   • In 1 John 3, the key word *love* could be marked with a red heart like this: ♡ If you want to distinguish God's love from man's, you could color God's heart yellow and man's red.
   • Every reference to the devil or evil spirits could be marked with a red pitchfork. ⨂
   • Every occurrence of covenant could be colored red and boxed in with yellow.

The *New Inductive Study Bible* (NISB) has a whole page of suggested markings for key words used throughout the Bible.

A WORD OF CAUTION

When looking for key words, sometimes the tendency is to mark too many words. For example, I rarely mark references to God and to Jesus Christ unless it is significant to understanding the message. For instance, the phrases "in Christ" and "in Him" are significant to understanding the message of Ephesians 1–3. If you marked every reference to Jesus in some of the gospel accounts, your Bible would be too marked up. So you need to use discretion. (I always mark every reference to the Holy Spirit because He is not referred to often, and there is much confusion about the person and ministry of the Holy Spirit.)

Remember to look for those words that relate to the foundational theme of the text. Sometimes a key word may not be repeated frequently, but you know it is key because without it you would not know the essence of what the author is talking about in that passage.

BE SURE TO MARK KEY-WORD SYNONYMS AND PRONOUNS

Synonyms for a key word would be marked the same way you mark the key word. For example, you would mark identically the word *devil* and the phrase "evil one" in Ephesians 6:10-18.

And be sure to mark pronouns (I, you, he, she, it, we, our, and so on) the same way you would mark the words to which they refer. In 1 Timothy 3:1-7, for example, you would mark the pronouns *he* and *his* in the same way you did the key word *overseer* in that passage.

For consistency, you may want to list on an index card the key symbols and colors you like using for certain words and keep that card in your Bible.

IMMEDIATE IDENTIFICATION

With a passage's key words marked in this way, you can look at the text and immediately spot the word's usage and importance. In the future you'll quickly be able to track key subjects and identify significant truths in any passage you've studied and marked.

CREATE LISTS FROM KEY WORDS

After you mark key words, you will find it helpful to list what you learn from the text by the use of the key word. For instance, once you mark the word *sin* in 1 John 3, you would make a list of what the text tells you about sin. As you look at each marked key word, list anything that would answer the questions *who, what, when, where, why,* or *how* about sin. You will be not only surprised but also delighted at the truths you can learn from this simple process of observation.

For more on how to mark your Bible and on the inductive Bible study approach, you may want to use the *New Inductive Study Bible* (from Harvest House Publishers), or you can reach us at Precept Ministries International by referring to the contact information in the back of this book.

GUIDELINES FOR GROUP USE

This study book, as well as all those in the "Lord" series, can be used for home Bible-study groups, Sunday-school classes, family devotions, and a great variety of other group situations. Here are some things to keep in mind as you use this study in a group setting to minister to others.

- Prayerfully commit the entire study to the Lord, seeking His direction for every step.

- As your group forms, encourage each member to purchase an individual copy of this book.

- If you have the companion audio or videotapes for this course, begin your first class by listening to or viewing the introductory lesson on the study. Each student should then do the study preparation for chapter 1 before the next class. (Encourage each student to do this faithfully week by week.)

- Beginning with your next meeting, your weekly pattern as you meet should be to first discuss what you have all studied and learned on your own during the preceding week. Then, if you so desire, you could have a teacher present an in-depth message on the material you just studied. Or you could listen to or watch on video the teaching tapes available on this series. Just make sure that the teaching tape follows the class discussion rather than precedes it. You want your group to have the joy of discovery and discussion.

- The group discussion questions following each chapter in this book are to aid you in leading a discussion of that week's material. However, merely having these questions will not be enough for a really lively and successful discussion. The better you know your material, the greater freedom you will have in leading. Therefore, Beloved, be faithful in your own study and remain dependent upon the ministry of the Holy Spirit, who is there to lead you and guide you into all truth and who will enable you to fulfill the good work God has foreordained for you. (As the group's leader, it would be ideal if you could either read the entire book first or do several weeks' study in advance, so you know where you're going and can grasp the scope of the material covered in this study.)

• Each week as you prepare to lead the group's discussion, pray and ask the Father what your particular group needs to learn and how you can best cover the material. Pray with pen in hand. Make a list of what the Lord shows you. Then create your own questions or select from the questions at the end of each chapter, which will help stimulate and guide the group members in the Lord's direction within the time you have.

• Remember that your group members will find the greatest sense of accomplishment in discussing what they've learned in their own study, so try to stick to the subject at hand in your discussion. This will keep the class from becoming frustrated. Make sure the answers and insights come from the Word of God and are always in accordance with the whole counsel of God.

• Strive in your group to create an atmosphere of love, safety, and caring. Be concerned about one another. Bear one another's burdens and so fulfill the law of Christ—the law of love (Galatians 6:2). We desperately need one another.

Please know that I thank our Father for you and your willingness to assume this critical role of establishing God's people in God's Word. I know that this process produces glory and reverence for Him. So press on, valiant one. He is coming, bringing in the kingdom in all its glory, and His reward is with Him to give to each one of us according to our deeds.

THE "LORD" SERIES: AN OVERVIEW

My burden—and calling—is to help Christians (or interested or desperate inquirers) see for themselves what the Word of God has to teach on significant and relevant life-related subjects. So many people are weak and unstable in their Christianity because they don't know truth for themselves; they only know what others have taught them. These books, therefore, are designed to involve you in the incomparably enriching experience of daily study in God's Word.

Each book has been thoroughly tested and has already had an impact on a multitude of lives. Let me introduce the full series to you.

Lord, I Want to Know You is a foundational study for the "Lord" books. In this seventeen-week study you'll discover how God's character is revealed through His names, such as Creator, Healer, Protector, Provider, and many more. Within the names of God you'll encounter strength for your worst trials, comfort for your heart's deepest pain, and provision for your soul's greatest need. As you come to know Him more fully—the power of His glorious name and the depth of His infinite love—your walk with God will be transformed and your faith will be increased.

Lord, Heal My Hurts is, understandably, one of the most popular studies in this series. If you're in touch with the world, you know that people around you are in great pain. We run to many sources for relief when we are in pain. Some of us turn to other people; many escape into drugs, work, further education, and even hobbies. But in God you can find salvation from any situation, from any hurt. In this thirteen-week study you'll see that, no matter what you've done or what's been done to you, God wants to become your refuge…He loves you and desires your wholeness…and He offers healing for your deepest wounds.

Lord, I Need Grace to Make It Today will reveal to you in fresh power the amazing truth that God's grace is available for *every* situation, no matter how difficult, no matter how terrible. You'll gain the confidence that God will use you for His glory, as His grace enables you to persevere regardless of your need, regardless of your circumstances, and despite the backward pull of your flesh. You will see and know that the Lord and His all-sufficient grace will always be with you. A highlight of this nine-week course is your study of the book of Galatians and its liberating message about our freedom in Christ.

Lord, I'm Torn Between Two Masters opens your understanding to the kind of life that is truly pleasing to God. If you've known discouragement because you felt you could never measure up to God's standards or if you've ever felt unbearably stretched by the clash of life's priorities, this nine-week study of the Sermon on the Mount will lead you into a new freedom that will truly clear your vision and fortify your heart. You'll be encouraged to entwine your thoughts, hopes, dreams, and desires around heavenly things, and you'll find your life transformed by choosing to seek first God's kingdom and His righteousness.

Lord, Only You Can Change Me is an eight-week devotional study on character that draws especially on the so-called Beatitudes of Matthew 5. If you've ever been frustrated at not being all you wanted to be for the Lord or at not being able to change, you'll find in this study of Christ's teaching the path to true inner transformation that is accomplished only through the work of the indwelling Holy Spirit. You will learn the achievable reality of a godly life and the fulfillment it can bring.

Lord, Where Are You When Bad Things Happen? is a critically important study in preparing you for times of trial. In this ten-week course you'll be grounded in the knowledge and confidence of God's sovereignty as you study especially the book of Habakkuk and see how God works in and through difficult and demanding situations. More than that, you'll learn what it means to live by faith…and to rest the details of your life in His hands.

Lord, Is It Warfare? Teach Me to Stand is a study that trains you for spiritual battle. God's Word tells us that our adversary, the devil, goes about like a roaring lion seeking whom he may devour (1 Peter 5:8, KJV). Many times we either don't recognize this enemy, or we're scared by his roar. We would like him to go away, but it's not that simple. In this eleven-week study you'll learn how to recognize Satan's tactics and how to be set free from bondage. As you focus your study especially on the book of Ephesians, you'll discover how to build an unshakable faith that makes victory yours for the taking. (This is the most challenging of the "Lord" books and requires an average of two to two and a half hours of weekly preparation to complete the assignments.)

Beloved, I have written these books so that you can have insight from God's Word on the pertinent issues of life—not only for yourself, but also for your ministry to others.

Know that you are on my heart because you are precious to God and I long to see you live as more than a conqueror, fulfilling God's purpose for your life.

ON-LINE RESOURCES

As you plant the seeds of God's Word in your heart in this study, I want you to know that you can now find immediate encouragement and help in a variety of ways just by connecting to our special "Lord" studies Web site at the address listed below.

Here's a sample listing of what you'll find at this site:

- Helpful information for guiding your individual study in this and other "Lord" books
- More detailed information on the exact study focus in all the "Lord" books
- Guidelines for group leaders and facilitators, both to get your group started and to keep it functioning in the best way
- Group study questions for you to download and reformat in a way that is most helpful for you and your group
- Additional insights on the topics in the "Lord" studies from the Precept Ministries International team
- Opportunities for you to join others in sharing your discoveries from God's Word

This information is continually updated to ensure that we're offering you the best support possible. Please e-mail and let us know what you find most helpful from this "Lord" studies Web site!

For more information on this and other "Lord" studies:
www.lordstudies.com

For other resources and information from Precept Ministries International:
www.precept.org

ABOUT KAY ARTHUR AND
PRECEPT MINISTRIES INTERNATIONAL

Kay Arthur, executive vice president and cofounder of Precept Ministries International, is known around the world as a Bible teacher, author, conference speaker, former missionary, and host of national radio and television programs.

Kay and her husband, Jack, founded Precept Ministries in 1970 in Chattanooga, Tennessee. Started as a fledgling ministry for teens, Precept today is a worldwide outreach that establishes children, teens, and adults in God's Word, so that they can discover the Bible's truths for themselves. Precept inductive Bible studies are taught in all 50 states. The studies have been translated into 60 languages, reaching 118 countries.

Kay is the author of more than 40 books and 27 inductive Bible study courses, with a total of over 5 million books in print. She is sought after by groups throughout the world as an inspiring Bible teacher and conference speaker. Kay is also well known globally through her daily and weekly television programs that air regularly on over 900 stations in 30 countries.

Contact Precept Ministries for more information about inductive Bible studies in your area.

Precept Ministries International
P.O. Box 182218
Chattanooga, TN 37422-7218
800-763-8280
www.precept.org